Sounding Out Pop

D1601043

TRACKING POP

SERIES EDITORS: LORI BURNS, JOHN COVACH, AND ALBIN ZAK

In one form or another, the sonic influence of popular music has permeated cultural activities and perception on a global scale. Interdisciplinary in nature, Tracking Pop is intended as a rich exploration of pop music and its cultural situation. In addition to providing much-needed resources for the ever-increasing number of students and scholars working in the field of popular culture, the books in this series will appeal to general readers and music lovers, for whom pop has provided the soundtrack of their lives over the past fifty years.

Sounding Out Pop

Analytical Essays in Popular Music

Edited by
Mark Spicer *and* John Covach

The University of Michigan Press • *Ann Arbor*

2013   2012   2011   2010   4   3   2   1

A CIP catalog record for this book is available from the British Library.

Library of Congress Cataloging-in-Publication Data

Sounding out pop : analytical essays in popular music / edited by Mark
    Spicer and John Covach.
        p.   cm. — (Tracking pop)
    Includes index.
    ISBN 978-0-472-11505-1 (cloth : alk. paper) —
    ISBN 978-0-472-03400-0 (pbk. : alk. paper)
    1. Popular music—History and criticism.   2. Popular music—
Analysis, appreciation.   I. Spicer, Mark Stuart.   II. Covach, John
Rudolph.
    ML3470.S635   2010
    781.64—dc22   2009050341

Contents

Preface

SOUNDING OUT POP contains nine new essays on pop and rock music, arranged chronologically by repertoire, which together are intended to mirror the aim of the Tracking Pop series, that is, to map the myriad styles and genres of the pop-rock universe through detailed case studies that confront the sounding music itself from a variety of perspectives. The three series editors of Tracking Pop—Lori Burns, John Covach, and Albin Zak—have each contributed essays especially for this volume. The other six chapters represent revised and expanded versions of essays commissioned by the volume editors from among what they considered to be the best papers on pop and rock music presented at national music theory and musicology conferences in North America over the past few years with an eye toward assembling a collection that explores a broad range of popular music repertories from the 1950s to the present day. While the book's subtitle touts these as "analytical" essays, the range of approaches taken by the authors—from historical to music-analytic, aesthetic to ethnographic, with several drawing liberally from ideas in other disciplines—is as vast and varied as the repertoire covered over the course of the book's nine chapters.

All of the essays in *Sounding Out Pop* deal with issues of musical style to some degree, yet three of the authors foreground style analysis as their central concern. In "'Only the Lonely': Roy Orbison's Sweet West Texas Style," Albin Zak offers a richly textured account of Roy Orbison's formative years as a songwriter and recording artist in the second half of the 1950s, showing how Orbison gradually developed a number of stylistic hallmarks that would crystallize in his 1960 breakthrough hit, "Only the Lonely." Jumping forward two decades, Mark Spicer tackles a seminal group that emerged at the height of the U.K. punk movement in his

" 'Reggatta de Blanc': Analyzing Style in the Music of the Police," adapting Leonard Ratner's theory of style topics to help him unravel the multiple stylistic threads—reggae, punk, and many others—that shaped the Police's musical idiolect. Jumping forward another two decades to the late 1990s, Rebecca Leydon also draws on Ratnerian topic theory in her "Recombinant Style Topics: The Past and Future of Sampling," demonstrating how eclectic artists such as Beck and Mr. Bungle have responded to the "digital aesthetic" of the late 1980s and 1990s by rejecting samples in their music in favor of newly composed stylistic allusions.

Three of the authors explore issues of race, gender, sexuality, and politics in the service of their analysis. In "Leiber and Stoller, the Coasters, and the 'Dramatic AABA' Form," John Covach challenges the oft-cited generalizations about "black" and "white" popular music in rock and roll's crucial first decade, revealing—through a close study of form and lyrics in Leiber and Stoller's records with the Coasters—a level of stylistic integration in 1950s pop that was in many ways at odds with the social segregation of the times. Andrew Flory, in "Marvin Gaye as Vocal Composer," sheds light on Marvin Gaye's working method through a close examination of several key tracks from the late 1960s and 1970s, showing how Gaye used his process of "vocal composition" to imbue his songs with sexual and political messages that often ran contrary to the ideals of Motown and ultimately led to Gaye's split from the record company in 1981. In "Vocal Authority and Listener Engagement: Musical and Narrative Expressive Strategies in the Songs of Female Pop-Rock Artists, 1993–95," Lori Burns draws on feminist theories of narrative authority in developing her own interpretive framework for analyzing vocal expression in songs by Tori Amos, PJ Harvey, Ani Difranco, and Alanis Morissette.

The remaining three authors also offer unique historical and music-analytic perspectives in their contributions. In "Ego and Alter Ego: Artistic Interaction between Bob Dylan and Roger McGuinn," James Grier explores the work of Roger McGuinn as the foremost interpreter of the songs of Bob Dylan, not only illuminating McGuinn's distinctive formula for reinventing Dylan's folk songs as rock tracks in his mid-1960s cover versions with the Byrds but also showing how McGuinn so thoroughly assimilated Dylan's idiolect that he would sometimes "sound more like Dylan than Dylan" in his subsequent work as a solo performer. In what is probably the most overtly music-analytical of all the chapters, "A Study of Maximally Smooth Voice Leading in the Mid-1970s Music of Genesis," Kevin Holm-Hudson uses techniques of neo-Riemannian transformational theory to explain keyboardist Tony Banks's highly chromatic harmonic language, which was so crucial in defining Genesis's new sound in the wake of Peter Gabriel's departure from the group in 1975. Finally, in "'I'm Not Here, This Isn't Happening': The Vanishing Subject in Radiohead's *Kid A*," the book's only chapter to concentrate on a single album, Marianne Tatom Letts offers a close analysis of Radiohead's controversial turn-of-the-millennium release, suggesting that *Kid A* is best understood as a "resistant" concept album that challenges conventional notions of narrative and thematic unity.

The analysis of popular music has now been a part of scholarly discourse for more than twenty years. One consequence of the increased growth and continued expansion of this kind of writing is that a younger generation of scholars has fully joined the conversation along the way, raising new kinds of questions, developing fresh approaches, and focusing on different repertoires and artists. The current collection not only sounds out pop but does so from many directions and employing a wide variety of tools. In celebrating this diversity of repertories and analytical approaches, our hope is that these nine new essays will make a further contribution to our understanding of rock and pop.

Acknowledgments

WE WISH TO THANK Ernie Jackson for his expertise in setting all of the musical examples in this volume, and Richard Covach for his preparation of the index. Mark Spicer thanks the Research Foundation of the City University of New York for providing a grant to support his initial stages of work on this project in the summer of 2004. During the final stages of production, the costs of preparing the musical examples and the index were generously supported by a 2009 Publication Subvention Grant from the Society for Music Theory. We owe a special debt of gratitude to Chris Hebert, our acquisitions editor at the University of Michigan Press, who has been a constant source of encouragement and guidance throughout this book's long gestation period. Finally, we wish to thank the publishers listed below for permission to use excerpts from the songs as indicated.

CHAPTER 3

CHAPTER 4

CHAPTER 5

CHAPTER 7

"Bells for Her"
Written by Tori Amos

ONE ※ Leiber and Stoller, the Coasters, and the "Dramatic AABA" Form

JOHN COVACH

THE HISTORY OF ROCK AND ROLL is filled with stories: everybody who was involved in any way, it sometimes seems, has a story to tell about some important figure or event in rock's past. There is little debate among popular music scholars that Jerry Leiber and Mike Stoller played a crucial role in the early history of rock and roll. They were among the most important songwriters in the first decade of rock and also pioneered and developed the idea of the independent record producer.[1] They were involved in rhythm and blues in the early 1950s before the style crossed over onto the pop charts, writing songs and running the independent label Spark out of Los Angeles. They enjoyed regional success with acts such as Big Mama Thornton and the Robins, the second of which would be the precursor to the Coasters. Working for Atlantic Records, they figured into rock's explosion later in the decade, writing songs for Elvis Presley and others, and helped develop the new style of sweet soul in the early 1960s, a style that enjoyed considerable commercial success until the advent of the British invasion in early 1964.

Leiber and Stoller like to tell stories, and a favorite has to do with their first major success. While the details tend to change somewhat as the years go by, the gist of it goes something like this: Leiber calls Stoller and says, "Hey, we've got a hit record." Stoller says, "Great, what song?" Leiber says, "Hound Dog." Stoller says, "Hound Dog, the Big Mama Thornton record?" and Leiber says, "No, a version by some kid named Elvis Presley." Stoller says, "Elvis who?!"[2] Of course, Leiber and Stoller went on to write several more tunes for Elvis, mostly for his movies ("Jail-house Rock" is the classic among these), and the sense that they had the "hit maker's touch" did much to establish their reputation and credibility in the burgeoning field of youth music. In the period between 1954 and 1964, Leiber and Stoller penned songs for a host of artists besides Presley, including the Coasters, the Drifters, Ray Charles, and Ruth Brown, and produced records for the Coasters, the Drifters, and Ben E. King, among others.[3]

In the midst of such broad success in pop songwriting and producing, Leiber and Stoller's most interesting work may well be the records they made with the Coasters. In fact, their partnership with the Coasters provides rich ground on which one can see many musical and cultural trends of the 1950s and even the 1960s coming together. Perhaps most obviously, we have two white men writing songs about African-American culture for a black doo-wop group or, as Jerry Leiber has described it, "a white kid's take on a black kid's take of white society."[4] The Coasters' lead singer, Carl Gardner, has remarked on how puzzled he was that these two white guys could get it right about black culture so much of the time:

> Leiber and Stoller were writing black music, and these were two Jew-ish kids [who] knew my culture better than I knew my culture. And I said, "How do they do that?" You know, and I wondered and I thought about it: "How do they know what we do?" 'Cause every song they wrote was in our culture.[5]

Regarding the nature of their working relationship with the group, Leiber and Stoller give a lot of credit to the Coasters, who had the right to reject or modify ideas that the songwriters brought to them and whose theatrically influenced performances vividly brought the songs to life. Jerry Leiber remarks, "When we hit on something that was really in the ballpark—which was, like, theater, fun, universal—they were the best."[6] As scholars have noted for many years, race plays a central role in the history of rock and roll; the partnership of Leiber and Stoller and the Coasters further underscores the notion that the meeting of black and white cultures in the 1950s could be a complicated and multifaceted exchange. Indeed, this topic could serve as the focus of an extended study of Coasters music considered from cultural and social perspectives, which could provide much insight into the nature of such collaborative endeavors.[7] The present chapter, however, will not focus on this dimension of Coasters records, at least not overtly; instead, it will survey the formal structure of these tracks, zeroing in on a formal type that I call the "dramatic AABA form," an exceptional form within rock music that arose, it will be argued, as a direct consequence of the short, often comical tracks Leiber and Stoller wrote for the Coasters, tracks they called "playlets." In order to better understand the playlet, and the various formal solutions Leiber and Stoller employed to realize it in a series of records, it will be useful to establish a bit more historical context.

What Is the Secret of Your Success? Leiber and Stoller, the Coasters, and Hit Singles

Jerry Leiber was born in Baltimore (1933) and Mike Stoller on Long Island (1933), but both relocated to Los Angeles in the late 1940s as youngsters. Leiber had an inclination toward the theater, hanging around the Hollywood studios whenever he could, while Stoller had studied piano and musical composition formally (his first composition teacher had been film composer Arthur Lange); despite these differences, they both loved rhythm and blues (R & B) fervently and felt themselves drawn to African-American culture and music. They had their first success as songwriters in the Los Angeles rhythm and blues scene of the early 1950s, pitching their songs to local singers such as Big Mama Thornton and working with established musicians such as Johnny Otis. The duo soon became associated with record promoter Lester Sill, and with Sill they formed a small independent label called Spark Records. It was during these early years that Leiber and Stoller first met members of a black vocal group called the Robins, the group that would later become the Coasters. It was also at about this time that they began to expand their role in the record business beyond the confines of songwriting, acting as producers in the studio with Leiber coaching the singers and Stoller handling the arrangements and often playing piano on the tracks. In establishing their own label, they gained greater freedom than they might otherwise have had, and their use of this freedom would have significant consequences for the future of rock and roll.

Leiber and Stoller began to enjoy a series of West Coast R & B hits, especially with the Robins, but they were not successful in getting these records distributed nationally, a perennial problem for a small label in those days. These singles would ultimately stall on the charts. The brother of Atlantic Records owner Ahmet Ertegun, Nesuhi Ertegun, was based on the West Coast, charged with keeping an eye out for regional hits that Atlantic could license for national distribution.[8] Nesuhi tipped off Atlantic's Jerry Wexler, and this led to Atlantic re-releasing the Robins' "Smokey Joe's Café" in late 1955.[9] As a Spark record, "Smokey Joe's Café" had hit number 122 on the national R & B charts, but as an Atlantic release it went to number 10 nationally and even placed as high as number 79 on the pop charts as well. Wexler had Atlantic buy Spark, with the larger label taking over the rights to the catalog; he then signed Leiber and Stoller to Atlantic as independent producers. The duo no longer had to worry about running a label; Wexler had given them a license to write and produce records. This new arrangement did not sit well with all of the Robins, however, and the group split up, with lead singer Carl Gardner and bass Bobby Nunn forming the Coasters (short for West Coasters) together with Billy Guy and Leon Hughes. Initially Leiber and Stoller recorded Coasters records at Master Recorders in Los Angeles, using many of the same studio musicians as before (including the master jazz guitarist Barney Kessel), but after the double-sided success of "Searchin'" and "Young Blood"—both of which hit number 1 on the R & B charts and broke into the Top 10 on the pop charts—they relocated to New York. The New York sessions, with Atlantic's Tom Dowd now behind the mixing board, produced a string of hit records starting with "Yakety Yak" in 1958, which topped both the pop and R & B charts and introduced the trademark sax playing of King Curtis. The follow-up singles "Charlie Brown" and "Poison Ivy" did almost as well in 1959, although subsequent records tended to cross over less forcefully with the exception of 1961's "Little Egypt," which hit number 23 on the pop charts and number 16 on the R & B charts.

How Do They Do That? Playlets, Form, and the Dramatic AABA

Not all of the Coasters sides recorded with Leiber and Stoller were playlets. The Robins had enjoyed a number 1 R & B hit in 1950 with "Double Crossing Blues," and it is thus easy to understand why the Coasters were unwilling to completely break with the R & B vocal group tradition.[10] Consequently, there are several Coasters tracks that seem to have little to do with their better-known playlet records. Having acknowledged such exceptions, however, it is fair to say that the Coasters are mostly remembered for the playlets. The term was coined by Leiber and Stoller, and they think of playlets as songs that act out a story in the manner of a radio play, often using a wide range of musical styles and sometimes even sound effects to enhance the drama and story, which is almost always humorous. The first playlet was "Riot in Cell Block #9," recorded by the Robins in 1954 and inspired by the radio drama *Gangbusters*. As its title suggests, the song tells the story of a prison uprising, sketching a colorful set of characters along the way and reinforcing the narrative with sirens and gunshots, presumably taken from standard sound effects recordings of the day. Given Leiber's interest in acting, Stoller's interest in film scores and concert music, and the gifts for comedic performance possessed by the Robins and Coasters, the playlet seems to have been almost inevitable. While Leiber and Stoller most often refer to the radio play as a model, in live performances (many of which survive on film) there was also a certain amount of Broadway and Hollywood performance practice in these songs, especially "Along Came Jones" and "What Is the Secret of Your Success?"

Figure 1.1 provides an overview of the different formal types that can be found among Coasters singles. The figure lists over twenty sides that range from 1954 to 1961, starting with some of the Robins songs and containing all the Coasters hits written by Leiber and Stoller.[11] Simple verse forms are listed first; these are songs that simply repeat a single verse structure over and over again, often with new lyrics but with no chorus. Simple verse forms often include a refrain, either at the beginning or end of the verse, serving as a kind of "minichorus" and often containing the song's hook.[12] In "Yakety Yak," for instance, the refrain is "yakety yak, don't talk back," placed at the end of each verse. The simple verse-chorus form is similar to simple verse except that now there is a chorus, although this chorus is sung over the same music as the verse. For those unfamiliar with the two songs listed in the example, consider Joe Turner's "Shake, Rattle, and Roll," which uses the same twelve-bar blues progression throughout as the harmonic structure of both verses and choruses. When the music supporting the chorus is not the same as in the verses, the resulting form is a contrasting verse-chorus form. Those unfamiliar with the songs listed in figure 1.1 might consider the Ronettes' "Be My Baby" or the Beatles' "Penny Lane," both of which have very clear choruses that contrast strongly with the verses.

The AABA form is a favorite among Tin Pan Alley composers, and the most conventional version of this form runs thirty-two measures in length, with four eight-bar phrases making up the four sections.[13] The AABA form consists of two verses, a bridge, and a verse (note that there is no chorus).[14] As in the simple verse form, a refrain is often found in the verses of AABA forms, especially in songs composed during the Brill Building days, and that refrain is often where the hook is located. Early

Simple verse (often with refrain)
> Riot in Cell Block #9 (Robins), Framed (Robins), Yakety Yak, What Is the Secret of Your Success?, The Shadow Knows, Turtle Dovin'* (refrain or chorus?)

Simple verse-chorus
> One Kiss (Robins), Keep On Rolling

Contrasting verse-chorus
> Wrap It Up (Robins), One Kiss Led To Another, Searchin', Along Came Jones, Run Red Run, [Turtle Dovin'*]

AABA
> Whadaya Want? (Robins), Charlie Brown, Sorry But I'm Going To Have To Pass, Three Cool Cats, This Is Rock and Roll, Young Blood* (refrain or chorus?)

Compound AABA (incipient)
> Poison Ivy, What About Us, [Young Blood*]

Dramatic AABA
> Smokey Joe's Café (Robins), Down in Mexico, Little Egypt

Figure 1.1. Formal types in Coasters/Leiber and Stoller songs

Beatles hits are overwhelmingly AABA forms, and noting this form is one way we can document the influence of American Brill Building pop on early Lennon-McCartney songs.[15] If a song has a chorus, that chorus is always the focus of the tune, but when a chorus is not present, as is the case with an AABA song, the focus is on the verses. The bridge in an AABA form is often so subordinate that it serves only as a way to get away from the verse and allow it to be reintroduced as fresh; consequently, many listeners cannot easily remember the bridges of AABA songs. Many who know the song, for instance, can easily recall the verses to "Charlie Brown," but most will have at least some difficulty recalling the bridge.

In the Coasters tracks listed under compound AABA in figure 1.1, each verse contains a refrain that resists being subordinated within the verse and seems to approach being a self-standing chorus. Full-fledged compound AABA forms employ a clear verse and chorus for each of the A sections, with contrasting music constituting the B section. Examples can be found in the 1960s—the Phil Spector/Righteous Brothers track "You've Lost That Lovin' Feelin'" is a good example—and the form became almost the default form of choice in much 1970s rock. In these Coasters tracks, however, one can see the AABA form beginning to pull away from the simpler thirty-two-bar model, mostly under the force of a refrain that seems to have outgrown its role within the structural confines of the verse. But the verses of these songs are not yet clearly compound AABA, so the term *incipient* is used to mark this distinction.

Figure 1.1 shows that the Coasters sides employ all of the typical forms associated with popular music. A few of the tracks—"Smokey Joe's Café," "Down in Mexico," and "Little Egypt"—employ a novel formal type not found elsewhere in rock (or if it can be found it is certainly not common). This novel form I call the "dramatic AABA" in part because it seems to arise out of the dramatic requirements of the playlet idea. As mentioned earlier, not all Coasters songs are playlets; it should be noted in addition that not all playlets employ dramatic AABA form. It will become clear, however, that the dramatic AABA form, when it is present, is employed in the service of the unfolding narrative of the song concerned and its structure presents an interesting twist on the well-worn AABA design. Perhaps most significant, the dramatic AABA form elevates the bridge section to greater prominence than it has in other AABA forms. A bridge section (or B section) is usually subordinate to the verses (or A sections), and even in a compound AABA the bridge (B) is subordinate to the verse-chorus pairs (A). But in a dramatic AABA form, the bridge emerges as the narrative climax of the song: the first two A sections develop the story, the bridge (B) is the culmination, and the last A section serves as a kind of epilogue. The dramatic AABA form thus inverts the relationship of the A sections to the bridge (B); rather than being a section that simply serves to provide contrast in order to make the return of the A section seem fresh, the bridge becomes the most important section in the tune. In order to see this more clearly, let us take a closer look at two instances of the dramatic AABA form, beginning with "Down in Mexico" from 1956.

A Dance I Never Saw Before: "Down In Mexico"

In a recording session at Master Recorders in Los Angeles on 11 January 1956, the Coasters were able to record four Leiber and Stoller songs. "Turtle Dovin'" and "Down in Mexico" were released on Atlantic's Atco label in February, while "One Kiss Led to Another" and "Brazil" were released in July.[16] Of these four songs, only "Down in Mexico" and "One Kiss Led to Another" can really be considered playlets. "One Kiss Led to Another" tells the story of a couple that cannot get much done but kissing despite their attempts to do otherwise, and the "Down in Mexico" story of adventure south of the border will be discussed subsequently. The lyrics to "Turtle Dovin'" do not develop a story line but rather explore various ways to describe a woman who prefers staying home with her lover to going out. "Brazil" is a somewhat traditional song, set to a Latin theme, that waxes nostalgic over happier romantic times in Brazil.[17] In terms of form, "Turtle Dovin'" has a simple verse form, while the form of "Brazil" is largely episodic, even if much of the music is based on a chromatic inner-voice figure that rises from perfect fifth to augmented fifth to major sixth and back down again above the roots of E-flat and F minor chords respectively. Of the playlets recorded in this session, "One Kiss Led to Another" is a contrasting verse-chorus form while "Down in Mexico" employs the dramatic AABA. The four songs from this single session underscore the idea that not all Coasters songs are playlets and not all playlets use the dramatic AABA form.

Carl Gardner handles the lead vocals on "Down in Mexico," backed by the other Coasters. The band for these sessions included jazz guitarist Barney Kessel and saxophonist Gil Bernal, as well as Mike Stoller on the piano. Figure 1.2 provides a formal diagram for the song and shows how "Down in Mexico" employs the dramatic AABA structure. The A sections are verses that consist of two eight-bar sections, both of which are built on a simple harmonic foundation. In the first of these sections, the harmony stays on the tonic of E-flat minor, moving to the dominant for bars seven and eight, and in the second verse section the harmony alternates between the tonic and subdominant. The lyrics for the first verse section change with each of the three verses, while the lyrics for the second section remain the same from verse to verse. The use of the same text in the second part of each verse suggests that this section might be thought of as a chorus. But in terms of the rhetoric of the song these second sections are neither the focus nor the hook of the song. Even if they are considered extended refrains—that is, "choruslike" without constituting a distinct section—one might still expect these sections to provide more of a focus point. Since such focus does not occur, this verse will be considered to be in two parts, with the second part acting as a refrain might but with none of the rhetorical effect within the form.

The lyrics in the first section of each verse move the story forward: in verse 1, we hear about a bar in Mexico run by a guy named Joe where both the food and the drinks are spicy. Gardner delivers the lead vocal as the other Coasters offer textless harmonic accompaniment and Kessel interjects bluesy guitar riffs. The second part of the verse features a change of texture, as the strummed nylon-string guitar comes to the front of the texture along with the maracas and a call-and-response arises between Gardner and the other Coasters. The lyrics tell us all about Joe, who wears a "red bandana" and plays a "blues piana." In the second verse, our protagonist asks Joe when the fun begins, and Joe winks and says, "Man, be cool." The second section of this second verse reprises the colorful description of Joe.

The focus of the song—the point to which everything leads dramatically—is the central B section. The percussion instruments now come to the fore, beating out an insistent rhythm as a low riff leading from B♭ to E♭ is repeated every two measures. It seems clear that a floor show has begun, as a woman emerges and begins to dance for our protagonist, who is taken somewhat by surprise. Gardner delivers each line, followed by the rest of the group chanting "in Mexico." The climax of the section occurs at the end of this bridge as the accompaniment stops and Gardner sings "and then she did a dance I never saw before." It is clear from the lyrics, as well as the primitive, almost ritualistic quality of the accompaniment, that something even hotter than the drinks and chili sauce has just transpired. The last verse acts as an epilogue. In the first half the protagonist recommends the club to anyone who might be down in Mexico, while the second half reprises the vivid description of Joe. The introduction to "Down in Mexico" establishes the atmosphere of a south of the border strip club in the song to follow, with languid sax riffs from Bernal answered by moaning guitar riffs from Kessel. The ending of the song picks up on these riffs again as Gardner goes into a speaking voice to urge listeners to "get your kicks in Mexico."[18]

As figure 1.2 illustrates, the AABA structure of this playlet is clearly delineated. As mentioned earlier, it is the way in which the B section (bridge) of this song is elevated to the point of focus that is exceptional. The verse sections in conventional AABA forms are the focus of the song, and these often feature refrains that act as the song's hook. The chorus in the verse-chorus pair found in the A sections of compound AABA forms are typically the focus of that kind of song. In AABA and compound AABA forms, bridges typically provide contrast and do not draw significant attention to themselves. But in the dramatic AABA form found in "Down in Mexico" the bridge is the focus of the song: the first two verses provide a buildup to the bridge while the last verse provides a wind-down from the climax provided at the end of the bridge. In "Down in Mexico," the moment when the dancer does the "special dance" at the end of the bridge is the dramatic goal around which the entire song is oriented. Leiber and Stoller take a familiar song form and invert its rhetorical structure in the service of the narrative.

	0:00–0:21 **Intro**	6 mm., 2 mm. rubato + 4 mm. in time
A	0:21–0:57 **Verse 1 w/refrain**	16 mm., 8 mm. verse + 8 mm. refrain
A	0:57–1:32 **Verse 2 w/refrain**	(same as verse 1)
B	1:32–2:06 **Bridge**	16 mm., eight 2 mm. phrases
A	2:06–3:13 **Verse 3 w/refrain**	16 mm., then vamp and fade on intro material

Figure 1.2. Formal diagram for "Down in Mexico"

Rhymes with "Row": "Little Egypt"

Another example of the dramatic AABA form can be found in "Little Egypt," a playlet recorded on 9 February 1961 in the Atlantic studios in New York, a little more than five years after "Down in Mexico" and on the other side of the country. By the time "Little Egypt" was recorded, the Coasters' membership had shifted somewhat. In 1956, Gardner was joined by Leon Hughes, Billy Guy, and Bobby Nunn. By 1961, Gardner and Guy were singing with Cornell Gunter, Earl "Speedo" Carroll, and Will "Dub" Jones. At least two other songs were recorded at the same session: "Keep on Rolling" (which was the B-side to "Little Egypt") and "Girls Girls Girls (Part II)." Neither of these is a playlet.

While "Little Egypt" is in the dramatic AABA form, "Girls Girls Girls (Part II)" is cast in a fairly conventional AABA form, with a short introduction and a partial reprise consisting only of a single A section that features a King Curtis saxophone solo.[19] The form of "Keep On Rolling" is an interesting blend of the simple verse-chorus and AABA forms. It employs the standard twelve-bar blues structure throughout. The first two verses use contrasting lyrics and feature the call-and-response interjection of "keep on rolling" by the backup vocalists. The third verse forgoes the call-and-response, using fresh lyrics and creating a sense of contrast. The fourth verse employs new lyrics but returns to the texture of the first two verses. The form thus suggests something like chorus, chorus, verse, chorus, although the use of the term *chorus* in this instance is very liberal. The insertion of a somewhat contrasting verse after two choruses suggests the AABA layout. As was the case with the session that produced "Down in Mexico," the songs recorded during these later sessions were not all of one type or design.

Figure 1.3 provides a formal diagram for "Little Egypt," and the dramatic AABA form is clearly in evidence. After an introduction featuring a carnival barker inviting patrons to see the show, accompanied by music

0:00–0:16	**Intro**	4 mm., spoken intro begins and then 4 mm. follow, ending with gong
A 0:16–0:58	**Verse 1 w/refrain**	24 mm., 16 mm. verse + 8 mm. refrain
A 0:58–1:39	**Verse 2 w/refrain**	(same as verse 1)
B 1:39–1:55	**Bridge**	8 mm., chromatic ascent @ 1 m.
A 1:55–2:50	**Verse 3 w/refrain**	24 mm., same as verses 1 & 2, plus fade on refrain

Figure 1.3. Formal diagram for "Little Egypt (Ying Yang)"

that is vaguely exotic and terminated by the striking of a gong, the song proper begins.[20] The lyrics revisit a similar story to the one we encountered in "Down in Mexico," but these turn out to have a few new twists. As before, the first two verses advance the story, leading to the focus of the song in the B section and a last verse that serves as an epilogue to round out the form. In this case, the second section of each verse is clearly a refrain. Harmonically, the first part of the verse moves from tonic in E major during the first four bars to subdominant in the next four and then dominant for four more bars; the refrain provides four bars of subdominant followed by four of tonic. The lyrics in the first verse describe the protagonist taking his seat as the show begins; the second verse describes the dancer's appearance and some of the suggestive dance moves. The action heats up in the B section, where the dance drives toward its climax as the accompanying series of chords rise chromatically in parallel motion from tonic toward the dominant. The last verse provides a surprise: we learn that the dancer and the protagonist are now happily married and living a life of domestic bliss with seven kids.[21]

In terms of the use of dramatic AABA form in "Little Egypt," the many close similarities to "Down in Mexico" can be seen clearly. The most important is the elevation of the bridge to the focal point of the song. But "Little Egypt" offers a few features we did not see in the other dramatic AABA song, perhaps the most prominent of which is the rhyme scheme that plays out in the lyrics. Leiber and Stoller structure the lyrics so that each line in all three verses rhymes with "row." Thus, in the first verse we get "low" and "bow." Initially there is nothing particularly noteworthy about the rhymes, but when the same rhyme continues in the second verse with "toe," "slow," and "show," the listener is alerted that something special is going on. Once one expects the rhymes to continue, the lyrics not only tell a tale but also play on the listener's expectations as he or she waits for the rhyme to align with the narrative unfolding of the story. In the last verse, Leiber and Stoller have as much fun with the rhymes as they seem to be having with the story: we get "anymo'," "sto'," and "flo'," all delivered in this abbreviated way to keep the game going.[22]

A second feature of the song underscores the good-natured fun and even corniness of the story. The group employs the "chipmunk" technique first developed by guitarist Les Paul and used most famously to create the voices of the cartoon Chipmunks. The technique involved recording a voice or instrument at half speed on a reel-to-reel tape recorder. When the tape is played back at full speed, the sound is sped up and sounds an octave higher.[23] The high voices at the end of "Little Egypt" are meant, of course, to portray the little children mentioned in the lyrics and were likely done by the Coasters themselves. These chipmunk voices sing along with the refrain and then trade licks with King Curtis's stuttering saxophone riffs, lending a sense of silliness to the ending that defuses any shock some listeners might have had with the sexy dancing described earlier.

Comparing "Little Egypt" to "Down in Mexico" in terms of formal design and story theme, one finds a lot of similarity. But there is also something there that is emblematic of the change that came over rhythm and blues as rock and roll developed out of it. "Down in Mexico" is close enough to hokum blues generally that it would have been tough to sell on white radio if it were not for the clearly comedic element, an element that also made it tough to produce a worthwhile cover version. But while "Down in Mexico" makes no effort to cover its tracks in terms of its sexual content, "Little Egypt" becomes thoroughly domesticated both literally and figuratively. In a kind of early 1960s version of the Beatles' later "Ob-La-Di, Ob-La-Da," a strong attraction born of wild nightlife results in a traditional, *Leave It to Beaver* kind of domestic bliss. Mike Stoller has remarked that even if "Little Egypt" was not as popular as the playlets "Yakety Yak" and "Charlie Brown" it was "more interesting in its construction." He adds that the track was the "epitome of the comic playlets" but also that it was "the last word in that bag."[24] While it might have been the last word for Leiber and Stoller in an aesthetic sense, it was not the historical last word. In fact, the idea of the playlet had already been taken up in teenage death-fascination records such as "Tell Laura I Love Her" and "Teen Angel." The most notorious of these so-called splatter platters or death disks was the Shangri-Las' "Leader of the Pack," which pushed the boundaries of good taste while topping the charts in late 1964. While this record was not produced by Leiber and Stoller (Shadow Morton has that dubious distinction), it was released on Red Bird, a label they established after leaving Atlantic in 1963.[25]

The form of "Leader of the Pack" is a slightly altered version of the dramatic AABA form that appears in the Coasters records discussed earlier. The change involves the presence of three verses before the focal B section rather than two verses as was seen in "Down in Mexico" and "Little Egypt." As figure 1.4 shows, the first verse starts off quietly with a call-and-response dialogue between the lead singer and the other Shangri-Las. By the end of this verse, guitar and drums have joined the piano and the sound of a revving motorcycle engine launches the track into full swing. The next two verses unfold the story of young lovers who are separated because the cycle-riding boyfriend is "from the wrong side of the tracks" and misunderstood by adults. The story reaches its climax in the central section as young Jimmy tears off on his cycle in a rage, only to be killed in an accident. The last verse, as was seen in the Coasters examples, acts as a kind of epilogue. The song created a scandal with its use of sounds depicting the crash and the screams that accompany them, which many found offensive and even disturbing. None of this outcry did much to dampen the song's commercial success, however, although the record was banned on several radio stations. This is a legacy Leiber and Stoller likely did not envision when they were developing their playlets with the Coasters, but "Leader of the Pack" has a clear claim to the playlet lineage nonetheless.

Probably the more important legacy of the Leiber and Stoller/Coasters partnership is the musical ambition the Coasters tracks embrace. Leiber and Stoller were not alone in raising the bar when it came to clever or sophisticated rock lyrics—Chuck Berry certainly deserves part of that credit—but when it comes to stylistic eclecticism nothing really compares to the playlets. Leiber and Stoller's use of orchestral instru-

A	0:00–0:32	**Verse 1 w/refrain**	16 mm., begins with spoken dialogue between lead vocal and backups, ends with motorcycle sounds
A	0:32–1:02	**Verse 2 w/refrain**	16 mm., now with full band
A	1:02–1:32	**Verse 3 w/refrain**	(same as verse 2)
B	1:32–1:53	**Bridge**	11 mm., leads to motorcycle crash
A	1:53–2:33	**Verse 4 w/refrain**	16 mm., quieter and dirgelike
	2:33–2:49	**Ending**	16 mm. and fade

Figure 1.4. Formal diagram for "Leader of the Pack"

ments in records they produced for Ben E. King and the Drifters in the early 1960s also showed an ambitious willingness to blend classical music ideas with rhythm and blues. The most oft-cited instance of this is the Drifters' "There Goes My Baby," which Atlantic's Jerry Wexler refused to release at first because he thought it sounded like a radio stuck between classical and R & B stations.[26] The use of tympani and strings—the latter playing classical-sounding thematic lines and not simply providing a soft background pad—pushed the boundaries of pop in its day.

Leiber and Stoller's work served as an example to the songwriters and producers who followed them, including Carole King and Gerry Goffin, Phil Spector, Brian Wilson, and the Beatles, demonstrating that rock music could be more than just disposable music. A line of development tracing pop and rock's increasing ambitions to musical sophistication can be followed from the Coasters' playlets to the Drifters' sweet soul, Phil Spector's Wall of Sound, Brian Wilson's ambitious surf music, the Beatles' *Sgt. Pepper's Lonely Hearts Club Band,* and beyond. As strange as it seems at first, the roots of the ambitious concept albums of the 1970s— albums such as Yes's *Tales from Topographic Oceans* (1973), Jethro Tull's *Thick as a Brick* (1972), or Emerson, Lake, & Palmer's *Tarkus* (1971)— can be traced back to "Riot in Cell Block #9." Ironically, the commercial successes for Leiber and Stoller were less frequent after the mid-1960s. Their songs continued to be performed by various artists, but they had less participatory influence in the new directions popular music was heading than they had experienced in rock and roll's first ten years. Their work endured even if their professional profile began to recede somewhat. One of their biggest hits of the later years was Peggy Lee's "Is That All There Is?," which went to number 11 in 1969. The duo went on to work with various musicians on various projects, producing the debut album by Stealer's Wheel in 1973, which contained the Top 10 hit "Stuck in the Middle with You." In 1994, Leiber and Stoller's songs were collected for a Broadway show called *Smokey Joe's Café.* The show debuted on Broadway in 1995 and in London the next year, and its continued success has brought the songs of Leiber and Stoller—including many Coasters songs—to the attention of a new generation.

NOTES

An earlier version of this chapter was presented at the International Association for the Study of Popular Music (U.S.) conference at the University of Virginia in Charlottesville, 16 October 2004. Thanks to Portia Maultsby and Venise Berry for their helpful reactions to that earlier paper.

1. Historical accounts of Leiber and Stoller can be found in Robert Palmer, *Baby, That Was Rock and Roll: The Legendary Leiber and Stoller* (New York: Harcourt Brace Jovanovich, 1978); and Ken Emerson, *Always Magic in the Air: The Bomp and Brilliance of the Brill Building Era* (New York: Penguin, 2005). The booklet that accompanies the two-compact-disc Coasters anthology *50 Coastin' Classics* (Rhino, 1992) contains a historical essay by Robert Palmer, as well as an interview with Leiber and Stoller by Randy Poe that features remarks from the duo on each song contained in this collection.

2. Mike Stoller tells this story in the second episode, "In the Groove," of the ten-part Public Broadcasting Service (PBS) series *Rock & Roll*, produced by the television station WGBH (South Burlington, VT: WGBH, 1995); this episode was written by Vicki Bippart and Daniel McCabe. Much of Leiber and Stoller's understanding of their roles in rock history can be drawn from the interview clips found in this episode, as well as in the other ten-part rock documentary of the same year, *The History of Rock 'n' Roll* (Time-Life Video, 1995). Perhaps as a result of these documentaries being made at almost the same time, the stories Leiber and Stoller tell are often contained in both series and are generally consistent on all points at which they intersect. With regard to this particular story, Ken Emerson reports that Stoller heard the news of the Presley hit on returning to New York from a belated honeymoon trip on the *Andrea Doria* in the summer of 1957. Stoller and his wife were among the over one hundred passengers that were rescued when the ship collided with another ship off the Nantucket coast (Emerson, *Always Magic in the Air,* 1).

3. Palmer, *Baby, That Was Rock and Roll*, provides a chronological list of records produced by Leiber and Stoller, beginning with the first sessions in 1953 and extending through 1976 (128–31).

4. Jerry Wexler and David Ritz, *Rhythm and the Blues: A Life in American Music* (New York: Knopf, 1993), 134.

5. "In the Groove," approximately 5:00 and forward.

6. Ibid., approximately 8:00 and forward.

7. In an essay contained in the booklet accompanying the Coasters' release *50 Coastin' Classics*, Robert Palmer offers a series of brief observations about Coasters songs, arguing that part of their charm lies in the way they gently and almost covertly criticize the social attitudes of their day. He mentions "Along Came Jones," "Run Red Run," and "Shoppin' for Clothes," among others, as songs that address issues of race. Leiber has remarked that each song tended to focus on some social issue even though this was done in a humorous and nonconfrontational manner. Ken Emerson provides an insightful and detailed discussion of this dimension of Leiber and Stoller's work with the Coasters and others in *Always Magic in the Air,* 3–12.

8. For a historical account of Atlantic Records, see Charlie Gillett, *Making Tracks: Atlantic Records and the Growth of a Multi-Billion-Dollar Industry* (New York: Dutton, 1974); and Justine Picardie and Dorothy Wade, *Atlantic and the Godfathers of Rock and Roll* (London: Fourth Estate, 1993). Gillett's book also provides an extended account of Leiber and Stoller's involvement with Atlantic (145–70).

9. Wexler and Ritz, *Rhythm and the Blues,* 133.

10. "Double Crossing Blues" debuted on the *Billboard* Rhythm and Blues Chart in February 1950, going to number 1, where it stayed for nine weeks (the

single remained on the chart for twenty-two weeks overall). The group's previous record, "If It's So Baby," debuted a week earlier and rose as high as number 10. The group did not chart again nationally until the Atco release of "Smokey Joe's Café" in late 1955.

11. The songs listed in figure 1.1 are drawn from *50 Coastin' Classics* and form a representative sample of the fifty songs contained in that anthology.

12. The formal types discussed here are explained in greater detail in my article "Form in Rock Music: A Primer," in *Engaging Music: Essays in Music Analysis*, ed. Deborah Stein (New York: Oxford University Press, 2005), 65–76.

13. In this discussion, my use of the terms *verse* and *chorus* differs significantly from their use in discussions of American popular song composed in the first half of the twentieth century. In writing on that repertory, an entire AABA form is often viewed as a chorus and the section that introduces the chorus is thought of as the verse. To distinguish this usage from the one employed here for the discussion of rock and pop in the second half of the century, I use the terms *sectional verse* and *sectional chorus* in place of *verse* and *chorus* in reference to the earlier music. See my *What's That Sound? An Introduction to Rock and Its History*, 2nd ed. (New York: Norton, 2009), 25–28.

14. Note that "Young Blood" is marked with an asterisk in figure 1.1 and appears in the next category, compound AABA, in brackets. The verses of "Young Blood" include refrains that some might want to consider chorus sections. That interpretation is not preferred here, partly because these refrains begin on the move to IV within a twelve-bar blues framework. This standard structural design binds the verses and the refrains into one section. Those who might take these refrains as choruses will view the form as an incipient compound AABA form, as the latter form is defined subsequently. A similar situation arises with "Turtle Dovin'," where the refrains occur with the move to IV. There again simple verse is the preferred analysis with contrasting verse-chorus as an alternative.

15. I discuss the Beatles' use of AABA form in detail in my article "From Craft to Art: Formal Structure in the Music of the Beatles," in *Reading the Beatles: Cultural Studies, Literary Criticism, and the Fab Four*, ed. Ken Womack and Todd F. Davis (Albany: State University of New York Press, 2006), 37–53.

16. At this time, it was standard practice to record four songs in a single three-hour session. Leiber and Stoller have remarked that "Searchin'" was done quickly at the end of one such session in February 1957 simply to have a fourth song that might be used as a B-side later. Of course, "Searchin'" became the Coasters breakthrough pop single along with "Young Blood," which was also recorded at that session (see the booklet enclosed with *50 Coastin' Classics*, especially 22–23). "Down in Mexico" debuted on the *Billboard* Rhythm and Blues Chart in late March 1956, rising to number 8, while "One Kiss Led to Another" debuted in September of that same year and hit number 11.

17. Leiber and Stoller claim that this song was written for Carl Gardner because he kept asking them for a "classy" number. One suspects that Leiber and Stoller's solution is something of a send-up of the Latin supper club number of the day, especially when the first rhyme in the lyrics is "moon" and "June" (see the booklet enclosed with *50 Coastin' Classics*).

18. Not surprisingly, the director Quentin Tarantino chose to use "Down in

Mexico" on the soundtrack for his 2007 movie *Death Proof* (one-half of the *Grind-house* double feature), where the song serves as the perfect backdrop for the scene in which the character of Arlene, nicknamed "Butterfly" (played by Vanessa Ferlito), performs a steamy lap dance for Stuntman Mike (played by Kurt Russell).

　19.　The A sections of this song are built on the standard twelve-bar blues structure. There is a clever overlap between the first two A sections that reduces the length of the first A section to ten measures while the second goes to twelve measures.

　20.　One can only suppose that the use of the gong, as well as the lyrics "ying yang," fit with the generally "Eastern" sense of exoticism created in this song.

　21.　The Beatles were enthusiastic fans of the Coasters' records, and perhaps Paul McCartney had this song in mind when he wrote "Ob-La-Di, Ob-La-Da." For the reggae influence on this song, see Mark Spicer, "Desmond Dekker and the Globalization of Jamaican Music," paper presented at the conference New World Coming: The Sixties and the Shaping of Global Consciousness, Queen's University, Kingston, Ontario, 14 June 2007.

　22.　Continuing the speculation on the influence of this song on the Beatles, the lyrics of George Harrison's "Taxman" play this same rhyming game as the rhymes get more and more absurd. The possible taxes are on "street," "seat," "heat," and "feet."

　23.　Such things have been done almost effortlessly on digital equipment for almost thirty years. Using analog gear, this kind of tape manipulation requires a certain degree of technical skill and much patience.

　24.　See the booklet enclosed with *50 Coastin' Classics.*

　25.　Alan Betrock's *Girl Groups: The Story of a Sound* (New York: Delilah, 1982) offers an extended discussion of Red Bird, as well as the circumstances surrounding the writing of "Leader of the Pack" (see chapter 7 especially). The song was written by George "Shadow" Morton along with Brill Building veterans Jeff Barry and Ellie Greenwich.

　26.　Wexler and Ritz, *Rhythm and the Blues,* 136–37.

TWO ❧ "Only the Lonely"

Roy Orbison's Sweet West Texas Style

ALBIN ZAK

IN THE SUMMER OF 1960, Roy Orbison reached a level of public acclaim that he would sustain for the next several years, during which he produced the body of work that gained him a place in rock's canon and its Hall of Fame. In June of that year, "Only the Lonely" (Monument 421), his third released single on the Monument record label, rose to number 2 on the *Billboard* charts, remaining in the Top 40 for fifteen weeks. The record eventually sold some three million copies worldwide and was followed over the next several years by a string of hits that included "Running Scared" (Monument 438), "Crying" (Monument 447), and "Oh, Pretty Woman" (Monument 851), which reached the number 1 spot in September of 1964. "Only the Lonely" was the result of a years-long process of development during which Orbison released tracks on four different record labels and worked with a series of collaborators: songwriters, musicians, arrangers, and record producers. The track represents the crystallization of a set of stylistic habits that would turn up again and again in Orbison's recordings of the early to mid-1960s. These include a taste for asymmetrical phrasing, shifting harmonic rhythm, avoidance of a stylized refrain, a narrative trajectory leading to a dramatic climax in Orbison's upper vocal register, and lyrics expressing a mixture of heartbreak and hope. While Orbison draws from this matrix of stylistic hallmarks in various ways on subsequent tracks, traces of such features are also present on many of his earlier recordings, suggesting a developing sensibility that achieved its first full expression with "Only the Lonely." This essay presents a brief style history outlining signature elements of songwriting, arranging, performance style, and sonic representation in Orbison's work during the period 1956–64.[1]

Orbison wrote "Only the Lonely" with Joe Melson, a frequent collaborator at the time and a fellow West Texan. Though presented in a guise suitable to the teenage audience that had helped to fuel the rise of rock and roll, the song's honky-tonk affinities are apparent in its themes of loneliness and yearning, staples of the honky-tonk country music that emerged after World War II, music Orbison had heard since childhood. Often in the evenings his father, Orbie Lee Orbison, an itinerant oil-field worker, would play his guitar and sing the country songs of the day. "My first music was country," Orbison told one interviewer. "I grew up with country radio in Texas."[2] In another interview he elaborated: "I was influenced by country music and by ballads I'd heard during the War, like 'Born to Lose' and 'No Letter Today'."[3] When he was ten years old, his father took young Roy to see a performance by Lefty Frizzell, another Texan singer-songwriter then on the verge of national success. The impression of Frizzell's singing, and his Cadillac, would prove indelible. In 1954, his senior year in high school, Orbison expressed twin aspirations in the caption under his yearbook picture: "To lead a Western Band / Is his after school wish / And of course to marry / A beautiful dish."[4] In a friend's yearbook he signed his name "Roy (Lefty Frizzell) Orbison," and decades later he would take the name Lefty as his pseudonym in the Traveling Wilburys. In his mid-1960s tributes to other honky-tonk influences, Orbison recorded an album devoted entirely to songs by Hank Williams and another to those of Don Dixon.[5]

The recurrent themes of loneliness, pain, fear, and longing in songs such as "I'm Hurtin'" (Monument 433), "Running Scared," and "In Dreams" (Monument 806) reflect, too, Orbison's experience of growing up in Wink, Texas, a small town in the arid Permian Basin oil country of which his lasting impression was "football, oilfields, oil, grease, and sand."[6] One can imagine the young Orbison, sensitive and physically unimposing, spending endless hours, as he did, watching the screened images in Wink's Rig Theater, transported in imagination to exotic realms he would evoke later in recordings of songs such as Cyndi Walker's "Shahdaroba" (Monument 806) and his own "Leah" (Monument 467), longing for an improbable escape from West Texas and a fantasy of erotic salvation.[7] A failure at school sports, the only assured path to social acceptance, he found refuge and a few friends in musical activities: playing baritone horn in the marching band and singing in the

Wink High School chorus, glee club, and boys quartet. Orbison's musical talent was apparent early on. Singing and playing the guitar since the age of six, he won a talent contest at ten, appeared on radio by the age of twelve, and was playing on local television shows at seventeen. He formed his first band, the country-styled Wink Westerners, when he was thirteen, followed by the rock and roll Teen Kings with whom he would make his first record at Norman Petty's studio in Clovis, New Mexico.

There is more to "Only the Lonely," however, than this sketch of Orbison's childhood suggests. The track's refined pop sound invokes associations far from the hard life of the West Texas oil fields and the stylings of either Lefty Frizzell or Hank Williams. The singing is consistently sweet and focused across an impressive pitch range. The arrangement includes the strings and soft backing vocals more typical of a major-label pop arrangement. The recorded sound is far clearer and more polished than most 1950s rock and roll records. And the track's narrative structure has a touch of the operatic, albeit on a diminutive scale. Indeed, without knowledge of Orbison's roots, the track can sound "curiously timeless and placeless," as Colin Escott has put it.[8] Yet the combination of elements that makes the track difficult to situate is perhaps its most rock-and-roll characteristic. Coming from a member of rock and roll's first generation, and one of its first songwriters, "Only the Lonely" illustrates the range of influences that fed the early rock-and-roll musicians. For while, on the one hand, the big beat and rough-hewn sound of early rock-and-roll records demonstrate obvious affinities with rhythm and blues (R & B) and country records, and a marked stylistic break with the pop music mainstream, as rock and roll began to emerge as a distinct idiom it also demonstrated a patent lack of stylistic discrimination. It asserted an independent identity through a willingness to borrow widely, practically without regard for boundaries of style or genre; that is, the more it absorbed from other musical idioms, including major-label pop, the more it became itself, the melting pot, pawn shop, collage, or junkyard depending on one's point of view. Among the music to be heard on radio and jukeboxes in the 1950s, major-label pop remained ubiquitous; it simply had the widest geographic distribution. According to a childhood friend, Bobby Blackburn, Orbison as a teenager was partial to the vocal stylings of Frankie Laine, Guy Mitchell, and Rosemary Clooney; he also "loved Mitch Miller arrangements, especially the French horns."[9] Such stars symbolized a success that could pluck a young, usually poor, musician from his or her situation as if in a fairy tale. Thus, in addition to contemporary country fare, Orbison's first band, the Wink Westerners, played pop standards; an audience favorite was Glenn Miller's "In the Mood."

Among rock and roll's stylistic and aesthetic strata can be found whatever music had made an impression on a young musician's imagination or had struck the entrepreneurial fancy of an opportunistic record producer or record label owner. And for Orbison, as for Buddy Holly in Lubbock, Johnny Ace in Memphis, and indeed for the king himself, Elvis Presley, the lure of the pop ballad was strong. In his first sessions at Sam Phillips's Sun studio in 1954, Presley recorded croonerly versions of such standards as "Harbor Lights" (RCA CPL1-1349) and "Blue Moon" (RCA LPM 1254).[10] Never released by Phillips, these tracks were not part of rock and roll's initial public identity, which was represented—fearfully by some, opportunistically by others—as transgressive of established aesthetic standards.[11] But they offer clear evidence, behind the scenes and from the outset, of a stylistic range that would become publicly apparent as Presley's success grew and he moved on to RCA. Two years after his first Sun session, Presley would have a number 1 hit with a ballad, "Love Me Tender" (RCA 47-6643), whose soft intimacy and utter lack of a rock beat would seem to place it comfortably within the mainstream pop sphere. Johnny Ace's 1955 recording of "Pledging My Love" (Duke 136), though possessed of a certain roughness in sound characteristic of independent labels in the 1950s, nonetheless bears specific pop affinities. Its arrangement (by Johnny Otis) includes harplike figures in a piano and vibraphone doubling and, in the bridge, cool jazz improvisational flourishes from the saxophone and vibraphone. The tempo is a lugubrious slow drag, and Ace's vocal is smoothly seductive. And Buddy Holly, in the short span of eighteen months (1957–59), moved from the thrash guitar of "Peggy Sue" (Coral 61885) to a string-drenched crooning rendition of "True Love Ways" (Coral 62210). As his contemporaneous "Apartment Tapes" sketches demonstrate, he was not leaving behind his rock and roll spunk but, rather, expanding his recorded expression to include more of the elements of his musical universe.[12]

Phrase Structure in "Only the Lonely"

One of the key elements of Orbison's stylistic language, which turns up repeatedly in his best-known songs, is an elastic metric sensibility that shapes both phrases and larger structural units. Orbison employs such techniques as dropped or added beats, shifting harmonic rhythm, and elision in ways that dilute strophic repetition and contribute to the development of the miniature dramas that so often unfold in his record-ings. The resulting flow of phrases often has an unpredictable proselike quality that focuses attention on the track's dramatic trajectory. In "Only the Lonely," the phrase proportions are set in motion innocently by the backup singers' opening phrase, "Dum-dum-dum-*dum*-be-do-wah," whose pickup motive previews Orbison's entrance (example 2.1a). Fol-lowing this introduction, Orbison's first line begins similarly ("Only the *Lone*-ly"), and the pickup motive continues for the rest of the line ("know the *Way* I feel to-*Night*"), downbeats falling in the middle and at the end. The backup singers answer each of the lead vocal's phrases with echoes of the introduction, displaced now by one measure. That is, while their pickup gesture leads initially to the downbeat of the introduction's *first* full measure, in the verse it leads into the *second* measure, shifting the larger metrical stress pattern for the backing vocals 180 degrees out of phase with the introduction. In effect, these responses pace the lead as Orbison waits to begin each succeeding phrase until the six-beat back-ing vocal figure is finished. The call-and-response pattern thus extends the first line to fill a five-measure unit and sets the stage for a shift of ac-cent in the song's second line from "lonely" to "only," probing the sense of the song's title from a different perspective (example 2.1b).

a) Initial pickup motive

b) Verse 1

c) Continuation of Verse 1

Example 2.1. "Only the Lonely"

While the second line begins with the same words as the first, the lead vocal, having followed the pacing of the backing vocals through the first line, is forced to drop its pickup orientation and start the line squarely on the downbeat. The backing vocals retain the same temporal relationship with the lead and, because the melodic rhythm remains unchanged, the voices appear now to be in a different metric orientation from the rhythm section. Adding to the metric disorientation is the false impression of a two-beat extension to the second line's initial call-and-response pattern (i.e., "Only the lonely / dum-dum-dum-dum-be-do-wah"), even though there is no added time after the backing vocal response. The sense of an interpolated 6/4 measure is created, rather, by a shift in harmonic rhythm as the bass remains on the dominant chord for an extra two beats, drawn into the temporal orbit of the backing vocals' six-beat pattern and apparently shifting the following lead vocal phrase ("know this feelin' ain't right") to begin once more as a pickup. But are the chord changes falling on a newly oriented first beat or have they only shifted momentarily to the third beat of the measure? The effect is delightfully ambiguous. One might be tempted to hear the passage in terms of mixed meter, but if we stick to 4/4, as the drummer does, the downbeat returns to its original place in time for the buildup to the verse's climax. In other words, whether or not we wish to shift the bar lines around, the number of beats overall is consistent with a steady 4/4 (example 2.1c). In addition to the apparent metric shift, the song's first two lines present an irregular, unbalanced phrase sequence, for, although the second line is the same length as the first, starting it on the downbeat results in a six-measure unit. The first half of the twenty-four-measure verse, then, fills eleven measures divided into two uneven time units (5 + 6).

The second half of the verse shifts course in a number of ways. The singsong backing vocals drop out, their responsive role taken by a new sound texture that includes strings and vibraphone. The rhythmic groove shifts to stop-time, intensifying the emotional melodrama as the voice delivers each phrase unaccompanied. Metric order has been restored, and the eight-measure stop-time section, driven by another pickup motive cast now in quarter-note triplets, involves both voice and instruments in a gesture of rising pathos whose climax is reached finally via an emphatic applied dominant. Following the peak of the emotional crescendo, the verse ends somewhat abruptly with a five-measure phrase whose final measure serves, too, as the pickup for a reiteration of the song's introduction, the cool detachment of the backing vocals returning the track to its initial emotional temperature. Following the verse's initial eleven measures, then, the verse's second half takes up thirteen measures, divided into 8 + 5, making for an overall phrase sequence of 5 + 6 + 8 + 5.

The song's second verse follows a similar plan, but, characteristically for Orbison, the melody is varied to reflect the differences in lyric content and the rising action in the emotional narrative. The eight-measure stop-time section begins at a higher pitch than in the first verse (scale degree 3 instead of 1) and continues ever higher until Orbison, in an unaccompanied falsetto, makes an ardent, fatalistic plea acknowledging the risks of passion yet longing for it nonetheless ("Maybe tomorrow a new romance / No more sorrow, but that's the chance / *You* got to take"). The melodic peak reaches scale degree 5 at a twelfth above the opening and closing tonic pitch, making for an overall vocal range of more than two octaves. The melodic and expressive variation in the second verse creates an overarching dramatic line—etched in the vocal melody, lyric, and performance—leading ultimately to a poignant moment of utter aloneness, the singer's exposed vulnerability reflected in the falsetto voice. The song's strophic elements are thus overlaid with a longer narrative gesture that reflects the protagonist's expression of rising pathos. The resulting superposition, a layering of two musical time frames, adds an element of tension to the musical drama that resonates, at the formal level, with the sense of the song's lyrics and their enactment.

Subsequent Monument tracks often feature such rhythmic and phrase irregularities, melodic variation, and goal-directed motion in varying configurations. "Blue Angel" (Monument 425), for example, is in two sections, the first of which is heard only once. The second occurs twice, but the repeat is varied, and the variation includes an unaccompanied falsetto climax in much the same place as in "Only the Lonely." The song's second section also contains shifts of harmonic rhythm that appear to move the bar lines around at the whim of the song's internal rhymes, yet, again, the whole fits into the time frame of a steady 4/4. "I'm Hurtin'" follows the technique used in "Only the Lonely" of pacing the lead vocal with the backing vocals, which results in harmonic shifts from the outset. The verses fall into twelve-measure units, but the harmonic rhythm seems to indicate ten measures, two of which are in 6/4. Also, like "Only the Lonely," the track has two stop-time sections in which the lead vocal melody traces a pair of rising arpeggio figures. The second of these sections is varied such that each of the arpeggios rises to a higher peak than in the first, again ultimately reaching a uniquely climactic pitch.

One final example, "Running Scared," derives its entire thematic substance from this conceit of stop-time coupled with rising emotional intensity mirrored by rising tessitura. The track is in stop-time throughout, driven by a bolero-style rhythm with a gradually rising melodic line that reaches its zenith on the voice's last note as the singer is finally overwhelmed by the psychological toll exacted by his increasing apprehension at imagined rejection turned, at the last moment, to ecstatic fulfillment. Again, the formal design is unconventional: a repeated sixteen-measure period (although the repeat is shortened to fifteen measures, a common Orbison technique, as we shall see) followed by ten measures of subdominant harmony leading to a climactic cadence. Clearly, by 1960 Orbison had developed a set of musical-dramatic techniques that suited his expressive purposes, both as a songwriter and performer, and were flexible enough to work in a variety of unconventional song forms. Let us turn now to the recordings made prior to "Only the Lonely" in search of stylistic clues to the origins of what appeared, at the time of the track's release, to be the work of what one writer has called a "mysterious figure who . . . seemed to come from nowhere."[13]

Clovis and Memphis

Orbison's first released recording appeared on the Je-Wel label (JE-101).[14] Its two tracks, recorded 4 March 1956 at Norman Petty's studio in Clovis, New Mexico, included "Ooby Dooby," a song written by two of Orbison's classmates at North Texas State University, and a cover version of a doo-wop song, "Trying to Get to You," which was recorded originally by the Eagles and then Elvis Presley.[15] The session was underwritten by Chester Oliver, an oil company executive, and Weldon Rogers, a honky-tonk singer and disc jockey, who were partners in Je-Wel. Both men were based in Seminole, Texas, and their aim was to capitalize on local West Texas bands playing the newly emergent style that presented country-flavored songs with a more insistent rhythmic feel driven by drum kits and quicker tempi, the as yet unnamed music that would come to be known as the West Texas version of rockabilly. Apparently this session was the first outside booking in Petty's studio, which he had built with the proceeds from recordings of his trio leased to ABC-Paramount. The Norman Petty Trio, which comprised Petty himself on organ, his wife,

Violet Ann, on piano, and guitarist Jack Vaughn (all three sang as well), had several modest hits, the most successful of which was a version of Duke Ellington's "Mood Indigo" (Nor-Va-Jak 1313, 1954). Petty thus joined the independent engineers, producers, and studio owners whose remote locations relative to the mainstream pop music axis of New York and Los Angeles fed into the burgeoning stream of rock and roll a steady supply of unknown and unconventional young performers and songwriters. Unlike other independents, however, most of whom specialized in some form of R & B or country music, Petty was a purveyor of mainstream pop. His trio's recorded sound is clean and relatively high fidelity; the arrangements abound with buttery, mildly chromatic harmonies; the vocal styling is sweet; and the rhythm is a stiff, slightly forced swing. With this musical orientation, Petty seems to have been an unlikely rock-and-roll producer, but his refined sense of musical arrangement and sound made for fruitful collaborations with young musicians exploring new kinds of stylistic crossover and fusion. In 1956, in addition to the Orbison tracks, he recorded "Party Doll" and "I'm Sticking with You" for Buddy Knox, Jimmy Bowen, and their Rhythm Orchids group, and the following year he would begin his most extended and successful rock-and-roll collaboration with Buddy Holly, yet another young West Texan whose pop music leanings were well served by Petty's production style.[16]

Orbison and the Teen Kings re-recorded both "Ooby Dooby" and "Trying to Get to You" about a month later at Sam Phillips's Sun studio in Memphis, and a comparison of the Clovis and Memphis recordings illustrates something of Petty's sonic sense and its affective influence. Although the musical arrangements for both sessions are more or less identical, the Petty productions are darker in hue, the result of a more prominent low end and a fuller midrange of the frequency spectrum. While the Sun recordings have a brighter, almost brittle sonic edge, the Clovis recordings have a soft textural depth that affords the tracks a touch of mystery. On "Ooby Dooby," the result is a warm, relaxed swing driven by a controlled drum part behind which the guitar, bass, and mandolin create a sonic wash. By contrast, the Sun version is thinner texturally and possessed of a rhythmic urgency in its quicker tempo and the added rhythmic elements of slap-back echo on the voice and slapped bass, both virtual trademarks of the Sun sound.[17] Measuring in terms of stylistic contrast with contemporary mainstream pop music, we might say that the Sun version is a more characteristic example of early rock and roll. The Clovis version of "Trying to Get to You," on the other hand, has a dreamlike sonic surrealism. The introduction features a texture of electric guitar combined with electric mandolin heavily processed with tremolo. The quivering mandolin hovers in the background throughout the track, lending a sense of fragility to the sound. The snare drum, played with brushes, is distant, and the steadily pulsing bass and kick drum provide the voice with a pillowy cushion. The Sun recording is, again, much brighter and thinner in its midrange, undercutting Orbison's haunting vocal by diminishing its fullness of timbral presence. The thinner sonic texture also removes the deep bass pocket inhabited by the tremolo mandolin on the Clovis version; the result is less sonic depth of field and a diminished sense of the mystery imparted by the Clovis recording.

Aside from the differences in sound, both the Je-Wel and Sun recordings of "Trying to Get to You" offer an instructive glimpse of Orbison's elastic phrase sense. The song is cast in a conventional thirty-two-measure AABA form, and in both the original version and Presley's cover each of the song's four sections consists of eight measures of 4/4 time. Orbison, however, drops two beats toward the end of each verse—in the sixth bar of the eight-measure unit—rushing the phrase ending and effectively mirroring the sense of anticipation in the lyrics ("I been traveling night and day / Running all the way baby, trying to get to you"). In the bridge, again eight measures in the original, Orbison adds the two beats back as an extension to the first phrase. He then complicates the bridge's second phrase with an irregular harmonic rhythm, anticipating the final chord change by two beats. Although the original version sounds like it is clearly in 4/4 time, we might strip away some of the complex quirkiness of Orbison's version by thinking of it in 2/4, which makes for fifteen-measure verses balanced by a seventeen-measure bridge. This reading is suggested by the rhythm section's *una battuta* feel, and it removes the complications of mixed meter and shifting harmonic rhythm to highlight simply the sense of irregular phrasing that seemed to come naturally to Orbison. Similar metric alterations to cover songs may be heard in the Teen Kings' version of "St. Louis Blues" and in Orbison's 1963 recording of Stephen Foster's "Beautiful Dreamer" (Monument 830).[18]

Orbison returned to Clovis in 1957 for sessions that yielded the unreleased tracks "A True Love Goodbye," "An Empty Cup," and "Cat Called Domino," all written by Orbison himself. On the first two of these, we hear early traces of his mature style both in the lyrics and in the musical elements. In the lyrics for "A True Love Goodbye," recorded on 26

August 1957, he evokes a young couple's sense of loss at parting mixed with hopeful yearning for reunion. Using metric presentation to sharpen the focus on the song's title, the verses are arranged so as to set off the lyric "this was a true love goodbye" in a two-measure extension added to the end of the preceding eight-measure period, forming altogether a ten-measure verse. Characteristically, however, the verse ending is treated differently from one verse to the next. The first verse ending is elided with the following interlude as the chord progression from the track's introduction returns abruptly, overlapping the lead vocal's phrase ending. At the analogous point in the second verse, the two-measure extension at the end of the verse is elongated to four measures, allowing the full sense of the tagline to sink in as the music transitions to the song's bridge. The bridge exhibits a couple of features common to many later tracks, especially in other bridge sections: a repeated bolero-type rhythmic motive and a goal-directed harmonic progression that reaches the dominant chord via its own applied dominant.[19] Again an unreleased recording of the song made later the same year at Sun exhibits differences in production style, most notably in the musical arrangement. The backing singers and soft clarinet obbligato of the Clovis version, the kinds of textural touches that would turn up on the Monument recordings, are stripped away on the Sun recording, and there is less melodic variation in the lead vocal part. As in the other comparisons, the Sun approach (produced in this case by Jack Clement and Bill Justis) leans toward a straightforward rock-and-roll style lacking the quirky hybrid nuances of the Petty productions.

The most complex track recorded in Clovis, "An Empty Cup," combines elision, mixed meter, and irregular phrase lengths in an early attempt at the sort of overarching drama encountered frequently in Orbison's later work. Other similarities include internal rhymes, a persistent bolero motive in the bass, and phrase climaxes approached via an applied dominant. The metric ambiguity begins with the lead vocal's opening phrases, four two-measure units forming apparently an eight-measure segment that turns around on the dominant in the eighth measure preparing for a repeat. The impression is confirmed by the vocal phrase beginning in the second half of the eighth measure ("She was to meet me"), which is similar to the pickup phrase that opened the verse. But instead of moving to the tonic in the next measure, as a repeat would indicate, the turnaround is delayed as the harmony remains on the dominant for an extra measure (example 2.2). The phrase's emphasis pattern is suddenly unclear, and the following seven measures turn out not to be

Example 2.2. "An Empty Cup," phrase design of the verse

the expected repeat of the first phrase but new material (one measure of which is extended from four to six beats, shown as $12/8 + 6/8$ in the example). (The metric extension, like those in "Only the Lonely," is dictated by the response of the backing singers.) Harmonically, this second part of the verse reaches its culmination via a V/V to V phrase ending followed by a reprise of the verse's opening music. The anticipated parallel period, then, turns out instead to be a slightly unbalanced ABA whose middle section represents an interruption and its third section a delayed resolution. Put another way, the B segment initially interrupts, but ultimately delivers, the expected repeat of the opening A.

Later in the track, the music from the B segment returns in a new context as the song's bridge passage, at which point an alternate interpretation of the verse is suggested retrospectively. The false turnaround, which causes the interruption, is in fact an elision, an overlap serving as both phrase ending and beginning. While the first verse appears to be an eight-measure opening followed by a deceptive continuation, the music now suggests that it might be heard alternatively as a seven-measure opening phrase followed by an eight-measure phrase that begins on the downbeat of measure eight. This is precisely how the same music is presented when it returns as the bridge, its metric sense clarified by the verse's final A, a closed eight-measure section that sets up the bridge's downbeat as an unambiguous new beginning. Having clarified that much, as an added twist Orbison alters the bridge a bit by adding a second extended measure of six beats, again paced by the responses of the backing vocals. Such variation would become common in Orbison's unusual narrative structures, where exact repeats are relatively rare and even refrains are treated with some degree of variation. These ambiguities and asymmetries create a sense of unpredictable, evolving development that reflects the sense of dramatic unfolding in the song's story line. The song's phrases respond to their changing surroundings: the sense of the lyric, the comment of the backing singers, an extra breath taken by the lead voice. Further, the ambiguity in the music mirrors the protagonist's uncertainty as he awaits his date at a drive-in movie while it gradually dawns on him that he has been stood up. Although the quality of the lyrics is not up to Orbison's later work (in a valiant but clumsy attempt at metaphor, the lyrics compare the empty cup to the protagonist's emotional emptiness, "Just like this Coke, my love is gone"), and he had yet to hit on his upper-register climax (the song ends, rather, in the low register), "An Empty Cup" is an instructive early instance of many of the techniques Orbison would refine over the next few years.

Orbison and the rest of the Teen Kings went to Memphis for their first Sun recording session hopeful of joining in the success of the stable of rockabilly stars Phillips had assembled: Carl Perkins, Jerry Lee Lewis, Johnny Cash, and the recently departed Presley. Their initial attempt, the re-recorded "Ooby Dooby" (Sun 242), scored an immediate if modest hit. Although "Trying to Get to You" was also recut, it was not released. Rather, the B-side for the "Ooby Dooby" single was another up-tempo song called "Go! Go! Go!," cowritten by Orbison and the Teen Kings' drummer, Billy Pat Ellis. The song, described by Ellis as a rocked-up version of Hank Williams's "Kaw-Liga" (MGM 11416, 1953), is a sort of blues boogie but with a combination of varying phrase proportions distributed among its three sections (verse, refrain, and instrumental solo). The first verse is a sixteen-measure unit divided evenly into fours, while the second verse drops the twelfth measure to form a fifteen-measure unit. The refrain ("Move on down the line") tumbles forth in a headlong nine measures, and the instrumental solos are twelve-bar blues patterns. So, even in what might be considered a formulaic B-side effort, Orbison's metric sense lends the song a touch of the unexpected. By contrast, in Jerry Lee Lewis's 1958 recording (Sun 288), the song, renamed "Down the Line," is presented in a strophic sixteen-bar blues pattern for verse, refrain, and solos alike.

Orbison's first release on Sun would be his only success there. The next record, another two-sided rocker featuring Harold Jenkins's song "Rock House" and Johnny Cash's "You're My Baby" (Sun 251), was a failure commercially. Orbison was clearly out of place at Sun. His sensibility tended toward a refinement and complexity in musical arrangement and song structure and an emotional introspection foreign to rockabilly. As Phillips withdrew increasingly from hands-on production, turning things over to Bill Justis and Jack Clement, who assured Orbison he had no future as a ballad singer, Orbison's sessions sometimes strayed toward the bizarre.[20] The Clement-Justis production of the single "Chicken Hearted," paired with "I Like Love" (Sun 284), is an especially appalling mismatch of performer and material. The songs, written by Justis and Clement, respectively, are mindlessly stupid, which, while not necessarily precluding rock-and-roll success, seems at least to require a special sort of performer, a rockabilly powerhouse such as Billy Riley, for instance, who could deliver "Flying Saucer Rock and Roll" (Sun 260) with a convincingly manic commitment.[21]

Two tracks recorded at Sun point to what seem to have been Orbison's true musical aspirations: "Sweet and Easy to Love" and "Devil Doll" (Sun 265), both Orbison's own songs. The tracks feature more lyrical melodies than any of his other Sun sides, as well as light, swinging rhythmic grooves and poplike backing vocals evoking an older and more cosmopolitan pop sound similar to Presley's 1957 hit recording of "(Let Me Be Your) Teddy Bear" (RCA 20/47-7000). Despite his insistence that nothing he did at Sun "was any good," "Sweet and Easy to Love"/"Devil Doll" is a fine record that might well have been a double-A-side hit.[22] But Orbison, on his own now, having split with the rest of the Teen Kings while making the record, was in a bind at Sun. For one thing, Phillips had no particular affection for the sound of mainstream pop. Early on he had rebuked Orbison, his reluctant rockabilly cat, for suggesting the possibility of cutting a ballad: "We're at the wrong stage of rock 'n' roll to come out and start croonin' like Dean Martin. . . . If I put you out singin' some damn ballad, the world will never hear of Roy Orbison again. That's not the tenor of what is going on in the United States of America as far as music and rock 'n' roll are concerned."[23] Still, Phillips was a businessman, and it seems likely that if "Sweet and Easy to Love"/"Devil Doll" had been successful he would have pursued this direction with Orbison. The more problematic factor was that Sun was not set up to either produce or market effectively this style of music. All of Phillips's success came from blues- and country-based tracks recorded by small combos with a sharp, raw sound. The electricity of Sun records emanated from their unrefined sonic intensity, not the stylized polish toward which Orbison was leaning.

Nashville

Late in 1957, two events occurred—one of artistic significance, the other commercial—that would prove to be turning points in Orbison's career. On returning to Texas, as he did routinely between periods of recording in Tennessee, seeking to earn a bit of money playing in local beer joints and to be near the support of family when the money ran out entirely, he met and eventually established a songwriting partnership with Joe Melson, another local musician whose stylistic sensibility complemented Orbison's beautifully. Orbison approached Melson after hearing one of Melson's songs, "Raindrops," which had several elements in common with Orbison's own efforts to this point. It relates a tale of fatalistic heartbreak—"I knew in my heart that it wouldn't be long / Until I looked up and you'd be gone"—made lovely by a sinuous melody cast in an asymmetrical verse of five measures answered by four. Although the song's musical form is an unremarkable ABAB, the lyrics unfold in a continuous narrative; the only repetition is the word "raindrops." The sixteen-measure B sections intensify the musings expressed in the corresponding A sections, leading deeper into the protagonist's mind and heart with words specific to their place in the overall narrative scheme.

The other significant boost to Orbison's career at this time was the placement of one of his songs, "Claudette," on the B-side of the Everly Brothers' "All I Have to Do Is Dream" (Cadence 1348), which early in 1958 held the number 1 chart position for five weeks. The Everlys were based in Nashville where doors now opened for Orbison, most auspiciously at the powerful Acuff-Rose publishing house. His new connections led to a recording contract with RCA under the production supervision of Chet Atkins. Orbison's time at RCA would be brief and unremarkable, however, resulting in only two released singles. Of seven songs recorded at three sessions (29 September 1958, 18 December 1958, and 23 April 1959), only two were Orbison's own ("The Bug" and "Paper Boy"), and neither of these is close to his best work. Perhaps the most important legacy of the RCA sessions was the genesis of a production situation—including studio, recording engineer, and musicians—that would carry over to Orbison's next label and all of his most successful tracks. This was RCA's Nashville studio (later named RCA Studio B), the birthplace of such rock-and-roll hits as Presley's "Now or Never" (RCA 1207, 1960) and the Everlys' "All I Have to Do Is Dream."

The head engineer at RCA was Bill Porter, who is also credited with the acoustic treatments that brought the room up to its full sonic potential.[24] The session musicians were the members of a group known as the A Team, which, like the Wrecking Crew in Los Angeles or the Funk Brothers in Detroit, contributed to the arrangements and overall feel of the tracks on which they were hired to play.[25] The A Team musicians included bassist Bob Moore, drummer Murrey "Buddy" Harman, guitarists Hank "Sugarfoot" Garland and Harold Ray Bradley, pianist Floyd Cramer, and saxophonist Homer Louis "Boots" Randolph. Altogether, the venue, the engineer, and the musicians made for a polished, professional sound and musical treatment, which finally allowed Orbison's stylistic inclinations free rein. When RCA decided not to release the tracks for a third single, publisher Wesley Rose, on Orbison's behalf, contacted Fred Foster, who had recently launched the Monument record label. Foster, a veteran of the record business—and the producer, coincidentally, of the Eagles' original recording of "Trying to Get to You"—was keen to sign Orbison and continue with the basic sound of the Nashville sessions. Orbison's first Monument session was scheduled for 3 June 1959 in the RCA studio with Porter and the A Team.

At this session, apparently at Rose's insistence, Foster re-recorded the Orbison-penned songs from the RCA sessions, but Orbison assured him that he had better songs in development back in Texas. He and Melson had by then been working together for over a year, their songs moving toward a pop sophistication that showcased the refinement and pathos in Orbison's voice in a way the rockabilly style numbers had not and exploring a deeper emotional introspection. A tape found among Orbison's effects after his death offers a glimpse of the developing sound in demos for the songs "I Guess I'm Lonely," "You Fool You," and "Velveteen Doll," performed by Orbison and Melson in soft harmonies similar to those of the Everly Brothers. According to Melson, among the conscious compositional choices the two made were the expanded use of Orbison's voice, both in terms of range and ornamentation, and the conception of a song's backing vocal parts as part of the songwriting rather than the arranging process. Melson recalls the song "Blue Avenue" as the one in which Orbison began to explore seriously his falsetto range, a contention confirmed by the complete lack of falsetto on the Je-Wel, Sun, and RCA tracks. Melson began the song on his own and was hesitant initially to bring it to Orbison. Although the pair had been unable thus far to place any of their songs through their association with Acuff-Rose and Melson was eager to move in a different stylistic direction, he was unsure whether Orbison would agree. In the end, unable to present the song face-to-face, he sang it to Orbison over the telephone. Melson need not have worried. The sketch, with its falsetto break on the opening word, "blue," struck Orbison immediately as "beautiful."[26] Of course, as we have seen, Orbison's falsetto would eventually play a more significant role than vocal ornament, providing the climactic moment in "Only the Lonely" and many other tracks.

The other notable feature of the falsetto plea, "you got to take," in "Only the Lonely" is its melismatic flourish. Melson recalls working with Orbison on the melismatic treatment of song lyrics, adding what he referred to as "curlicues"; this technique is also probably what Orbison meant when he spoke of being impressed by the way Frizzell would "slid[e] syllables together."[27] The musical evidence with which to unpack Melson's "curlicues" comment is in Orbison's recording of "Raindrops." According to Melson, he asked Orbison, "Do you remember the phrasing in 'Raindrops'? It doesn't stay on straight notes, Roy. It *curls.* You've got to wind around inside them."[28] Indeed, the melody is filled with decorative turns, which, again, are unlike anything Orbison had recorded to that point but are common in later performances.

Melson's claim about including backing vocal figuration in the songwriting process—"the backups were integrally incorporated into the writing from the start"—highlights the songwriting duo's concern for an element that, although it might be considered secondary from a compositional standpoint, is in fact key both structurally and affectively.[29] We have already noted the role that backing vocals might play in pacing a song's phrase structure. But the sound of Melson's soft, airy voice leading the Anita Kerr singers also set the intimate tone of such tracks as "Only the Lonely" and "Blue Angel," creating an effect much like what we hear on the demos of "I Guess I'm Lonely," "You Fool You," and "Velveteen Doll." The backing figures have a whispered quality, as if the singers are leaning in close to the microphone to impart a secret to the listener. On the one hand, the cool softness serves as a foil to Orbison's powerful delivery, a contrast the two cultivated consciously.[30] But the intimacy also provides an affective context for the lead voice, drawing it in seductively such that its strength appears to be imbued with a certain fragility.

The effect extends implicitly to the entire mix. According to Bill Porter, prior to the "Only the Lonely" session Orbison asked that Melson's backing figures serve as the track's central sonic theme. Porter was skeptical; the backing vocals were sung so softly that their microphones would have to be set at a high input level, and with all the musicians playing in one room microphone leakage was bound to be a serious problem. Porter's normal mixing technique was to build a mix in what he likened to the shape of a pyramid, starting with a foundation of bass, drums, piano, and guitar. In order to highlight the backing vocals, his solution was to reverse this process. As he told an interviewer for the *Journal of Country Music,* he "took the vocal sound, the 'dum, dum,' and started and mixed *down* from that. The drums sound almost like an overdub because they're so quiet. There's not much . . . rhythm [section], because I took that soft sound—and that was my top—and mixed down from that. But that became a trademark with him."[31]

Orbison's second Monument session, which took place on 18 September 1959, featured three songs that represented his and Melson's newly emerging style, each with elements in common with "Only the Lonely": Melson's "Raindrops"; "Orbison's "Pretty One"; and the collaboration "Up Town," which they had written together in an Odessa motel room earlier that year. "I hit a melody line on the guitar," recalled Melson, "and Roy really liked it. He said, 'That's a real uptown melody.'" Here, again, was a turning point for the two young songwriters. "We wrote 'Up Town' that night," recalled Melson. "We moved from rock 'n' roll to class rock right then."[32] Not surprisingly, one element of the class rock "Up Town" exemplifies is unusual phrase lengths. The song has the conventional AABA structure of a thirty-two-bar form, but the first two A sections are each twelve bars, the B section a standard eight, and the final A section is seven (the result of a foreshortened phrase much like that in "Trying to Get to You"), making altogether a quirky thirty-nine-bar form. It also has a persistent chromatic motive in the vocal melody and a new level of sophistication in the lyrics, which frame erotic fantasy in terms of class status and its symbolic trappings. Orbison's "bellhop" protagonist, ignored by the woman in "penthouse number three," dreams of wealth in the form of a "big car" and "fine clothes," which he imagines will one day catch her attention, melt the barrier between them, and translate into sexual fulfillment.

Another important style feature that emerges at this session for the first time is the string writing on the three tracks. Indulging his fondness for pop arrangements, Orbison asked Foster if he would provide the extra musicians and arranger. Foster obliged with three violinists and arrangers Jim Hall ("Raindrops") and Anita Kerr ("Up Town," "Pretty One"). By 1959, strings had joined rock and roll's timbral palette, notably through the efforts of arrangers and producers at Atlantic (the Leiber and Stoller production of the Drifters' "There Goes My Baby," for example). But for Orbison they must also have held an association with the earlier mainstream pop records whose remoteness from his situation in West Texas made them, like the films in the Rig Theater, particularly attractive. On hearing playbacks at the session, Melson recalled, the two "thought it was the most beautiful sound in the world."[33] The sustained harmonic colors interrupted by distinctive, fragmentary flourishes add to the tracks both a timbral complexity and a resonant touch of melodrama that reflected Orbison's own. With Foster's cooperation, Orbison's sound was to become an idiosyncratic hybrid of rock-and-roll combo and orchestral pop, complementing both his unusual songwriting and his exceptional vocal performances. All but a small handful of Orbison's tracks recorded for Monument would feature string arrangements, most by Hall or Kerr, who also provided the Anita Kerr singers for background vocals.

The last of the three songs recorded that day—"Pretty One," which would be the B-side of "Up Town"—comes closest, both in its topic of romantic loss and in its musico-dramatic conception, to a preview of "Only the Lonely," which would be recorded at Orbison's next session six months later. The significant difference is in the lyrics; "Pretty One" lacks a progressive narrative. Since the song's two verses have the same words, all of the dramatic action is in the music, with the vocal melody varied considerably from one verse to the next. The second verse begins an octave higher than the first and then, halfway through, the key moves up a step from C to D, pushing the song to an emotional climax in Orbison's falsetto voice. At this point, the meter stops for a brief vocal cadenza with minimal accompaniment that serves both as the track's moment of ultimate pathos and its point of musical and dramatic arrival. The emotional crescendo, then, is expressed in a rising tessitura, spurred on by the key change, leading to a timbral and textural break at the climactic moment. While the track's musical design clearly prefigures "Only the Lonely," it is also something of a prototype that turns up often on Orbison's later tracks. Other examples include "Running Scared," "Blue Angel," "Crying," "The Crowd" (Monument 461), and "It's Over" (Monument 837). The strategy, of course, is flexible. The specific course of the drama varies from track to track and the high-pitched climactic moment is rendered in different ways—falsetto or full voice, a cappella or with accompaniment—depending on the affective context.

As we have seen, one result of the dramatic conceit embodied in such overarching emotional crescendos, enacted with a rising vocal line spinning out a melodic variation, is to loosen a song's strophic design and create a sense of continuous dramatic unfolding. On occasion, however,

Orbison also uses this technique to fashion a track that is entirely
through composed. The remarkable track "In Dreams"—which Orbison
wrote on his own shortly after his partnership with Melson ended—un-
folds in a sequence of four nearly equal length sections, achieving its
episodic, proselike effect through continuous variation of harmonic progression, melody, and lyric (example 2.3). The track begins with the
same sort of haunted rubato introduction as "Pretty One," with Orbison's low-register voice bathed in reverberant ambience and accompanied only by single-strum iterations of each chord in a I–vi–IV–V sequence. The full texture of a large rhythm section (including several
guitars) follows, accompanying a verse made up of two musically identical eight-bar phrases. Orbison, still in his low register and joined in that
timbral, affective space by the low violins, evokes a drowsy descent into
the realm of dreams, intoning inwardly a "silent prayer" as he slips into
unconsciousness and the promise, once again, of erotic fantasy. Porter's
stereo mix is expansive, accommodating the large ensemble on a wide
soundstage. The pacing is appropriately relaxed, with each vocal phrase
fragmentary and the harmonic rhythm moving at a leisurely pace.

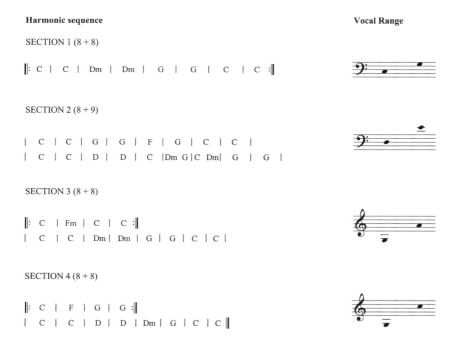

Example 2.3. "In Dreams"

The track's second section, seventeen measures (8 + 9) in length, finds the protagonist inside the dream. The music now is different both in melody and harmonic progression. Moreover, unlike the first section, the second has no repetition. Its two metric units differ not only in length but in harmony and melody as well. This acceleration of the song's formal unfolding is accompanied by a gradually hastening and irregular harmonic rhythm. The sound brightens as the voice and strings rise into a higher register and the singer sketches a scene of eternal union with the beloved ("in dreams you're mine / all the time"). This section, which rises gradually to a new vocal height (scale degree 3 [E], a tenth above the tonic touched on in the opening verse), might well be the song's refrain. It sounds the part, and it would work quite well if it were to return later in the track. Like everything else heard thus far, however, it will not be heard again.

Following the second section, where conventionally one would expect a return to by now familiar music, the song's unusual form begins to dawn. As the dreamer emerges from sleep, finding the beloved gone, the vocal line picks up at the new high point of E and continues to inch upward, accompanied by new music inflected with a minor subdominant harmony whose effect is intensified by the string flourishes that answer the vocal phrases. These eight measures of apprehension lead to a second eight-measure unit, again of a completely different character. While this unit repeats the chord sequence of the first section (I–ii–V–I), there is no sense of return for the rhythmic texture is now in stop-time and the melody is utterly unlike that in section 1. As the protagonist cries three times "I can't help it," his helpless agitation reaches into a breaking register a thirteenth (A) above the warm and drowsy opening tonic.

In the song's final section, a waking acknowledgment that blissful union "can only happen in dreams," the two eight-measure units are, again, different from any previous music and from one another. While the general pitch range is similar to that established in section 3, the high G, only touched on before, is now sustained with a straining intensity. Finally, in the song's swooning final eight measures, the voice rises to the tonic pitch two octaves above the opening. The moment, enacting the song's title with a climactic mingling of ecstasy and desperation, is typical Orbison, yet it is also fresh and moving. Manipulating the fairly limited set of resources that he and Melson had used repeatedly, Orbison manages once again to avoid the formulaic. Rather than placing familiar syntactic features into a ready mold of conventional pop song form, he uses them as elements of language to craft a unique narrative.

No less than his extraordinary voice, then, it is Orbison's rhetoric, his continual recasting of a basic set of elements and techniques, that makes his Monument tracks such exceptional pop records.

"There was a lot of loneliness in West Texas where I grew up," Orbison mused in a 1987 interview. "We used to say it was the center of everything, five hundred miles from anything."[34] Melson expressed a similar sentiment: "In the beginning, the dust of West Texas was in our eyes and mouths, and music seemed as far away as China."[35] If music itself seemed remote, the elegant "Only the Lonely" seems an especially unlikely product of such a place. Yet in a sense the song is the pair's metaphoric portrait of West Texas, a picture of bleakness permeated with a desperate hope for transcendence. It was also, for Orbison, his permanent ticket out. Once the song hit, he settled in Hendersonville, Tennessee, outside of Nashville, where he lived for most of the rest of his life. The song's success made it something of a paradox, an anthem of community for the abandoned and the isolated. Paradoxical as well, at least on its face, is its sweet style born in a hard place, evoking a hardscrabble memory in beautifully polished tones. But as we've seen, the roots of that style run deep and point us to Orbison's formative years. In his mature style, we hear traces of the eclectic range of musical characters that shaped his imagination and, in turn, helped to shape rock and roll. The musical and topical elements that come together in such finely honed fashion in "Only the Lonely," yielding a perfect pop record, were sown in the soil of Orbison's and Melson's West Texas experience, but they developed in a virtual world of broader horizons influenced by the passing voices on the mass media highway.

NOTES

1. All the Orbison recordings cited in this essay are contained in the seven-CD collection *Orbison, 1955–1965,* on Bear Family Records (BCD 16423, 2001).

2. Orbison is quoted (from an unpublished interview with David Booth) in Colin Escott, "Orbison," an essay that accompanies *Orbison, 1955–1965,* 5.

3. Ibid., 36, quoted from an Orbison interview with Roy Trakin published in *Hits,* 20 July 1987. Both songs appeared on the same record (Okeh 6706), and both were hits in 1944 for Ted Daffan's Texans. "Born to Lose" was written by Daffan and "No Letter Today" by Frankie Brown.

4. The yearbook inscription under Orbison's school photograph is reproduced in Ellis Amburn, *Dark Star: The Roy Orbison Story* (New York: Carol, 1990), facing p. 88.

5. *Roy Orbison Sings Don Gibson* (London 8318, 1967); *Hank Williams the Roy Orbison Way* (MGM Se-4683, 1971).

6. Escott, "Orbison," 5.

7. In "Leah," the protagonist is a pearl diver who lives on a tropical beach. *Shahdaroba* is an ancient expression of optimism, the song explains, that comes from "where the Nile flows." The word's provenance is underscored by the arrangement's oboe timbre. In both tracks, mild chromaticism serves as an exotic symbol.

8. Escott, "Orbison," 3.

9. Amburn, *Dark Star,* 19.

10. "Harbor Lights," Jimmy Kennedy and Wilhelm Grosz (aka Hugh Williams), 1937; "Blue Moon," Richard Rodgers and Lorenz Hart, 1934. While Presley's "Blue Moon" appeared on his first RCA album in 1956, "Harbor Lights" was not released until 1976 on *Elvis: A Legendary Performer, Vol. 2* (CP1-1349).

11. In the film *Blackboard Jungle,* for example, teenage hooliganism is identified with rock and roll, specifically the music of Bill Haley and the Comets, in contrast to the cultural refinement represented by the jazz records of high school teacher Richard Dadier (played by Glenn Ford).

12. The so-called Apartment Tapes, recorded in Holly's New York City apartment at 11 Fifth Avenue, include such songs as "Peggy Sue Got Married" and "Smokey Joe's Café." The tracks were released after his death in various versions with overdubbed band backing. There are also extant, though less readily available, bootleg versions of the unadorned demos.

13. Peter Lehman, *Roy Orbison: The Invention of an Alternative Rock Masculinity* (Philadelphia: Temple University Press, 2003), 1.

14. In 1955, Orbison and the Teen Kings recorded an audition demo for Columbia Records at Jim Beck's studio in Dallas, Texas. The local Artists and Repertoire man at the time, Don Law, passed on the group.

15. These Eagles, of course, are not to be confused with the later supergroup of the same name.

16. Examples are Holly's "Everyday" (Coral 61885, 1957) and "Words of Love" (Coral 61852, 1957).

17. Initially, however, it appears that Phillips sought to emulate the sound of the Clovis recording. According to Weldon Rogers, Phillips, unable to duplicate the sound of the original, called Rogers asking to purchase the master tape. Rogers, who had lost the rights to the Teen Kings' record in a contract dispute (instigated by Phillips) regarding the underage status of the musicians, demanded eleven hundred dollars, a price Phillips was unwilling to pay (Escott, "Orbison," 13–15).

18. The "St. Louis Blues" recording is from a 1956 television appearance.

19. These features turn up repeatedly, both singly and, as in this example, in combination. A particularly good example, aside from "Only the Lonely," is "I'm Hurtin'." What I am calling the bolero-type gesture is simply a rhythmically subdivided pickup motive, not the triple meter of the traditional Spanish bolero. Fred Foster, the founder of Monument records, claims to have introduced Orbison to this rhythmic idea via a recording of Ravel's *Bolero,* which resulted in Orbison's "Running Scared" (Escott, "Orbison," 40). Clearly, however, the technique was already part of Orbison's lexicon.

20. According to Clement, Orbison "was ahead of what we could do there in

Memphis, really. He was thinking orchestrations, choirs—big production stuff. He wanted production numbers, like he ultimately wound up doing. I told Roy he'd never make it as a ballad singer. He never let me forget that, either" (quoted in John Floyd, *Sun Records: An Oral History* [New York: Avon, 1998], 78).

21. Billy Riley and His Little Green Men, "Flying Saucer Rock and Roll" (Sun 260, 1957).

22. Colin Escott with Martin Hawkins, *Good Rockin' Tonight: Sun Records and the Birth of Rock 'n' Roll* (New York: St. Martin's, 1991), 151.

23. Phillips, quoted in Amburn, *Dark Star,* 49.

24. Jim Cogan and William Clark, *Temples of Sound: Inside the Great Recording Studios* (San Francisco: Chronicle, 2003), 60–61.

25. Musicians from the Wrecking Crew played on tracks by such groups as the Ronettes, Sonny and Cher, the Beach Boys, and the Byrds. The Funk Brothers were the house band at Motown's Hitsville U.S.A. studio.

26. Melson's recollection of Orbison's response is quoted in Amburn, *Dark Star,* 83.

27. Orbison, quoted (from an unpublished interview with David Booth) in Escott, "Orbison," 5. Listen, for example, to Frizzell's "I Want to Be with You Always" (Columbia 20799, 1951).

28. Melson, quoted in Amburn, *Dark Star,* 89.

29. Ibid., 70.

30. Melson recalled, "We used [my voice] to do the soft backups to contrast with his hard driving instrument—the soft against the piercing made for a lovely contrast" (quoted in ibid., 69).

31. Porter, quoted in John W. Rumble, "Behind the Board: Talking with Studio Engineer Bill Porter," *Journal of Country Music* 18, no. 2 (1996), 22, emphasis in the original.

32. Melson, quoted in Escott, "Orbison," 32.

33. Ibid.

34. Orbison, quoted in ibid., 36.

35. Melson, quoted in Amburn, *Dark Star,* 70.

THREE ⁘ Ego and Alter Ego

Artistic Interaction between Bob Dylan and Roger McGuinn

JAMES GRIER

FOR OVER FORTY YEARS, Roger McGuinn has been the foremost interpreter of the songs of Bob Dylan behind only the songwriter himself. First as a member of the Byrds and subsequently as a solo performer, McGuinn created distinctive versions of several Dylan songs that differ markedly from the composer's own renditions. The Byrds, for a short time in the mid-1960s, stood among the foremost American rock bands, with a string of hit single releases and several critically acclaimed albums. Bob Dylan, meanwhile, was arguably the most important American singer-songwriter of popular song to emerge from the decade. Dylan and McGuinn are active professionally today, and throughout their careers each has responded to the other by imitating and sharing musical styles.

Both midwesterners, they were installed in New York's Greenwich Village by the early 1960s. Dylan was discovered and signed to Columbia by John Hammond, the label's maverick executive, in 1961. He proceeded to make a series of commercial albums that increasingly showcased his original songs and moved gradually toward embracing the rock idiom.[1] McGuinn backed up several prominent commercial folk artists on guitar and banjo, including Bobby Darin, Chad Mitchell, and Judy Collins. By 1964 he had moved to Los Angeles and formed a rock band with several other experienced folk musicians.[2] On 12 April 1965, the Byrds burst onto the national popular music scene with the release of their rock version of Dylan's "Mr. Tambourine Man," their first release on Columbia, Dylan's label.[3]

Other artists had covered Dylan songs by this time, principally Peter, Paul and Mary, but the style remained firmly within the commercial folk idiom.[4] From the very first note of the Byrds' recording of "Mr. Tambourine Man," played by McGuinn on his distinctive chiming Rickenbacker electric twelve-string guitar, however, the Byrds gave notice that they were exploring uncharted territory in the interpretation of Dylan's songs.[5] After two bars, McGuinn's guitar introduction is supplemented with a booming electric bass guitar, and then drums and a second electric guitar enter simultaneously with the vocals to complete the rock accompaniment. Above the rock instrumentation, the vocal timbres contrast strikingly with Dylan's sharply nasal vocal production, clearly reminiscent of traditional folk and country singers, and his sometimes variable intonation. In the chorus, the Byrds sing in harmony with a fuller, more rounded vocal quality dominated by David Crosby's clear tenor, although McGuinn, singing solo during the verse, allows some nasal overtones to enter his voice.

Two details of this version show that, beyond creating a rock arrangement of the Dylan original, they were imposing a personal style on the song. The first is the guitar introduction, which also occupies the song's fadeout. It is one of the most distinctive in the rock repertory and the first of many that McGuinn created.[6] Its extraordinary sound derives from several factors, including the unique timbre of the Rickenbacker guitar he plays and the richness of sound generated by the doubling of the strings at the octave (or unison for the highest two strings), the chief design feature of the twelve-string guitar. He also divides the melody across more than one string and allows the plucked strings to ring while moving to another string (see example 3.1). McGuinn links the introduction to the guitar accompaniment of the vocals by using an arpeggiated style that breaks the chords across several strings.

The second detail that contributes to the Byrds' distinctive treatment concerns the harmonic rhythm. Both chorus and verse employ for the

Example 3.1. The Byrds, "Mr. Tambourine Man," twelve-string guitar introduction

most part one chord per bar. In the published sheet music, each half of both sections ends with a single bar that uses two chords. This progression anticipates the dominant chord that occupies the last two bars of the section (the first half of the chorus and both halves of the verse) or just the penultimate bar (at the end of the chorus).[7]

```
 I D /  /  /   IG / Em /   I A ///I A ///I
   I              IV   ii        V
```
I'm not sleepy and there is no place I'm goin' to.

or

```
 ID /  / /   IG  /  Em  /   IA ///ID ///I
   I            IV   ii       V      I
```
In the jingle jangle morning I'll come followin' you.

The Byrds alter this scheme in both halves of both the opening and closing choruses and at the end of the first half of the single verse they sing by retaining the subdominant throughout the second bar of the phrase.[8]

```
 ID ///IG ///IA ///IA ///I
   I      IV      V
```

or

```
 ID ///IG ///IA ///ID ///I
   I      IV     V     I
```

At the conclusion of the verse, however, they extend the subdominant harmony for an extra bar.[9]

```
 ID ///        IG ///IG ///     IA ///IA ///I
   I              IV                V
```
Cast your dancing spell my way, I promise to go under it.

This extension provides a dramatic climax for the song. It broadens the end of the phrase, sung by McGuinn alone, and makes an effective transition back to the chorus that concludes the song and the reentry of the full vocal harmony.

These details combine to create an entirely unique approach to the performance of Dylan songs and the entire repertory of commercial folk music. Contemporary journalists (or, as Dave Swaney put it, "Someone in the label department at 'Billboard' work[ing] overtime") named the style folk rock.[10] Elements of both traditions are audible, but it is the rock instrumental ensemble that makes this version so different from Dylan's and places the Byrds' distinctive imprint on the song. As if to make a claim for the authenticity of their rock arrangements of "Mr. Tambourine Man" and other Dylan songs, Columbia and the Byrds printed, on the back cover of the Byrds' first album, a photograph of Dylan visiting them onstage during a live performance.[11] The album is entitled *Mr. Tambourine Man* and includes three other Dylan songs. Table 3.1 gives a complete list (to date) of commercial recordings of songs by Dylan performed by McGuinn as a member of the Byrds or as a solo performer.[12]

The Byrds' second single, their arrangement of another Dylan song, "All I Really Want To Do," features a characteristic that became a signature for their interpretations of his songs: the conversion from 3/4 meter to duple meter.[13] (The footnoted songs in table 3.1 employ this conversion.) Dylan's use of triple meter reflects the pervasive influence of the Anglo-American ballad tradition, in which many songs exhibit this meter, and which constituted one of his principal sources for musical

TABLE 3.1.   Commercial Recordings by Roger McGuinn as a Member of the Byrds or as a Solo Performer of Songs Written by Bob Dylan

Title	Single	Album	Date
"Mr. Tambourine Man"	4-43271	*Mr. Tambourine Man* CS 9172	1965
"All I Really Want To Do"ª	4-43332	*Mr. Tambourine Man*	
"Spanish Harlem Incident"		*Mr. Tambourine Man*	
"Chimes of Freedom"ª		*Mr. Tambourine Man*	
"Lay Down Your Weary Tune"		*Turn! Turn! Turn!* CS 9254	1965
"The Times They Are A-Changin'"ª		*Turn! Turn! Turn!*	
"My Back Pages"ª	4-44054	*Younger than Yesterday* CS 9442	1967
"You Ain't Goin' Nowhere"	4-44499	*Sweetheart of the Rodeo* CS 9670	1968
"Nothing Was Delivered"		*Sweetheart of the Rodeo*	
"This Wheel's on Fire"		*Dr. Byrds and Mr. Hyde* CS 9755	1969
"Lay Lady Lay"	4-44868		1969
"It's Alright, Ma (I'm Only Bleeding)"		*Easy Rider* Dunhill DSX-50063	1969
"It's All Over Now, Baby Blue"	4-45071	*Ballad of Easy Rider* CS 9942	1969
"Positively 4th Street"		*(Untitled)* G 30127	1970
"Knockin' on Heaven's Door"		*Roger McGuinn and Band* KC 33541	1975
"Up to Me"		*Cardiff Rose* KC 34154	1976
"Golden Loom"		*Thunderbyrd* PC 34656	1977
"Paths of Victory"		*The Byrds* C4K 46773	1990

Note: All releases are on Columbia, except *Ballad of Easy Rider*.
ªSongs composed by Bob Dylan in triple meter and converted to duple meter by the Byrds.

styles.[14] The Byrds certainly had the ability to play in 3/4 time, as the B-side of "Mr. Tambourine Man," the modally ambiguous "I Knew I'd Want You," shows.[15] In my discussion of their 1967 recording of Dylan's "My Back Pages," I will demonstrate that the Byrds chose duple meter in order to place the rhythmic complexion of these Dylan songs more fully in the rock idiom.

I offer the following transcriptions of this song in 2/4 rather than 4/4, the standard duple meter in rock music, principally because of the harmonic rhythm of two passages in the chorus and bridge, which I discuss later. In each, the chord changes every two beats three times, thus necessitating either one bar of 2/4 within the customary 4/4 meter or a single bar of 3/2 that absorbs the entire pattern. Either solution would disrupt the visual flow of the transcription. A transcription in 2/4, however, permits an orderly visual progression that mirrors the musical flow yet does not substantively contradict the prevailing duple meter in simple or compound form. When the drummer strikes the snare drum in a simple backbeat pattern, as is the case in "All I Really Want To Do," it makes no difference whether we place those notes on beats 2 and 4 of a 4/4 bar or beat 2 of two successive 2/4 bars. (Some drum patterns differentiate the halves of a 4/4 bar with afterbeats on the snare or different patterns on the bass drum, but these, too, could be transcribed with equal felicity in 2/4 or 4/4.)

Again, as in the case of "Mr. Tambourine Man," the Byrds alter the chord progression, this time in the chorus. Dylan's version and the published music use only the three primary triads and end with a perfect cadence, V–I.[16] The Byrds, compressing one bar of 3/4 into one of 2/4, add a chord on the submediant and replace the dominant with a subdominant.[17]

Dylan: 3/4 | A // | A // | D // | D // | A // | D // | A // | E / / | E / / | A // |
         I   IV   I   IV I   V   I
      All I   really want to do   is baby be friends with you.

Byrds: 2/4 | A / | A / | D / | D / | A / | F♯m / | D / | D / | D / | A / |
        I   IV   I   vi   IV   I
        All   I really want to do   is baby be friends with you.

The submediant chord provides some harmonic variety and permits a conjunct descending bass line in contrary motion to the rising vocal line.

The substitution of the subdominant for the dominant softens the cadence, meanwhile, in a gesture typical of a great deal of rock music.[18]

More strikingly, they completely recompose what stands as the last verse in Dylan's version to create a bridge. The bridge was a staple of the American popular song throughout the twentieth century and usually fulfills the simple function of providing contrast with the stanza and chorus of a song.[19] Songwriters usually achieve this contrast by two means: new melodic material and a passing modulation to a new key. The latter is often balanced at the end of the bridge by a prolonged dominant harmony in the principal key to prepare for the simultaneous return of the tonic and the verse or chorus. The Byrds' bridge for "All I Really Want To Do" certainly introduces a previously unheard melody, as well as fresh harmonic directions. Those harmonies, however, do not establish a new key even in a passing sense. Instead they introduce a harmonic vocabulary that strongly contrasts with the diatonic harmony of the verse and chorus.[20]

| G / | G / | G / | G / | Bm / | Bm / | Bm / | Bm / |
♭VII   ii
I don't want to fake you out, Take or shake or forsake you out

| E / | E / | A / | A / | C / | C / | F / | D / | D F | D / | D / |
V   I   ♭III   ♭VI   IV   ♭VI IV
I ain't look' for you to feel like me,   See like me or be like me.

The bridge begins abruptly on a major triad built on G, a tone below the tonic, which then moves smoothly, because of common tones, to the supertonic. The harmonic rhythm slows at this point by a factor of four times compared to the verse to give the listener more time to absorb the new harmonic direction, I believe. The supertonic leads just as smoothly to the dominant and tonic chords midway through the bridge. Neither the harmonic rhythm nor the melody, however, allows us to apprehend this progression as a cadence, but the progression retains A major as the principal key in the background. The harmony then moves quickly on to other chords outside the key, namely, major triads built on the lowered third and sixth. The bridge closes on the subdominant chord with one further embellishment on the lowered sixth.

The major chords built on G and C, the lowered seventh and third, respectively, introduce a new harmonic palette. The major chords built on the notes of the pentatonic scale often identified as the blues scale (first, lowered third, fourth, fifth and lowered seventh degrees) appear frequently in rock songs. For example, the Kinks' "All Day and All of the Night" and "Till the End of the Day" use no other harmonies.[21] In the Byrds' adaptation of this scheme for "All I Really Want To Do," the chord built on F, the lowered sixth degree, seems to function as ♭III/IV, as it embellishes the subdominant harmony. The harmonic vocabulary of the bridge, then, moves Dylan's squarely diatonic harmonies into the more idiomatic language of rock music.

Because the bridge does not modulate, there is correspondingly less need to reestablish the tonic by ending on a prolonged dominant. Moreover, the verse, which immediately follows the bridge, begins with the subdominant harmony instead of the tonic. Although the progression V–IV is common in rock music, the Byrds chose not to end the bridge on the dominant but rather to retain the subdominant harmony, embellished with the triad built on F (the subdominant's ♭III, as suggested earlier) to create a hint of tonicization, as the close of the bridge. Thus, they effect a smooth transition back to the verse and the rest of the song.

After one further verse and chorus, sung and played in the same way as the first two, the Byrds close the song by repeating the second line of the chorus ("Baby be friends with you") as a hook over a plagal extension. In comparison with their arrangement of "Mr. Tambourine Man," the Byrds' version of "All I Really Want To Do" radically transforms several aspects of Dylan's original. I would isolate the incorporation of the bridge and the use of the hook, in particular, as elements that significantly increase the song's commercial appeal. The bridge adds contrast to maintain interest in the song while the hook concludes it with the repetition that creates familiarity. In combination with the instrumentation and vocal styles, these elements produce a distinctive rock arrangement of the song.

The Byrds added two more Dylan songs to their debut album, a cursory rendering of "Spanish Harlem Incident," noteworthy simply for its fidelity to Dylan's original version and for the fact that they sing all the verses, and "Chimes of Freedom," which bears further brief comment.[22] Again, they convert the song from triple to duple meter and change the chord progression in several places, most notably substituting the subdominant chord for the dominant in the opening and penultimate phrases of the verse. But, more important, they add an interlude between the last two verses of the three they sing (Dylan sings six in all) and again at the end. The interlude restates the principal harmonies of the song below textless vocal harmonies. This technique has its precedents, in the Byrds arrangement of "The Bells of Rhymney," for example. In both songs, these passages serve to articulate and highlight poignant lyrics (Idris Davies' plaintive poem about a Welsh mining disaster, set by Pete Seeger, and Dylan's hymn to "each and every underdog") and emphasize the poetic message.

With this corpus of four songs, including two successful single releases, the Byrds redefined the way the audience for popular music consumed Dylan's songs. Without sacrificing his directness of expression, they enhanced the commercial appeal of his output by adding rock instrumentation and vocal harmonies and by introducing novel arrangements, sometimes subtle, as in "Mr. Tambourine Man," sometimes more radical, as in the bridge of "All I Really Want To Do." They recorded and considered releasing as a third single "It's All Over Now, Baby Blue" but shelved the project in deference to "Turn! Turn! Turn!," the title song of their second long-playing (LP) release.[23] I discuss this recording later in comparison with their 1969 release of the song.

Nevertheless, their program of recording Dylan songs continued in the album tracks of *Turn! Turn! Turn!* which includes two of his songs. "Lay Down Your Weary Tune" had been recorded but not yet released by Dylan, and the Byrds created a richly ironic version of "The Times They Are A-Changin'."[24] The latter, another example of the conversion from triple to duple meter, also undergoes a radical simplification of the chord progression that restricts the harmonic language to the three primary triads, probably to achieve a more commercial sound as they did with their modifications to "Chimes of Freedom" but in contrast with the harmonic scheme they introduced to "All I Really Want To Do." More important, however, is the tone of the performance, in which McGuinn draws out the humor implicit in Dylan's rendition.[25] The group then frames the song with a brief guitar introduction and conclusion, punctuated each time with unanticipated accents by Michael Clarke on the drums. Both features animate their whimsical interpretation of Stephen Foster's "Oh! Susannah," which ends the album.[26] On repeated hearings of the album, the blatant humor of the latter cannot avoid coloring one's perception of the Dylan song.

With the release of *Turn! Turn! Turn!*, the Byrds began to express anxiety about their public image as a cover band of Dylan songs. Their publicist Derek Taylor (formerly and again later press agent for the Beatles) addressed the issue in the liner notes for their second album: "Anyone ungenerous enough to suggest that The Byrds rely on Dylan—and, surprisingly, there are one or two mean people in show business—will be disappointed to see that of the eleven numbers within this gorgeous sleeve, six are by Byrd-members, one is by Pete Seeger, one by S. Foster, another is an old country standard. Only two are by Dylan."[27]

The Byrds' solution was to avoid recording Dylan's material for a period. Between the release of "All I Really Want To Do" in June 1965 and March 1967, when they issued "My Back Pages" (on which more later), the Byrds produced six singles on which all but one side are original songs.[28] (The one exception is "Turn! Turn! Turn!," Pete Seeger's setting of a passage from the Old Testament book of Ecclesiastes.) The one album they recorded in 1966, *Fifth Dimension,* contains no song at all by Dylan, although, as I discuss later, his overt influence as a songwriter is present.[29]

In 1967, then, after not having recorded a Dylan song for over a year, and more than a year and a half after their last single featuring one of his songs ("All I Really Want To Do"), the Byrds released their version of "My Back Pages," Dylan's 1964 autobiographical renunciation of the didactic tone of his earlier work.[30] Yet again, they significantly alter the melody and chord progression and convert Dylan's triple meter into duple. The latter offers a good illustration of their method and possible motivation for performing the conversion. First, the melody line features greater rhythmic syncopation in keeping with the surface rhythms of rock songs in general (see example 3.2).[31] The Byrds' version creates a more striking setting of the key words "older" and "younger." These receive the same surface rhythm and occur in the same metrical position when sung by Dylan. The syncopation employed by the Byrds, however, shifts "older" off the beat and thereby prepares the stronger metrical declamation of the phrase "I'm younger," with "I'm" falling on the upbeat and the first syllable of "younger" on the following downbeat.

But second, and more important, the drum part becomes more characteristic. When the Byrds perform a rock song in 3/4, the snare drum

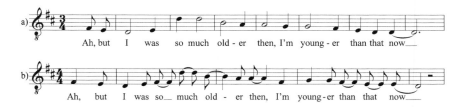

Example 3.2. "My Back Pages," (a) sung by Bob Dylan, (b) sung by the Byrds

accent falls on the first beat of every second bar, coincident with its principal metrical accent, while the right hand strikes the cymbal in steady
quarter notes analogous to the steady eighth notes on the cymbal in a
conventional 4/4 drumming pattern.[32] One might argue that because
the drummer strikes the snare on every second downbeat one could con-
strue the meter as 12/8, with the cymbals being struck on steady eighth
notes and the snare drum accents occurring on beats 2 and 4 in a typical
backbeat pattern. The tempo of the three examples I cite from the
Byrds, however, is too slow to permit the pattern from coalescing into the
larger 12/8 meter just proposed, and the snare accents invariably sound
like downbeats. By shifting to 4/4, the Byrds retain the typical rock backbeat with snare drum accents on the metrically weak second and fourth
beats (see example 3.3). Thus, McGuinn and the Byrds transform the
song from a commercial folk tune drawing on the Anglo-American ballad tradition into an idiomatic rock song.

This memorable recording was the last made of a Dylan song by the
original personnel of the Byrds. McGuinn periodically returned to Dylan's material with later manifestations of the group and as a solo artist,
as noted in table 3.1. *Sweetheart of the Rodeo,* on which Chris Hillman performs along with McGuinn, begins and ends with Dylan songs that the
songwriter had not yet released, "You Ain't Going Nowhere" (discussed
later) and "Nothing Was Delivered."[33] Similarly, *Dr. Byrds and Mr. Hyde,*
the first on which McGuinn alone appears among the original members
of the band, begins with "This Wheel's On Fire," cowritten by Dylan and
Rick Danko of the Band.[34]

They recorded two additional songs in 1969, both of which deserve
further comment. In May 1969, the Byrds released their recording of
"Lay Lady Lay" just a month after Dylan's own on *Nashville Skyline.*[35] The
Byrds' version opens dramatically with a female choir, which was added
by producer Bob Johnston apparently without the group's knowledge.[36]

Example 3.3. Rock drumming patterns in (a) 3/4, (b) 12/8, AND (c) 4/4

When the song was reissued on compact disc, the chorus was removed.[37] Nevertheless, I believe it makes a significant contribution to the effect of the song. First, it markedly distinguishes the Byrds' version from Dylan's nearly contemporaneous release, just the type of distinction they sought with many of the alterations they had previously made to Dylan songs, from "All I Really Want To Do" to "My Back Pages." Second, it adds a dramatic element to the performance that is not only lacking in Dylan's version but is perhaps antithetical to it. One might compare the difference to that which exists between the competing versions of "All Along the Watchtower" released by Dylan and Jimi Hendrix.[38]

Third, and most important from a purely historical point of view, the use of the choir on "Lay Lady Lay" anticipates by some months the appearance of choral performing resources on two significant recordings. In July 1969, the Rolling Stones issued "You Can't Always Get What You Want," and in November "Superstar," the initial conceptual single release from the musical *Jesus Christ Superstar* by Andrew Lloyd Webber and Tim Rice, appeared, sung by Murray Head.[39] Both songs enjoyed significantly more success than the Byrds' release, and some of that success may be attributed to their distinctive use of the choir. As happened often in the Byrds' career, they anticipated the curve, even if on this occasion they did so without their knowledge or consent and failed to derive the fullest benefit from their innovations.

The second recording of a Dylan song by the Byrds from 1969 is "It's All Over Now, Baby Blue," previously recorded in 1965 by the band's original personnel but not released, as mentioned earlier.[40] The Byrds' original recording of the song captures much of the anger and outrage of Dylan's own recording.[41] As such, it is perhaps a closer reading of Dylan than any of the band's early recordings of his material with the possible exception of "Spanish Harlem Incident" on *Mr. Tambourine Man,* as noted earlier. But the 1969 recording has a completely different effect, and in my opinion it remains a highly original interpretation of the song. By slowing the tempo considerably, using a subdued instrumental accompaniment, and delivering the words in somber ensemble harmony, the Byrds successfully bring out the profound pathos of Dylan's lyric. The song becomes melancholy and brooding, the outrage perhaps all the more moving because of its being understated. The chorus, from which the song's title is taken, emerges as a statement of resignation instead of a searing recrimination, as it seems to be in Dylan's version.

These 1969 recordings of "Lay Lady Lay" and "It's All Over Now, Baby Blue" are, in my opinion, the last effective interpretations to date of Dylan songs by the Byrds or McGuinn as a solo artist. Perfunctory readings of "Positively 4th Street" by the Byrds among the live tracks on *(Untitled)* and of "Knockin' on Heaven's Door" on McGuinn's third solo album were not redeemed by McGuinn's spirited performance of "Up To Me" on *Cardiff Rose,* his next album release. This last admirably compliments the other strong material on this album, but he was unable to match it with his interpretation of "Golden Loom" on *Thunderbyrd,* his last album release on Columbia to date.[42]

The Byrds made a remarkable beginning, then, with one of the most successful recordings in rock history, "Mr. Tambourine Man" (still a staple of "classic rock" radio programming along with "Turn! Turn! Turn!"), and several other aesthetically and commercially successful recordings of Dylan songs. With the breakup of the original personnel of the group, however, and the variety of directions McGuinn has taken in his subsequent solo career, the project to interpret Dylan, to offer fresh and original readings of his material, has faded. The much anticipated but commercially disappointing reunion album by the original Byrds included no songs by Dylan (although they did record two by Neil Young and one by Joni Mitchell).[43] During the brief reunion of McGuinn, Crosby, and Hillman in 1990, when they made four new recordings for inclusion in the archival boxed set entitled *The Byrds,* they laid down an enthusiastic performance of Dylan's "Paths of Victory," written in the early 1960s and not released by Dylan until 1991.[44] This was the first recording of a Dylan song by McGuinn for well over a decade, and, until recently, the last (see note 12).

Although this corpus of Dylan songs forms a central part of the Byrds' recorded legacy and includes some of their most memorable accomplishments, it would be wrong to judge the success of their career by these songs alone and especially to question their failure to continue the project. They established a reputation as innovators based on the significant amount of original material they composed, as the list of singles from 1965 to 1967 given earlier suggests (although it provides only a glimpse of their original output). Along the way, and alongside other bands, most notably the Beatles, they embraced a number of styles, including jazz, and Indian influences. In the case of country music, the Byrds produced a new fusion for the rock audience just as evocative as the genre of folk rock they fashioned with "Mr. Tambourine Man." Perhaps they made their most indelible mark by creating and recording original interpretations of Dylan's material, but that accomplishment stands as one of many they achieved.

Ironically, the Byrds' rise to national prominence in the spring of 1965 coincided with Dylan's own extremely controversial adoption of rock accompaniments in both live and recorded performance.[45] His first hit single with rock backup, "Like a Rolling Stone," was released in June, only two months after the Byrds' release of "Mr. Tambourine Man."[46] His performance at the Newport Folk Festival backed by a rock band, which enraged Pete Seeger and after which Peter Yarrow (of Peter, Paul and Mary) pleaded with him to complete his set with some acoustically accompanied songs, took place on 25 July.[47] (Curiously, no such furor greeted his earlier experiments with rock accompaniment on recordings made in 1962–63, perhaps because they took place in the studio and not in the forum of a high-profile public performance.)[48] Despite persistent rumors, and despite recording on the same label, Dylan never recorded with the Byrds during this era, nor did he borrow any of the stylistic conventions they had developed in their adaptations of his songs.[49] Dylan's rock songs cultivate a style based on urban blues, particularly with respect to guitar timbres and the use of keyboard instruments.

Nevertheless, Dylan could not avoid acknowledging the Byrds' contributions to his success as a songwriter. They anticipated Dylan by recording a country rock version of "You Ain't Goin' Nowhere," as mentioned earlier. When Dylan recorded his own version in 1971 for the album *Bob Dylan's Greatest Hits, Vol. II,* he changed the words to include the invocation, "Pack up your money, Pull up your tent, McGuinn, you ain't goin' nowhere."[50] Dylan later participated in two performances of his songs, with McGuinn, Crosby, and Hillman in the first case and with McGuinn alone among the original members of the Byrds in the other, at commemorative concerts. In both performances, the Byrds' arrangements of his material formed the accompaniment to his singing.

At a Roy Orbison tribute on 24 February 1990, Dylan joined three of the original Byrds onstage for a performance of their first hit, "Mr. Tambourine Man."[51] The arrangement is the Byrds', of course, and Dylan sings the second verse, the only one present on the Byrds' original 1965 recording. When he comes to the end of the verse, he and the band do not employ the extension of the harmonic rhythm on the subdominant, mentioned earlier, that the Byrds used on their recording to create anticipation for the ensuing dominant. Thus, the Byrds' instrumental accompaniment combines with the harmonic rhythm Dylan himself used on his own recording of the song to create a conflation of the two versions. More poignant, however, was the concert in honor of Dylan's thirtieth anniversary of recording, 16 October 1992. When the assembled guest artists, including McGuinn, came to sing "My Back Pages," they used the Byrds' rock arrangement in 4/4. McGuinn and Dylan each sang a verse, and in so doing, McGuinn came very close to matching Dylan's nasal vocal timbre. And so we hear first McGuinn sounding very much like Dylan and then Dylan singing McGuinn's arrangement of Dylan.[52]

To say that Dylan exerted an extraordinary influence on songwriting in the 1960s, and indeed for some time afterward, is certainly an understatement. In the case of McGuinn, however, that influence takes on a heightened significance because of the degree to which some members of the audience identified McGuinn and the Byrds primarily as interpreters of Dylan. They evince some self-consciousness about this identity, as is indicated by the comment of their publicist Derek Taylor in the liner notes for *Turn! Turn! Turn!*, quoted earlier. The Byrds, after all, had expended considerable effort to transform Dylan's songs into their own distinctive style, as I try to show here, while simultaneously exploring a plethora of other styles, often in an innovative manner. Therefore, when McGuinn consciously imitates Dylan's style, as he does in some cases, those songs carry an extra dimension of irony.

A small group of songs in McGuinn's oeuvre use 3/4 meter. This feature, of course, would not be of great import were it not for the fact that he habitually changes Dylan's songs in this meter to duple meter, as noted earlier. And, to a lesser degree, McGuinn sometimes imitates Dylan's vocal timbre, as in "Mr. Tambourine Man" and the 1992 version of "My Back Pages." Although small in number, these songs in triple meter occupy important positions in McGuinn's output. The song "5D (Fifth Dimension)" is the first one on the LP of the same title, released in 1966.[53] It is their third album and the first not to include a song by Dylan. Simultaneously, then, the group and McGuinn declared their emancipation from their public perception as a cover band for Dylan tunes while embracing the most distinctive elements of the songwriter whose works had pushed them into prominence.

The song begins with a lilting surface rhythm characteristic of ballads and Dylan songs in 3/4. McGuinn sings solo, again with the same mildly nasal timbre we have remarked in the two Dylan songs. And the lyrics, a questioning of the physical and temporal limits of reality, could be construed as Dylanesque. More concretely, one line, "And I saw the great blunder my teachers had made," echoes "the mongrel dogs who teach" in Dylan's "My Back Pages." Moreover, after three stanzas set strophically,

McGuinn supplies a bridge that moves toward the dominant and ends with a prolonged dominant preparation for the return of the tonic at the beginning of the fourth stanza.

I mentioned earlier the role of the bridge in American popular song of the twentieth century in connection with the one the Byrds added to "All I Really Want To Do." Here I would point out that it becomes a significant marker in rock music of this period. The conventional bridge, with modulation and concluding with a lengthy preparation on the dominant, creates a strong connection with commercial songwriting in the style of Tin Pan Alley instead of the folk and ballad repertory or the African-American blues tradition, the other principal sources for rock music. It was just at this time, however, that Dylan himself began to introduce the bridge into his songs with some frequency in precisely this way, particularly on the album *Blonde on Blonde,* also released in 1966.[54] And so, although McGuinn's bridge in "5D" is no innovation, it could well be a reflection of exactly contemporary developments in Dylan's songwriting.

But the assimilation ends with these structural features, the 3/4 meter and the use of the bridge. The Byrds retain the rock instrumentation that had become their trademark, dominated by McGuinn's electric guitar with ample complement from Chris Hillman's electric bass guitar and here supplemented with keyboards, principally electronic organ, played by Van Dyke Parks. More telling is the use of vocal harmony, first in the bridge but even more distinctively in the fifth stanza, which repeats the text of the first stanza. In the reprise, David Crosby supplies a characteristic high harmony that completes the transformation of the song from a Dylan-inspired triple-meter ballad to an idiomatic Byrds song.

Even more conspicuous, both in its similarities to Dylan's compositions and in its position in McGuinn's output, is the song "I'm So Restless." By 1973, the Byrds had dissolved, and McGuinn decided to strike out as a solo artist, releasing an eponymous album the same year.[55] "I'm So Restless" occupies the first position on that album, and so it sets the tone for the persona McGuinn wishes to define for himself in the post-Byrds era. And that persona is the solo folksinger-songwriter epitomized during the 1960s by Bob Dylan. McGuinn was no stranger to the role, as his performance of Dylan's "It's Alright, Ma (I'm Only Bleeding)" on the soundtrack of the 1969 film *Easy Rider* or, even more compellingly, the song "Chestnut Mare," which became a staple of his performances during the 1970s, demonstrates.[56] The definition of persona dominates the lyrics of "I'm So Restless." Each stanza addresses a different figure in rock music, identified by his initial, Dylan, John Lennon, and Mick Jagger. McGuinn discusses points of intersection between himself and the public persona each addressee projects. By extension, therefore, McGuinn treats these three musicians in order to supply a mirror for the presentation of his new persona.

McGuinn makes his musical point in two ways. First, the song is in 3/4 meter, which by this time had achieved iconic status in McGuinn's songwriting. And it uses strophic form, with the last line of each stanza serving as a refrain, a form common to the Anglo-American ballad and frequently met in Dylan's songs, "My Back Pages," for example. But the most striking aspect of the song is the array of timbres, each a powerful signifier in the context, that McGuinn assembles for the song. He accompanies himself on acoustic guitar, and Dylan, in a measure that echoes his appearance in the photograph on the back cover of the *Mr. Tambourine Man* album, plays harmonica on the track, to complete the identification and authentication.[57] And, once again, McGuinn sings with a somewhat nasal vocal production. In short, he evokes pre-electric Dylan, pre-Newport Folk Festival Dylan, even authentic Dylan.

To be sure, McGuinn did not sustain that persona even as far as the rest of the songs on his debut solo album, although he did tour alone in 1974, singing and accompanying himself on acoustic and electric guitar, banjo, and harmonica, the archetypal modern troubadour.[58] The other songs on that first album embrace a plethora of styles, some of which McGuinn had already essayed with the Byrds, including jazz ("My New Woman"), Beach Boys–influenced doo-wop ("Draggin'"), country ("Bag Full of Money"), and a sea shanty ("Heave Away").[59] But by launching the album with "I'm So Restless" McGuinn creates a link between his original songs and the songs of Dylan so as to sound more like Dylan than Dylan and to submerge his identity as a songwriter within the larger ethos and iconic power of Dylan's musical persona.

NOTES

An earlier version of this essay was presented at the annual meeting of the Sonneck Society for American Music in Fort Worth, 10 March 1999.

1. Among the compendious bibliography on Dylan (on which see William McKeen, *Bob Dylan: A Bio-Bibliography* [Westport CT: Greenwood, 1993]), see, on his early career, Anthony Scaduto, *Bob Dylan* (London: W. H. Allen, 1972; rpt., London, 1996), 51–230; Robert Shelton, *No Direction Home: The Life and Music of Bob Dylan* (New York: Beech Tree, 1986; rpt., New York, 1997), 87–304; Bob Spitz, *Dylan, a Biography* (New York: McGraw-Hill, 1989), 113–368; Clinton

Heylin, *Bob Dylan: Behind the Shades Revisited* (New York: Morrow, 2001), 58–243; and Bob Dylan, *Chronicles, Volume One* (New York, 2004), 3–104, 225–93.

2. On McGuinn's early career and the formation of the Byrds, see Johnny Rogan, *The Byrds: Timeless Flight Revisited*, rev. ed. (London: Rogan House, 2001), 23–44. See also John Einarson, Mr. *Tambourine Man: The Life and Legacy of the Byrds' Gene Clark* (San Francisco: Backbeat, 2005), 33–66.

3. The Byrds, "Mr. Tambourine Man" (Columbia 4-43271, 1965). As is well known, McGuinn alone, among the Byrds, plays on the instrumental backing track of the A- and B-sides of the single ("I Knew I'd Want You" is the B-side), while he, Gene Clark, and David Crosby sing, and the other instruments are played by studio musicians. See Rogan, *The Byrds*, 61–63; and Christopher Hjort, *So You Want to Be a Rock 'n' Roll Star: The Byrds Day-by-Day, 1965–1973* (London: Jawbone, 2008), 24b–c. Nevertheless, the arrangement itself is the Byrds', as attested by their 1964 recording of the song on *Preflyte* (Together Records ST-T-1001, 1969), side 2, track 5. Subsequently, all the band members played their respective instruments on all Byrds recordings, including the album tracks for *Mr. Tambourine Man*.

4. For an overview, see McKeen, *Bob Dylan*, 221–29. See also the list in Bob Dylan, *Bob Dylan Song Book* (New York: Witmark, 1966), 138–41.

5. McGuinn's choice of instrument, a Rickenbacker 360-12 electric twelve-string guitar, was undoubtedly influenced by George Harrison's use of the same model beginning in 1964, particularly in the film *A Hard Day's Night*. See Andy Babiuk, *Beatles Gear* (San Francisco: Backbeat, 2001), 110–12, 118, 120–22; Rogan, *The Byrds*, 46; and Hjort, *So You Want to Be a Rock 'n' Roll Star*, 20a–b.

6. Examples include "The Bells of Rhymney," "All I Really Want To Do," and "Don't Doubt Yourself, Babe" on the Byrds, *Mr. Tambourine Man* (Columbia CS 9172, 1965) alone (side 1, track 6, and side 2, tracks 1 and 4, respectively). The 1964 version of "Mr. Tambourine Man," released on *Preflyte*, uses the same introduction but is accompanied by a pseudo-military drum part.

7. Bob Dylan, *The Definitive Dylan Songbook*, ed. Don Giller and Ed Lozano (New York: Amsco, 2001), 438–39.

8. Dylan also prolongs the subdominant chord and suppresses the supertonic in his version of "Mr. Tambourine Man," on *Bringing It All Back Home* (Columbia CS 9128, 1965), side 2, track 1. This harmonic scheme is reproduced in the verse only of the sheet-music version of the song in *The Byrds Complete* (New York: Amsco, 1973), 83–85 at 84–85.

9. This alteration is not reproduced in the notation for the second verse (the only one sung by the Byrds) in *The Byrds Complete*, 85, where the subdominant chord occupies one bar only.

10. Dave Swaney, liner notes for the Byrds, *The Byrds' Greatest Hits* (Columbia CS 9516, 1967). See also Richie Unterberger, *Turn! Turn! Turn! The '60s Folk-Rock Revolution* (San Francisco: Backbeat, 2002); and *Eight Miles High: Folk-Rock's Flight from Haight-Ashbury to Woodstock* (San Francisco: Backbeat, 2003).

11. Rogan, *The Byrds*, documents other early meetings with Dylan (54–56, 68–69) and his approval of their recording of "Mr. Tambourine Man" (65–66).

12. Appearing too late for inclusion in table 3.1 is McGuinn's cover of "One More Cup of Coffee" with Calexico on the soundtrack for the 2007 Bob Dylan

biopic *I'm Not There* (Columbia 712038, 2007), originally released by Dylan on *Desire* (Columbia KC 33894, 1976).

13. The Byrds, "All I Really Want To Do" (Columbia 4-43332, 1965). It also appears on *Mr. Tambourine Man,* side 2, track 1. Cher, who recorded the song at about the same time (Imperial 66114, 1965), similarly converted it to duple meter, and it bears other resemblances to the Byrds' version. See Rogan, *The Byrds,* 81–83.

14. See, for example, the songs collected in Bertrand Harris Bronson, *The Traditional Tunes of the Child Ballads with Their Texts According to the Extant Records of Great Britain and America,* 4 vols. (Princeton: Princeton University Press, 1959–72).

15. The Byrds, "I Knew I'd Want You" (Columbia 4-43271, 1965), also on *Mr. Tambourine Man,* side 2, track 2.

16. Bob Dylan, "All I Really Want To Do," on *Another Side of Bob Dylan* (Columbia CS 8993, 1964), side 1, track 1; Dylan, *The Definitive Dylan Songbook,* 28.

17. The progression | A / | F#m / | D / | carries the effect of three bars of 2/4, which therefore dictates the choice I made to transcribe in 2/4 throughout.

18. See Ken Stephenson, *What to Listen for in Rock: A Stylistic Analysis* (New Haven and London: Yale University Press, 2002), 113–14.

19. Ibid., 137–38.

20. The progression | F / | D / | D F | moves as three bars of 2/4.

21. The Kinks, "All Day and All of the Night" (Pye 7N-15714, 1964); and "Till the End of the Day" (Pye 7N-15981, 1965). Stephenson (*What to Listen for in Rock,* 90–92) identifies these chords as part of the "chromatic-minor" system; he admits, however, that the tonic chord in this system can be either major or minor, and his examples use harmonies that combine a number of modal orientations. Walter Everett offers a more cogent analysis of what he calls the "triad-doubled or power-chord minor-pentatonic systems" in "Making Sense of Rock's Tonal Systems," *Music Theory Online* 10, no. 4 (December 2004), http://mto.societymusic theory.org/issues/mto.04.10.4/mto.04.10.4.w_everett_frames.html, paragraphs 19–22.

22. The Byrds, "Spanish Harlem Incident" and "Chimes of Freedom," on *Mr. Tambourine Man,* side 1, track 3, and side 2, track 5, respectively; Bob Dylan, "Spanish Harlem Incident" and "Chimes of Freedom," on *Another Side of Bob Dylan,* side 1, tracks 3 and 4, respectively.

23. Rogan, *The Byrds,* 123–24. It was eventually released on the Byrds, *Never Before,* variously identified as Re-Flyte MH 70318 and Murray Hill/CBS Special Products A21143 (1987), side 1, track 4. Two versions of this recording are now available: The Byrds, *The Byrds* (Columbia/Legacy C4K 46773, 1990), disc 1, track 8; and the Byrds, *Turn! Turn! Turn!* (Columbia CK 64846, 1996), track 15.

24. The Byrds, *Turn! Turn! Turn!* (Columbia CS 9254, 1965), side 1, track 4, and side 2, track 4, respectively. Dylan first issued a previously unreleased 1963 recording of "Lay Down Your Weary Tune" on *Biograph* (Columbia C5X 38830, 1985), side 4, track 1.

25. Bob Dylan, "The Times They Are A-Changin'," on *The Times They Are A-Changin'* (Columbia CS 8905, 1964), side 1, track 1.

26. The Byrds, "Oh! Susannah," on *Turn! Turn! Turn!* side 2, track 6.

27. Derek Taylor, liner notes for the Byrds, *Turn! Turn! Turn!*

28. The Byrds, "Turn! Turn! Turn!" / "She Don't Care about Time" (Columbia 4-43424, 1965); "Set You Free This Time" / "It Won't Be Wrong" (Columbia 4-43501, 1966); "Eight Miles High" / "Why" (Columbia 4-43578, 1966); "5D (Fifth Dimension)" / "Captain Soul" (Columbia 4-43702, 1966); "Mr. Spaceman" / "What's Happening?!?!" (Columbia 4-43766, 1966); "So You Want To Be A Rock 'n' Roll Star" / "Everybody's Been Burned" (Columbia 4-43987, 1967).

29. The Byrds, *Fifth Dimension* (Columbia CS 9349, 1966).

30. The Byrds, "My Back Pages" (Columbia 4-44054, 1967), also on *Younger than Yesterday* (Columbia CS 9442, 1967), side 2, track 3; Bob Dylan, "My Back Pages," on *Another Side of Bob Dylan*, side 2, track 2.

31. For the sake of comparison, I have transposed the Byrds' version from E major to D to agree with the pitch of Dylan's published version in Dylan, *The Definitive Dylan Songbook*, 444–45.

32. The Byrds, "I Knew I'd Want You"; "If You're Gone," on *Turn! Turn! Turn!* side 2, track 3; "5D (Fifth Dimension)."

33. The Byrds, "You Ain't Going Nowhere" and "Nothing Was Delivered," on *Sweetheart of the Rodeo* (Columbia CS 9670, 1968), side 1, track 1, and side 2, track 5, respectively. Dylan recorded both songs with the Band in 1967 and released them in 1975: Bob Dylan and the Band, "You Ain't Going Nowhere" and "Nothing Was Delivered" on *The Basement Tapes* (Columbia C2X 33682, 1975), side 4, tracks 1 and 3, respectively.

34. The Byrds, "This Wheel's on Fire," on *Dr. Byrds and Mr. Hyde* (Columbia CS 9755, 1969), side 1, track 1; Bob Dylan and the Band, "This Wheel's on Fire," on *The Basement Tapes,* side 4, track 6. The song is perhaps best known from the recording by the Band, on *Music from Big Pink* (Capitol ST-2955, 1968), side 2, track 5.

35. The Byrds, "Lay Lady Lay" (Columbia 4-44868, 1969); Bob Dylan, "Lay Lady Lay," on *Nashville Skyline* (Columbia CS 9825, 1969), side 2, track 1, later released (in August 1969) as a single (Columbia 4-44926, 1969).

36. Rogan, *The Byrds,* 289–90; Hjort, *So You Want to Be a Rock 'n' Roll Star,* 208b–c, 209a.

37. The Byrds, *The Byrds,* disc 3, track 11; the Byrds, *Dr. Byrds and Mr. Hyde* (Columbia CK 65113, 1997), track 12.

38. Bob Dylan, "All Along the Watchtower," on *John Wesley Harding* (Columbia CS 9604, 1967), side 1, track 4; Jimi Hendrix, "All Along the Watchtower" (Reprise 0767, 1968), also on *Electric Ladyland* (Reprise 2RS-6307, 1968), side 4, track 3. See also Albin J. Zak III, "Bob Dylan and Jimi Hendrix: Juxtaposition and Transformation 'All Along the Watchtower'," *Journal of the American Musicological Society* 57, no. 3 (Fall 2004): 599–644.

39. The Rolling Stones, "You Can't Always Get What You Want" (Decca F 12952, 1969), the B-side of "Honky Tonk Women," also on *Let It Bleed* (Decca SKL 5025, 1969), side 2, track 4; Murray Head, "Jesus Christ, Superstar" (MCA MKS 5019, 1969), also on *Jesus Christ Superstar* (MCA MKPS 2011/2, 1969), side 4, track 3.

40. The Byrds, "It's All Over Now, Baby Blue," on *Ballad of Easy Rider* (Co-

lumbia CS 9942, 1969), side 2, track 2, also issued as the B-side of "Jesus Is Just Alright" (Columbia 4-45071, 1969).

41. Bob Dylan, "It's All Over Now, Baby Blue," on *Bringing It All Back Home,* side 2, track 4.

42. The Byrds, "Positively 4th Street," on *(Untitled)* (Columbia G 30127, 1970), side 1, track 2; Roger McGuinn, "Knockin' on Heaven's Door," on *Roger McGuinn and Band* (Columbia KC 33541, 1975), side 1, track 2; Roger McGuinn, "Up To Me," on *Cardiff Rose* (Columbia KC 34154, 1976), side 2, track 1; Roger McGuinn, "Golden Loom," on *Thunderbyrd* (Columbia PC 34656, 1977), side 2, track 3. Also included in this group is the tentative recording of "Just Like a Woman" made during the sessions for *(Untitled)* in 1970 and eventually released on the Byrds, *The Byrds,* disc 4, track 5.

43. The Joni Mitchell song "For Free" is on the Byrds, *Byrds* (Asylum SD 5058, 1973), side 1, track 4. The Neil Young songs "Cowgirl in the Sand" and "(See the Sky) About to Rain," are on side 2, tracks 2 and 6, respectively.

44. The Byrds, "Paths of Victory," on *The Byrds,* disc 4, track 19. Dylan released a 1963 recording of "Paths of Victory" on *The Bootleg Series, Volumes 1–3* (Columbia C3K47382, 1991), disc 1, track 15.

45. Scaduto, *Bob Dylan,* 187–90, 211–21; Shelton, *No Direction Home,* 266–339; Spitz, *Dylan,* 297–310; Heylin, *Bob Dylan,* 167–260.

46. Bob Dylan, "Like a Rolling Stone" (Columbia 4-43346, 1965). Paul Williams, in *Bob Dylan: Performing Artist, 1960–1973, the Early Years* (London: Omnibus, 1990), 288, gives a release date of 20 July 1965, just five days before Dylan's stormy appearance at the Newport Folk Festival, by which date the song was already receiving a great deal of radio play. See Scaduto, *Bob Dylan,* 213.

47. Scaduto, *Bob Dylan,* 212–15; Shelton, *No Direction Home,* 301–4; Spitz, *Dylan,* 300–10; Williams, *Bob Dylan,* 156–57; Heylin, *Bob Dylan,* 206–16; Mike Marqusee, *Chimes of Freedom: The Politics of Bob Dylan's Art* (New York: New Press, 2003), 141–47; Lee Marshall, "Bob Dylan: Newport Folk Festival, July 25, 1965," in *Performance and Popular Music: History, Place, and Time,* ed. Ian Inglis (Aldershot: Ashgate, 2006), 16–27; Ronald D. Cohen, *A History of Folk Music Festivals in the United States: Feasts of Musical Celebration,* American Folk Music and Musicians, no. 11 (Lanham, MD: Scarecrow, 2008), 93–99.

48. Bob Dylan, "Mixed Up Confusion" and "Corrina, Corrina" (Columbia 4-42656, 1962). The latter also appears on *The Freewheelin' Bob Dylan* (Columbia CS 8786, 1963), side 2, track 5. The sidemen are identified in the liner notes by Nat Hentoff, who also claims that "Don't Think Twice, It's All Right" (side 2, track 1), used a rock accompaniment (as does Shelton, *No Direction Home,* 156). This is untrue, as Andy Gill, in *Classic Bob Dylan, 1962–1969: My Back Pages* (London: Carlton, 1998), 31b, notes. Williams, *Bob Dylan,* 62, claims that "Corrina, Corrina" is "the only song on [*Freewheelin'*] that features musicians other than Dylan," but Heylin, *Bob Dylan,* 104, states that Bruce Langhorne played the guitar accompaniment for "Don't Think Twice, It's All Right." In fact, the guitar playing on that track is noticeably cleaner than on the other tracks on *The Freewheelin' Bob Dylan.* On Dylan's use of the backup band in general, see Shelton, *No Direction Home,* 154–57; and Heylin, *Bob Dylan,* 103–4.

49. For McGuinn's narrative of the supposed collaboration between the Byrds and Dylan, see Ed Ward, "Roger McGuinn: So You Want to Be a Rock and Roll Star," in *The Rolling Stone Interviews*, vol. 2, ed. Ben Fong-Torres (New York: Warner Paperback Library, 1973), 100–101 (first published in *Rolling Stone*, October 1970). See also Rogan, *The Byrds*, 308.

50. Bob Dylan, "You Ain't Goin' Nowhere," on *Bob Dylan's Greatest Hits, Vol. II* (Columbia KG 31120, 1971), side 4, track 6. In the first stanza of this performance, Dylan conflates and alters the published lyrics of the first and second stanzas. The passage on which the quotation is based reads "Pick up your money / And pack up your tent / You ain't goin' nowhere." See Dylan, *The Definitive Dylan Songbook*, 776.

51. The Byrds, *The Byrds*, disc 4, track 17.

52. Bob Dylan, "My Back Pages," on *The 30th Anniversary Concert Celebration* (Columbia C2K 53220, 1993), disc 2, track 12. McGuinn performs "Mr. Tambourine Man" on disc 2, track 10.

53. The Byrds, "5D (Fifth Dimension)," on *Fifth Dimension*, side 1, track 1, also released as a single (see note 27).

54. See, for example, Bob Dylan, "I Want You," "Just Like a Woman," "Most Likely You Go Your Way (And I'll Go Mine)" (where the bridge ends on the dominant, but the subsequent verse begins on the supertonic), "Temporary Like Achilles," and "Absolutely Sweet Marie," on *Blonde on Blonde* (Columbia C2S 841, 1966), side 2, tracks 1 and 4, side 3, tracks 1–3, respectively.

55. Roger McGuinn, *Roger McGuinn* (Columbia KC 31946, 1973). "I'm So Restless" is on side 1, track 1.

56. Roger McGuinn, "It's Alright, Ma (I'm Only Bleeding)," on *Easy Rider* (Dunhill DSX-50063, 1969), side 2, track 4; The Byrds, "Chestnut Mare," on *(Untitled)*, side 3, track 1.

57. Identified in the liner notes on the insert.

58. Rogan, *The Byrds*, 360–61.

59. McGuinn, "My New Woman," "Draggin'," "Bag Full of Money," and "Heave Away," on *Roger McGuinn*, side 1, tracks 2 and 4, side 2, tracks 1 and 4, respectively.

FOUR ❧ Marvin Gaye as Vocal Composer

ANDREW FLORY

IN JANUARY 1981, Marvin Gaye's method of making music was at the center of a heated debate that led to his break from the famous Motown Record Corporation.[1] It had been more than two years since the release of Gaye's last Motown album, *Here, My Dear* (1978), and the gaps between his highly anticipated releases had grown larger throughout the 1970s. Thus, without Gaye's permission, Motown finalized and released the album *In Our Lifetime* after procuring the master tapes from a recording engineer who had worked on the project.[2] Gaye was not only furious that Motown had not waited for his approval but also upset about the way in which the album was mixed and the addition of new instrumental parts. His major complaint was the inclusion of the song "Far Cry." Years later Gaye recalled his feelings to biographer David Ritz:

> I hadn't completed it. . . . The song was in its most primitive stage. All I had was this jive vocal track, and they put it out as a finished fact. How could they embarrass me like that? I was humiliated. They also added guitar licks and bass lines. How dare they second guess my artistic decisions! Can you imagine saying to an artist, say Picasso, "Okay Pablo, you've been fooling with this picture long enough. We'll take your unfinished canvas and add a leg here, an arm there. You might be the artist, but you're behind schedule, so we'll finish up this painting for you. If you don't like the results, Pablo, baby, that's tough!"[3]

Gaye's reference to Picasso is telling, for it reveals that he viewed his process of making music as nonlinear. There are several aspects of the released version of "Far Cry" that illustrate his working method (an abbreviated transcription is provided in example 4.1).[4] Most noticeably, the tentatively enunciated words throughout the track show how Gaye developed lyrical content. These words were most likely improvised while singing through the chord changes over an already completed backing track.[5] Consequently, the melody does not have a structural hierarchy

Example 4.1. Marvin Gaye, "Far Cry"

and there are no established formal sections such as a verse, chorus, or refrain. The rhythm of the melody, while potentially interesting for its consistent syncopation, is also mostly invariable. The tone collection in the vocal line and the manner in which these pitches are used are also extremely limited. For the most part, the tune simply alternates between two short motives that incorporate scale degrees 7 and 1 and scale degrees 4 and 3. Finally, it is clear that the formal structure of this song was partially determined through postproduction editing, most likely without Gaye's approval. By cutting much of the original improvised track and inserting a spliced copy of the first minute and a half of the song after the bridge as a "return" to the opening material, the form of the piece was altered after Gaye recorded his vocals.[6] In comparison with Gaye's contemporaneous work, "Far Cry" was, in fact, very primitive.

Throughout this essay I will use the term *vocal composition* to refer to Gaye's process of documented improvisation as songwriting.[7] This term acknowledges Gaye's ability to blur the lines between performing, recording, and composing. Although he was certainly not the first artist to use the recording studio in this fashion, this method of crafting a song was vital to his creative process and is therefore fundamental to a basic understanding of his work. My exploration of Gaye's work as a vocal composer begins with an account of his career at Motown in Detroit during the 1960s, exploring first his background as a singer, then documenting an important early example of his compositional process. Following a discussion of some critical approaches to vocal composition, the final section of the essay includes historical and analytical readings of three songs that clearly illustrate Gaye's vocal composition during the 1970s.

While the rhythm and blues (R & B) tradition has a formidable history of appropriating technology to capture unrepeatable performances, establish and shift power structures, and liberate nontraditional composers, Gaye was a product of Motown, a company whose streamlined creative process is often regarded as the antithesis of individualist creativity.[8] Gaye's association with Motown was deep seeded, encompassing both his creative and professional lives. Thus, the impact of Motown on all facets of Gaye's life was at the core of his vocal composition process.

Motown's operations were housed in several converted homes on Detroit's West Grand Boulevard, where founder Berry Gordy presided over a micromanaged system of creating art that functioned as a musical "assembly line."[9] Gordy and Motown controlled all aspects of a performer's career, administering or owning everything from management, wardrobe, and etiquette to publishing, songwriting, and musical production. Using dedicated songwriters, producers, studio musicians, arrangers, studio engineers, professional development specialists, and a quality-control board, this process helped to produce the majority of Motown's well-known hits between 1959 and 1972 and has famously been compared to the assembly line processes used in Detroit's many automobile plants.[10]

As one of Motown's biggest stars, during the 1960s Gaye found it difficult to assert any sort of creative control, and for nearly a decade he worked mostly as a singer. He first wanted to be a romantic balladeer in the tradition of Nat King Cole and Frank Sinatra. After this proved unpopular, he turned to upbeat rhythm and blues, singing on nearly thirty hit songs during the first seven years of his career from 1961 to 1968.[11] In addition to his solo recordings, Gaye perfected the role of the romantic male in duets with Mary Wells, Kim Weston, Tammi Terrell, and later Diana Ross, collaborations that resulted in nearly twenty songs that charted in *Billboard*. Simply put, Gaye thrived at Motown; he was the company's most popular male soloist and duet partner throughout the majority of the 1960s and was arguably at the center of Motown's creative output throughout the decade.

In addition to his vocal duties Gaye also experimented with behind-the-scenes roles at the company. He performed as a drummer in the early 1960s after arriving in Detroit as a member of the new Moonglows and later worked as a writer and producer (often for his own recordings).[12] Between July 1962 and August 1967, he received credit for writing or cowriting seven charting singles and many more album tracks and B-sides released by Motown (see appendixes 1 and 2).[13] This activity foreshadowed Gaye's involvement in the creative process during the 1970s.

The trajectory of Gaye's career changed dramatically in the fall of 1968, when disc jockeys helped to popularize his album track "I Heard It Through the Grapevine," which had been produced by Norman Whitfield almost a year earlier and promptly rejected for release as a single by Berry Gordy.[14] "Grapevine" was released as a single in November 1968, becoming the first Gaye song to top the pop chart and the best-selling disc in Motown's decade-long history.

Although Gaye was at his artistic peak as a vocalist, in the wake of "I Heard It Through the Grapevine" he did not perform live for several years, becoming increasingly involved in production.[15] The producer was arguably the most powerful role in the Motown assembly line, and—in keeping with the philosophy of dividing the creative process among various specialists—most performers were not given access to this level of creative control.[16] During the late summer of 1968, Gaye enlisted the help of a lesser-known Motown producer, Richard Morris, and arranged a recording session to produce a song called "The Bells," which he had cowritten with his wife Anna (the sister of Motown president Berry Gordy).[17]

The yearlong production effort that followed clearly exhibited Gaye's emerging method of vocal composition. In June and August 1968, Gaye and Morris coproduced two preliminary versions of "The Bells" for the vocal group Bobby Taylor and the Vancouvers.[18] One by one, Motown Quality Control rejected both of these recordings.[19] Without re-recording any instrumental parts, Gaye continued to work on the project by rewriting the lyrics and melody.[20] With a new set of lyrics, the track was transformed from "The Bells" into "Baby, I'm For Real," with re-recorded vocal parts by the Originals. In August 1969, "Baby, I'm For Real" was released by Motown as a single and reached the number one position on the *Billboard* "Best Selling Soul Singles" chart.[21]

Because "The Bells" and "Baby, I'm For Real" use exactly the same musical background, the differences between their vocal parts help to illustrate how vocal composition was used to write two original songs from the same backing track (see example 4.2).[22] The melody of the verse in "Baby, I'm for Real" resides on an axis that lies consistently a third below that of the verse of "The Bells." Additionally, the vocal rhythms of these

Example 4.2. Bobby Taylor and the Vancouvers, "The Bells" (1968), and the Originals, "Baby, I'm For Real"

two verse sections emphasize different parts of the measure: "The Bells" contains heavy activity on the downbeats, while "Baby, I'm For Real" stresses the off beats. This contrary rhythmic emphasis is so stark that, when superimposed, the two verse melodies nearly fit together in a perfect call-and-response pattern. Finally, using a series of eighth-note quartuplets, one of which even occurs over the bar line, "Baby, I'm For Real" also illustrates the rhythmic fluidity that occurs frequently in Gaye's works created through vocal composition.[23] In its time, the success of "Baby I'm For Real" from within Motown's merit-based assembly line system gave credence to Gaye's creative methods as a producer and set the stage for his move toward extended vocal composition techniques. Although the 1968 version of "The Bells" was not released for another thirty-five years, we may now view this piece as a harbinger of Gaye's creative methods in the 1970s.

Gaye's use of vocal composition ventured even farther outside of the Motown norm as he gained greater control of his productions during the late 1960s. Beginning with the 1971 album *What's Going On*, Gaye started to produce his own recordings, which allowed him to compose important elements of the music during a session, perform his original compositions directly to tape, and continually edit and refine his work through the process of "punching in" and overdubbing. Although he still relied heavily on the assembly line to create his music, he often used his vocal performances to inspire new material.

During this period Gaye also started to create dense vocal composites by combining multiple recordings of his own voice. Throughout the majority of *What's Going On*, for example, there are two simultaneous Gaye vocal tracks that assume the lead, performing at times in unison, heterophony, parallel motion, and call-and-response. The two existing "final mixes" of this album—one completed in Detroit and the other in Los Angeles—approach the spatial placement of these voices in the stereo field much differently, arguably offering different perspectives on the musical material.[24]

These contrasting versions of *What's Going On* are a reminder of the growing importance of the vocal element in Gaye's music of the 1970s. By developing material directly to tape in the studio, Gaye captured tapestries of unrepeatable utterances in fixed form for posterity and superimposed the acts of composition and documentation in a manner that shifted the power structure of his creativity. This methodology allowed Gaye, who had an otherwise limited ability to create a song in a standard compositional setting, to play a much greater role in the com-

positional process. He sang duets with himself, re-created doo-wop textures by singing every part, highlighted the contrast between the different timbres and ranges of his voice, and included spoken word elements.
In fact, after *What's Going On* Gaye rarely used a solo voice to represent
the sung portion of his music.

There is a growing body of musicological work that acknowledges the act
of recording as akin to the practice of composing. Scholars as diverse as
Albin Zak, Mark Katz, Walter Everett, and Joseph Schloss have explored
the commonalities of, and inherent differences between, composing directly to tape (or disc) and traditional written composition.[25] For example, Zak reminds us that through recording a composer (or what Zak
calls a "recordist") has the ability to dictate elements that are difficult to
notate such as spatial arrangement and timbral manipulation. Zak also
recognizes that by composing directly to tape "the syntax and structural
shape of songs and arrangements are absorbed in their material form,
that is, in their utterance and its sonic presentation as it appears in our
loudspeakers and headphones."[26]

It is also important to consider how African-American vernacular performance practice may have informed Gaye's methodology. In *The Power
of Black Music,* Samuel Floyd writes, "Aesthetic deliberation about African-
American music requires a perceptual and conceptual shift from the idea
of music as an object to music as an event, from music as written—as a
frozen, sonic ideal—to music as making."[27] Thus, in vocal composition,
we witness a process of composition and "notation" that has the capacity
to reveal and incorporate ultraspecific performative details as well as a vocal performance tradition that occurs while recording, resulting in a marriage between Zak's acknowledgment of the permanence of composing
in the recording studio and Floyd's "music as making."

Although Gaye was experimenting with greater creative indepen-
dence during this time, it is still important to remember that vocal composition often required a delicate balance between the ideas of many
other collaborative authors. The ways in which Gaye's originality was supported through collaboration is quite complex but nevertheless important to consider when analyzing his work from the 1970s. For example,
in a study of *What's Going On,* Travis Jackson investigates the complicated
process of collaborative authorship, offering many important ideas for
consideration.[28] Drawing from the ideas of Howard Becker, Nicholas
Cook, and Zak, Jackson's work gives credit to the behind-the-scenes musicians who made significant contributions to Gaye's creative process. He

specifically cites the work of arranger David van de Pitte, songwriter (and member of the Four Tops) Renaldo "Obie" Benson, bassist James Jamerson, and the "47 other instrumentalists and vocalists who participated in the recording of the [*What's Going On*] L.P." Jackson's overall argument—that we need to acknowledge the creative personnel who were "standing in the shadows"—is important and rapidly gaining popularity in the mainstream media.[29] Gaye's collaborative pattern is clear, and Jackson's study could certainly be expanded to include each Gaye album of the 1970s by identifying the importance of collaboration in nearly every project after *What's Going On*.[30] To clarify, I do not seek to discredit the collaborative efforts of others at Motown. Instead, I wish to focus on Gaye's often cited but rarely defined role in the creation of his music.[31]

From Gaye's extensive 1970s catalog, I have chosen to discuss three groups of songs that reflect various elements of his vocal composition. The issues discussed earlier—including Gaye's personal and professional relationships with Motown, his collaborative process, and the act of simultaneous recording and performance—will pervade the analyses of these pieces. In the first example, the interpretive potential of vocal composition is evident in a comparison of two recorded versions of the Frank Loesser standard "I Wish I Didn't Love You So." In contrast to Gaye's highly sexualized image during the 1970s, this example demonstrates his obsession with a more conservative style of vocal music that was in concert with Motown's uplift ideology of the previous decade. A second example discusses Gaye's alteration of the song "Let's Get It On." The process of creating this song demonstrates how political and personal concerns were often infused into Gaye's music, and how he used vocal composition to collaborate with producer Ed Townsend. Finally, Gaye's method of utilizing the technological advancements of the recording studio to create contrasting vocal composites will be explored in the last example, which considers two songs from Gaye's 1978 album *Here, My Dear*.

In viewing Gaye's process through these three types of creative activity (interpretation, collaboration, and utilization), this study is presented in a nonteleological manner. What follows are three snapshots of Gaye's process seen equally from the analytical and contextual levels. Taken as a group, these examples form a complex picture of a process of creating music that encapsulates the many political, artistic, and personal aspects of Gaye's music during the 1970s.

Although Gaye's attempts to record standards during the early 1960s were all financially unsuccessful, he remained optimistic about working with this style throughout his career, often pushing Motown to let him pursue what he called "ballads."[32] His public interest in standards waned after an unsuccessful set of performances at New York's Copacabana in August 1966 and a failed attempt to begin recording a new studio album several months later.[33] He did not release standards after this but continued to rehearse and record cabaret music through the end of the 1970s. Gaye's personal interest in romantic balladry during this decade led to many inventive recordings that specifically highlight the interpretive range of vocal composition.

Gaye was largely preoccupied with one particular group of ballads during the 1970s, a group of arrangements created years before by multi-instrumentalist and composer Bobby Scott.[34] Gaye first worked with these pieces in January 1967, several months after the run at the Copacabana, when backing tracks and vocals were recorded for all six of Scott's arrangements. In the end, however, both Gaye and Motown considered these vocals unusable. Although it was increasingly evident that the odds were against Gaye becoming the "black Sinatra," he continued to study the unfinished Scott arrangements for more than a decade, amassing a variety of radically different interpretations of each song in this set.[35] During downtime of sessions for his more popular music (or sometimes as a means of procrastination), Gaye would experiment with the vocal elements of the Scott recordings, adding layers, changing melodies, and interpreting and reinterpreting the material.[36] The varying vocal performances for the Frank Loesser song "I Wish I Didn't Love You So," for example, are notable for their wide range of interpretation. Motown has subsequently released three different versions of this song—all of which were probably recorded during the late 1970s—two on a 1997 album entitled *Vulnerable* and one on the 1990 *Marvin Gaye Collection* boxed set.[37]

The original Loesser melody and changes for "I Wish I Didn't Love You So" are shown in example 4.3.[38] In his arrangement, Scott used only a single appearance of the thirty-two-bar refrain of Loesser's tune—in a swung compound meter rather than cut time—framed by a four-measure prelude and a three-measure postlude that fades out in both versions.[39] Scott followed Loesser's basic harmonic scheme with some alterations in the first four bars of the verse, where the original changes are replaced by an oscillating I–ii progression over a tonic pedal in the bass. In the second half of each A section, Scott's arrangement briefly tonicizes the IV and iii chords, respectively, via local secondary dominants, then moves through a diatonic circle-of-fifths progression (starting at iii), essentially preserving Loesser's original harmonic scheme.

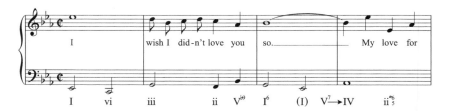

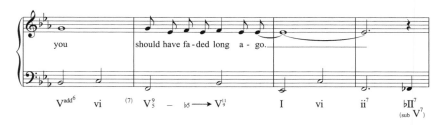

Example 4.3. Frank Loesser's "I Wish I Didn't Love You So," mm. 1–8 (changes and melody)

Gaye recorded three different voices over this backing arrangement, which comprise two interpretive "strains" (see example 4.4). The first (strain 1) is a vocal duet using Loesser's text whose melody, rhythm, and phrasing are traceable to Loesser's tune. For example, the parallel descending contour of the vocal duet matches the original melody, which descends an octave from tonic to tonic in the first eight measures. Gaye similarly derived and altered Loesser's rhythms in this strain, using extended note values for the words "I" and "so" and eighth notes to accompany the words "didn't love you so" in a declamatory fashion. There are also some significant alterations to Loesser's original tune in these performances. Most important, the two melodic strands of the Gaye duet emphasize different scale degrees and encompass a significantly smaller range than the original melody. In the key of D-flat major, Gaye begins on scale degrees 3 and 7 (the pitches F and C) and descends downward only two notches in the thirdwise vertical space of the tonic seventh chord, cadencing on scale degrees 7 and 3 (C and F), respectively.[40] So, while the linear descent in the duet is clearly derived from the original melody, a much smaller intervallic space exists in the individual voices.[41]

The second strain (strain 2) is a solo vocal performance that preserves virtually none of the melodic, textual, or rhythmic elements from the original. There is a completely new set of words throughout this strain. Gaye also adopts a single rhythmic motive for the first sixteen

Example 4.4. Two of Marvin Gaye's interpretations of "I Wish I Didn't Love You So" (four-bar prelude and eight-bar A phrase)

measures of the arrangement (comprising the prelude and first A section), most likely a result of improvising in the studio. This repeated figure consists of three eighth notes followed by a syncopated accent on the eighth note that precedes each strong beat (1 and 3). Even as the arrangement continues past six sets of oscillating I–ii chords (in the prelude and beginning of the verse) into the section of greater harmonic motion that contains the circle-of-fifths progression, Gaye's new melody remains focused on this four-syllable motive.

In terms of interpretive distance, it is crucial to remember that these standards were recorded at a time when audiences knew Gaye best for his pioneering "hyper-sexualized soul" (discussed later in connection with "Let's Get It On"). Gerald Early provides an interesting perspective on the phenomenon of the singer's continuing interest in light, vocal styles.

> It is one of the peculiar and penetrating gestures of "crossover" in American culture that in the 1960s, Marvin Gaye could fantasize about being an Italian ballad singer, making four ballads-and-standards albums for Motown between 1961 and 1965, while the Italian singers of the Rascals could fantasize about being black soul singers with such songs for Atlantic as "Good Lovin'" (1966) and "Groovin'" (1967).[42]

Gaye's continuing interest in the Scott arrangements betrays how this "fantasy" of being a ballad singer persisted well beyond the 1960s. Accordingly, "I Wish I Didn't Love You So" and the rest of the Scott ballads became Gaye's only connection to this failed aspect of his career. He once claimed that it was his maturity and life experiences that finally made it possible for him to interpret these songs to his liking, but it is also relevant that his fully developed vocal composition process facilitated his work with these pieces.

Although Gaye recorded many interpretations of the Scott ballads and did not preside over the mixing of any of this music, it is unclear which of his many performances of "I Wish I Didn't Love You So" he would have included in a final mix.[43] The three commercially available versions of the song complicate this issue even further because each includes a different combination of these vocal tracks. The two versions included on *Vulnerable* keep the vocal strains distinct from one another, with the first version using strain 1 and the second (called an alternative vocal performance) using strain 2, while a third version, released on the 1990 *Marvin Gaye Collection* boxed set, mixes the two strains together, superimposing the higher voice of strain 1 over that of strain 2. Through the lens of vocal composition, it is clear that these vocal performances simply represent a sketch pad of ideas for the track, not a finished or completed work. Therefore, just like "Far Cry," "I Wish I Didn't Love You So" cannot be considered compete. (As far as commercial releases are concerned, it may be most revealing simply to include all three of these vocal tracks to help the listener understand the process that these unfinished performances inhabited.) Nevertheless, for the purposes of this study, "I Wish I Didn't Love You So" offers a clear instance of the interpretive potential of Gaye's compositional technique.

While Gaye was secretly rehearsing cabaret music in the recording studio, his most popular music was far more corporeal. Perhaps the most famous example of this was the song "Let's Get It On." The first sessions for "Let's Get It On" occurred in California during the spring of 1973, after Motown had settled on the West Coast.[44] On 13 March, producer and songwriter Ed Townsend ran a session to record the backing track for this song, which at the time had only a tentative melody and lyrics that Townsend had written himself.[45] A demonstration recording was also made on 13 March, which allows us to hear the state of the song when Gaye entered the creative process. The final lead vocal take was recorded nine days later, on 22 March, and Gaye completed his vocal element on 4 April when he added a set of layered background vocals. A comparison of the demonstration vocals and final lead vocals illustrates the extent to which Gaye acted as a vocal composer after the song's conception.

The harmonic content of the background instrumentation consists mostly of a churning four-chord progression in E-flat major (I–iii–IV–V). This cycle is repeated throughout the majority of the backing track, underlying what would become the verse and chorus sections.[46] The flexibility of using a repeated progression for the bulk of the harmonic material enabled Gaye to improvise on the basic lyrics and melodic ideas presented by Townsend and eventually piece together a concrete melody and lyric. As example 4.5 shows, there are notable differences between Gaye's demonstration and final vocals. The first important change involves the song's phrase design. In the demo version, Gaye enters with the catchphrase "let's get it on" after three harmonic cycles, creating an asymmetrical 6 + 10 hypermetric design. This irregular hypermeter is

Example 4.5. Marvin Gaye, "Let's Get It On" (demo) and "Let's Get It On" (final)

Example 4.5. (continued)

"corrected" in the final vocals, which feature an 8 + 8 structure for the first verse and subsequent chorus. The change in phrase design is easy to explain, as both the chorus and the verse are based on four repetitions of the basic two-measure harmonic progression. In the demo version, Gaye simply shifted the entrance of the chorus one cycle earlier, but he also compensated for this by extending the chorus to span five repetitions of the two-bar unit, maintaining a square sixteen-bar pattern for the verse and chorus combined.

There is a second set of differences between the two versions in the melodic ranges of these two performances during the verse. In the demo version, Gaye tends to work mainly between the pitches C_4 and G_4, with the upper note G (and the blue G♭, ♭$\hat{3}$) serving as a kind of "goal tone" for many of the subphrases. On the contrary, the pitch content of the finished vocals resides mostly a third above the demo version, exploring the range between E♭$_4$ and B♭$_4$, with the upper note B♭ likewise serving as the goal tone of subphrases. A good example with which to illustrate these differences occurs at the opening of the song when Gaye sings the phrase "I've been really trying baby" (and "I've been tryin'"). In the demo version Gaye's vocal line outlines what is essentially a C minor triad over the E♭–Gm progression that begins the song. In the same section of the finished version, however, Gaye sings a stepwise melody that begins on G, climbs to B♭ and then vacillates between G♭ and F for nearly two full beats over the subdominant chord (giving particular emphasis to the blue note G♭) in anticipation of the movement to V, where, after moving through the lower neighbor E♭, the melody eventually rests on F (the structural fifth of the chord).

A third and final difference has to do with the text, and offers a clear instance of the editorial latitude that existed between Gaye and Ed Townsend.[47] Townsend wrote the song after completing rehabilitation for alcoholism, and his original lyrics, which occur in the demo vocals, use the phrase "let's get it on" to refer to "moving on" with life after a struggle with the bottle. Accordingly, the lyrics of the verse—directed back at the protagonist—speak of peace, love, understanding, and brotherhood while the chorus refers to the collective "we." Gaye altered the perspective of the song for the finished version, situating the catchphrase as a pickup line of a libidinous fantasy, and including in the lyrics another person, the potential partner. More important, this alteration is accompanied by a vast amount of sexual energy, infusing the vocal performance with a new series of grunts, groans, and growls that are conspicuously absent in the demo version.[48]

Michael Eric Dyson argues that this movement toward "hyper-sexual-ized soul" was a rebellion against the singer's strict religious upbringing:

> In his erotic exultation, Gaye struck a symbolic blow against sexual prisons built on narrow religious belief. As the son of a strict Pente-costal preacher, Marvin had plenty of cells to unlock. . . . His sensual strivings took on political meaning because they decried the spiritual claustrophobia that smothered erotic freedom.[49]

During the making of *Let's Get It On,* Gaye's sexual exploration was far more than musical. At the recording studio, he was especially attracted to a young woman named Janis Hunter, who was the daughter of one of Ed Townsend's guests, and after the 22 March session Gaye began an intense physical relationship with Hunter, who was then only sixteen years old. Gaye summarized the conflict that arose:

> I was a thirty-three-year-old man married to a fifty-year-old woman. Wasn't that something? My wife was seventeen years older than I was and this girl was seventeen years younger. I was worried about how everyone would react—my friends, my family, my fans.[50]

Thus, the aural exploration of sexuality in "Let's Get It On" mirrored an intense period of both turmoil and excitement in Gaye's personal life. In contrast to the cabaret music and middle of the road R & B Gaye recorded during the 1960s, "Let's Get It On" reflected a much deeper, and more accurate, portrait of life as a celebrity singer. By looking closely at these two different recordings through the lens of vocal composition, we are able to actually see and hear the process through which Gaye "sex-ualized" his music.

The two songs that form the focus of the final part of this study, "Here, My Dear" and "Everybody Needs Love," come from Marvin Gaye's last official studio album for Motown, *Here, My Dear,* which was released in December 1978.[51] Gaye's relationship with Motown was far from favor-able at the time, and he created this album in an unusually autonomous setting. Gaye wrote eleven of the tracks on the album, recorded it in his own studio in Los Angeles, and produced the sessions.[52] Using these pieces, it is possible to show how Gaye created two discrete works with contrasting lyrics, melodic characters, and vocal composites over a single backing track.[53]

It is critical to understand the context surrounding the production of these songs before analyzing them in greater depth since their subject matter—the theme of the larger *Here, My Dear* album—governs their musical similarities and differences.[54] Although Marvin and Anna Gaye had been separated since the 1973 completion of *Let's Get It On,* the two did not officially divorce until March 1977. In the interim, Marvin Gaye and Janis Hunter had parented two children, which caused the tension of the divorce proceedings to rise considerably. Marvin's lack of financial prudence, combined with an extremely expensive drug habit, left the singer without acceptable funds with which to settle the divorce. The two parties made an unorthodox arrangement: Marvin would provide a cash payment for about half of the settlement of six hundred thousand dollars, and Anna would receive the remainder from his next record advance. In essence, Gaye would make an album to settle the financial terms of his divorce.[55]

The resulting album, *Here, My Dear,* is a magnum opus on the trials and tribulations of a failing marriage. Gaye would later discuss his thought process concerning the album:

> I figured I'd just do a quickie record—nothing heavy, nothing even good. Why should I break my neck when Anna was going to wind up with the money anyway? But the more I lived with the notion, the more it fascinated me. Besides, I owed the public my best effort. Finally, I did the record out of deep passion. It became an obsession. I had to free myself from Anna, and I saw this as the way. All those depositions and hearings, all those accusations and lies—I knew I'd explode if I didn't get all of that junk out of me. So I had [studio engineer] Art [Stewart] open up the mikes and I just sang and sang until I'd drained myself of everything I'd lived through.[56]

It was in this setting that Gaye created the songs "Here, My Dear" and "Everybody Needs Love," tracks whose multitude of vocal performances offer examples of Gaye's emotional investment in the *Here, My Dear* project (see example 4.6).[57] One clear example of this conflict lies in the texts of these songs, which are at odds. Although they deal with the same subject matter, Gaye's discussion of the divorce is approached from two very different perspectives, which show the range of emotions experienced during his trying separation. The text of "Here, My Dear," the album's opening track, reveals immediately that the album will be entirely about the singer's divorce in a tongue-in-cheek fashion, remarking "this is what you wanted, here, my dear, here it is." The contrasting text of "Everybody Needs Love" recalls how love benefits everybody and everything; Gaye claims that his mother and father "need love" and he "needs love, too." He continues with the revelation that the object of the song, the "you" (presumably Anna), also needs love. Finally, in a remarkable turn he claims that he needs *her* love. In other words, Gaye asks for a most unlikely source of comfort and compassion: the support of his former wife.

The music of these songs reflects these different perspectives. In the second verse of "Here, My Dear," Gaye speaks of the past, projecting memories of discontent using a lazy, inward vocal style that centers on $\hat{2}$ (F) for four utterances, only moving to $\flat\hat{3}$ (G♭) and $\hat{5}$ (B♭) as the harmony progresses to the V chord at the end of the phrase. In the corresponding section from the second verse of "Everybody Needs Love," he includes a wide range of vocal expression, using three tracks of his voice. One of these voices sings the texted lead, a second performs the role of the functional bass for the first four measures of the example (altering the harmony to a root position I–iii–ii–V progression), and the third maintains a constant repeating pattern of scale degrees 5–6–5.[58] In contrast to the lethargic vocal melody of "Here, My Dear," the swelling tension of the vocals in "Everybody Needs Love" reaches a peak at the poignant moment when Gaye confesses that his father, the man who would eventually take Gaye's life, "needs love."[59] This marks one of the most harmonically active points in the song, when, over a G half-diminished chord in third inversion (analyzed in example 4.6 as part of an expanded V^9 of IV), the melody lands on a dissonant nonchord tone (C) and jumps up an octave before resolving downward.

Gaye's vocal composites help to achieve a difference of affect in these two songs, providing a fascinating case study in aural representation. Nearly every song on *Here, My Dear* contains a thickly textured vocal composite, often to a staggering effect. It is clear that Gaye performed historical roles through these vocal arrangements, re-creating aural memories of the past to cleanse himself of the difficult reality of the present. The doo-wop groups of the 1950s, the gospel choirs and shouting preachers of his religious youth, the seductive spoken rap of his hypersexualized soul, and his many sung solo voices across the timbral spectrum all combine to create this historicizing effect.[60] Gaye was at his artistic peak during this tumultuous time of his life, creating dense vocal

Example 4.6. Marvin Gaye, "Here My Dear" and "Everybody Needs Love"

Example 4.6. (continued)

compositions that highlighted the wide range of his vocal capabilities and allowed him to mix myriad types of singing on one album.

It is important to clarify that Gaye's *process* is not necessarily unique. When I asked him about Gaye's technique, David Ritz, who has written collaborative biographies (and composed) with many important rhythm and blues artists, acknowledged that it was representative of a common methodology in rhythm and blues and "beat-based" music:

> In R & B, [as] far as I've seen, the melody-lyric is usually done after the basic tracks. Even today, hip-hop producers make tracks and give [th]em to vocalists for melodies/words. That's how Janet Jackson works w[ith] [Jimmy] Jam and [Terry] Lewis. [That's] certainly how Barry White and Isaac Hayes worked. . . . I genuinely don't think MPG [Marvin Pentz Gaye] was that different. His vocals, of course, were astoundingly inventive and daring, but his methodology pretty much standard.[61]

In other words, this methodology—whether we call it vocal composition or something entirely different—is clearly at the backbone of the processes used to create an enormous amount of modern popular music.

Even though Gaye's use of technology wasn't novel, his use of vocal composition is still very revealing. Gaye's life experiences during the 1970s often imbued his musical content, and the context of his personal and professional relationships help to paint a full picture of his method of vocal composition. Close readings of vocal composition provide a fresh perspective on how and why Gaye's vocals were "astoundingly inventive." Through analysis that offers evidence of Gaye's input into the creative process, it is clear that the freedom offered by the modern recording studio enabled this all-star vocalist to compose some of the most enduring works of his time.

Gaye was primarily a vocal composer during the last decade of his career—from *What's Going On* in 1971 until his death in 1984—and it is virtually impossible to analyze these works in any detail without taking this process into account. While the release of "Far Cry" may have been an embarrassment to Gaye, it ultimately opened an invaluable window into the creative world of this seminal rhythm and blues artist. It is, of course, ironic that an unfinished, unflattering song in part provides the key to understanding the depth of the late work of Gaye and his methods of musical creation.

APPENDIX 1

Motown Single A-Sides Written or Cowritten by Marvin Gaye, 1962–70

Song	Chart	Artist	Author	Release Date
Beachwood 4-5789	17p, 7r	Marvelettes	William Stevenson Berry Gordy Marvin Gaye	7/11/62
Stubborn Kind of Fellow	46p, 8r	Marvin Gaye	Marvin Gaye William Stevenson George Gordy	7/23/62
Hitch Hike	30p, 12r	Marvin Gaye	Marvin Gaye William Stevenson Clarence Paul	12/19/62
Pride and Joy	10p, 2r	Marvin Gaye	Norman Whitfield Marvin Gaye William Stevenson	4/18/63
Dancing in the Street	2p, 2r	Martha and The Vandellas	William Stevenson Marvin Gaye Ivy Joe Hunter	7/31/64
Pretty Little Baby	25p, 16r	Marvin Gaye	Marvin Gaye Clarence Paul Dave Hamilton	6/18/65
If This World Were Mine	68p, 27r	Marvin Gaye	Marvin Gaye Tammy Terrell	8/29/67
Baby, I'm for Real[a]	14p, 1r	The Originals	Anna Gordy Gaye Marvin Gaye	8/12/69
The Bells[b]	12p, 4r	The Originals	Anna Gordy Gaye Marvin Gaye Elgie Stover Iris Gordy	1/9/70
We Can Make It Baby[b]	74p, 20r	The Originals	Marvin Gaye James Nyx	7/7/70

Note: p = *Billboard* Hot 100 (7/7/62–12/27/70). r = *Billboard* Hot R & B Sides (7/7/62–10/28/62), *Billboard* Hot R & B Singles (11/3/62–11/23/63), *Cash Box* Top 50 in R & B Locations (11/30/63–1/23/65), *Billboard* Hot Rhythm and Blues Singles (1/30/65–5/29/65), *Billboard* Top Selling Rhythm and Blues Singles (6/5/65–4/2/66), *Billboard* Top Selling R & B Singles (4/9/66–1/6/68), *Billboard* Best Selling R & B Singles (1/13/68–3/30/68), Best Selling Rhythm and Blues Singles (4/6/68–8/16/69), Best Selling Soul Singles (8/23/69–12/27/70)

[a]Produced by Marvin Gaye and Richard Morris
[b]Produced by Marvin Gaye

APPENDIX 2

Motown Album Tracks and B-Sides Cowritten by Marvin Gaye, 1962–69

Song	Original Artist	Author	Release Date
Whistling About You[a]	Harvey	Mel Kanar Marvin Gaye Harvey Fuqua	3/31/62
It's Now or Never[b]	Johnny Powers	Bob Kayli Marvin Gaye George Gordy Johnny Powers	12/90 recorded 4/62
I've Got a Story[b]	Mary Wells	Marvin Gaye William Stevenson Henry Cosby	9/93 recorded 6/62
It Hurt Me Too	Marvin Gaye	Marvin Gaye William Stevenson Ricardo Wallace	7/23/62
Get My Hands On Some Lovin'	Marvin Gaye	Marvin Gaye William Stevenson	1/31/63
My Two Arms – You = Tears	Mary Wells	Marvin Gaye William Stevenson Clarence Paul	1/31/63
Soul Bongo	Stevie Wonder	Clarence Paul Marvin Gaye	5/31/63
It's Got to Be Love[b]	Marvin Gaye	Marvin Gaye Clarence Paul	4/95 recorded 1/64
Need Your Lovin' (Want You Back)	Marvin Gaye	Marvin Gaye Clarence Paul	1/21/65
Stepping Closer to Your Heart	Marvin Gaye	Marvin Gaye Harvey Fuqua	1/21/65
Loving and Affection[b]	Marvin Gaye	Marvin Gaye Clarence Paul Cornelius Grant	3/86 recorded 8/63
Hey Diddle Diddle	Marvin Gaye	Harvey Fuqua Marvin Gaye Johnny Bristol	5/23/66
I Love You[c]	Chris Clark	Marvin Gaye Anna Gordy Gaye Margaret Johnson	2/23/67
Change What You Can	Marvin Gaye	Marvin Gaye Elgie Stover Harvey Fuqua	12/21/67
At Last (I Found a Love)	Marvin Gaye	Marvin Gaye Anna Gordy Gaye Elgie Stover	12/21/67
Court of the Common Plea[b]	Marvin Gaye	Marvin Gaye Anna Gordy Gaye Elgie Stover	6/94 recorded 8/68
I Can't Help but Love You	Marvin Gaye Tammi Terrell	Robert Gordy Thomas Kemp Marvin Gaye	8/26/68

Motown Album Tracks and B-Sides Cowritten by Marvin Gaye, 1962–69

Song	Original Artist	Author	Release Date
You're the One[d]	The Originals	Ivy Jo Hunter Elgie Stover	1/16/69
When You Are Available	Shorty Long	Marvin Gaye Anna Gordy Gaye Elgie Stover Shorty Long	8/28/69

[a]Released on the Tri-Phi label
[b]Not released contemporaneous to recording
[c]Produced by Marvin Gaye
[d]Produced by Marvin Gaye and Ivy Jo Hunter

DISCOGRAPHY

Recordings are listed in order of release. Sources include the liner notes to *Marvin Gaye: The Master, 1961–1984,* http://www.bsnpubs.com/motown/motown story.html, www.allmusic.com, www.dftmc.info, and www.hip-oselect.com. The abbreviation "b/w," commonly used in the 1960s, stands for "bundled with."

Clark, Chris. "I Want to Go Back There Again," b/w "I Love You" (V.I.P. 25041, February 1967).

Gaye, Marvin. *The Soulful Moods of Marvin Gaye* (Tamla TM-221, June 1961).

Gaye, Marvin. "Stubborn Kind of Fellow," b/w "It Hurt Me Too" (Tamla 54068, July 1962).

Gaye, Marvin. "Hitch Hike," b/w "Hello There Angel" (Tamla 54075, December 1962).

Gaye, Marvin. *That Stubborn Kind of Fellow* (Tamla TM-239, January 1963).

Gaye, Marvin. "Pride and Joy," b/w "One of These Days" (Tamla 54079, April 1963).

Gaye, Marvin. *When I'm Alone I Cry* (Tamla TM-251, April 1964).

Gaye, Marvin. *Hello Broadway* (Tamla TM-259, November 1964).

Gaye, Marvin. *How Sweet It Is to Be Loved By You* (Tamla TM-258, January 1965).

Gaye, Marvin. "Pretty Little Baby," b/w "Now That You've Won Me" (Tamla 54117, June 1965).

Gaye, Marvin. *A Tribute to the Great Nat King Cole* (Tamla TM-261, November 1965).

Gaye, Marvin. *Moods of Marvin Gaye* (Tamla TM-266, May 1966).

Gaye, Marvin. "Your Unchanging Love," b/w "I'll Take Care of You" (Tamla 54153, June 1967).

Gaye, Marvin. "You," b/w "At Last I Found Love" (Tamla 54160, December 1967).

Gaye, Marvin. "You," b/w "Change What You Can" (Tamla 54160, December 1967).

Gaye, Marvin. *In the Groove* (also issued as *I Heard It Through the Grapevine*) (Tamla TS-285, August 1968).

Gaye, Marvin. "I Heard It Through the Grapevine," b/w "You're What's Happening (In the World Today) (Tamla 54176, November 1968).

Gaye, Marvin. "What's Going On," b/w "God Is Love" (Tamla 54201, January 1971).

Gaye, Marvin. *What's Going On* (Tamla TS-310, June 1971).

Gaye, Marvin. *Trouble Man* (Tamla TS-322L, December 1972).

Gaye, Marvin. "Let's Get It On," b/w "I Wish It Would Rain" (Tamla 54234, June 1973).

Gaye, Marvin. *Let's Get It On* (Tamla T-329V1, August 1973).

Gaye, Marvin. "Come Get to This," b/w "Distant Lover" (Tamla 54241, October 1973).

Gaye, Marvin. "You Sure Love to Ball," b/w "Just to Keep You Satisfied" (Tamla 54244, January 1974).

Gaye, Marvin. *I Want You* (Tamla T6-342S1, March 1976).

Gaye, Marvin. *Here, My Dear* (Tamla T-364LP2, December 1978).

Gaye, Marvin. "Ego Tripping Out," b/w "Ego Tripping Out (Instrumental)" (Tamla 54305, September 1979).

Gaye, Marvin. *In Our Lifetime* (Tamla T8-374M1, January 1981).

Gaye, Marvin. *Midnight Love* (Columbia 38197, October 1982).

Gaye, Marvin. "Sexual Healing," b/w "Sexual Healing (Instrumental)" (Columbia 03302, October 1982).

Gaye, Marvin. *Romantically Yours* (Columbia 40208, 1985).

Gaye, Marvin. *Motown Remembers Marvin Gaye* (Motown 6172, March 1986).

Gaye, Marvin. *The Marvin Gaye Collection* (Motown MOTD4-6311, September 1990).

Gaye, Marvin. *In Our Lifetime* (Motown 374636379-2, 1994).

Gaye, Marvin. *Love Starved Heart: Rare and Unreleased* (Motown 31453 0319 2, June 1994).

Gaye, Marvin. *The Master, 1961–1984* (Motown 31453 0492 2 April 1995).

Gaye, Marvin. *Vulnerable* (Motown 314530786-2, March 1997).

Gaye, Marvin. *Midnight Love and The Sexual Healing Sessions* (Columbia/Legacy C2K-65546, November 1998).

Gaye, Marvin. *What's Going On (Deluxe Edition)* (Motown 440-013-304-2, February 2001).

Gaye, Marvin. *Let's Get It On (Deluxe Edition)* (Motown 440-014-757-2, September 2001).

Gaye, Marvin. *Love Songs: Bedroom Ballads* (Motown B00005UNBG, January 2002).

Gaye, Marvin. *I Want You (Deluxe Edition)* (Motown B0000467-02, July 2003).

Gaye, Marvin. *Marvin Gaye at the Copa* (Hip-O Select/Motown B0003629-02 DG02, April 2005).

Gaye, Marvin. *In Our Lifetime (Expanded Love Man Edition)* (Hip-O Select/Motown B0008082-02, May 2007).

Gaye, Marvin. *Here, My Dear* (expanded edition) (Hip-O Select/Motown B0010315-02, December 2007).

Gaye, Marvin, and Tammi Terrell. "If I Could Build My Whole World Around You," b/w "If This World Were Mine" (Tamla 54161, November 1967).

Gaye, Marvin, and Tammi Terrell. *You're All I Need* (Tamla TS-284, August 1968).

Knight, Gladys, and the Pips. "I Heard It Through the Grapevine," b/w "It's Time to Go Now" (Soul 35039, September 1967).

Long, Shorty. "A Whiter Shade of Pale," b/w "When You Are Available" (Soul S 35064, August 1969).

Martha and the Vandellas. "Dancing in the Street," b/w "There He Is (At My Door)" (Gordy 7033, July 1964).

Marvelettes, the. "Beachwood 4-5789," b/w "Someday, Someway" (Tamla 54065, July 1962).

Originals. "Green Grows the Lilacs," b/w "You're the One" (Soul 35061, May 1969).

Originals. "Baby, I'm For Real," b/w "Moment of Truth" (Soul 35066, August 1969).

Originals. "The Bells," b/w "I'll Wait For You" (Soul 35069, January 1970).

Originals. "We Can Make It Baby," b/w "I Like Your Style" (Soul 35074, July 1970).

Powers, Johnny. *Can't Resist the Rock 'n' Roll* (Roller Coaster ROLL2017, 1990).

Various artists. *Motown Classics: Dancing in the Street* [karaoke] (The Singing Machine G-8851, September 2003).

Various artists. *Motown Classics: Let's Get It On* [karaoke] (The Singing Machine G-8855, September 2003).

Various artists. *Motown Sings Motown Treasures, Volumes 1 and 2*. Hip-O Select B0003619-02, January 2004).

Wells, Mary. *Two Lovers* (Motown MT-607, January 1963).

Wells, Mary. *Looking Back* (Motown 37463 6253 2, September 1993).

Wonder, Stevie. *The Jazz Soul of Little Stevie Wonder* (Tamla TM-233, July 1963).

Young Rascals. "Good Lovin'," b/w "Baby, Let's Wait" (Atlantic 2321, February 1966).

Young Rascals. "Groovin'," b/w "Sueno" Atlantic 2401, May 1966).

NOTES

An early version of this chapter was presented at the annual meeting of the Society for Music Theory in Madison, Wisconsin, in November 2003. More developed presentations were later given at the Center for the History of Recorded Music at Royal Holloway, University of London, and the University of Surrey in April 2008. Thanks especially to John Covach, Tim Hughes, Adam Krims, Jocelyn Neal, and David Garcia for their comments during the early stages of this research. Travis Stimeling and John Brackett read early drafts of this chapter and offered innumerable insightful comments. Thanks to David Ritz and Bill Schnee for their advice and willingness to answer questions about the life, work, and recording legacy of Marvin Gaye. Harry Weinger and Keith Hughes also helped immeasurably with discographical and historical concerns. During the final stages of revision, Mark Spicer's editorial comments (especially on the transcriptions) were extensive and extremely helpful, and two anonymous readers provided insightful and useful comments and suggestions.

1. By the late 1970s Motown had lost faith in Gaye as a marketable performer as he fled from Los Angeles to Hawaii and then Belgium to avoid paying taxes and a divorce settlement. It is difficult to determine which party eventually took action and severed the business relationship. However, Gaye was vocal in the press concerning his feelings for Motown. In a 1981 interview with *Blues and Soul* magazine, for example, he said, "As far as I'm concerned [*In Our Lifetime*] is definitely my last album for Motown—even if Berry [Gordy] does not release me from my existing recording obligations and I am in fact, under obligation to record for the rest of my natural life for Berry. If he refuses to release me, then you'll never hear any more music from Marvin Gaye. . . . *I'll never record again!*" (emphasis in original). Bob Killbourn, "In Marvin's Lifetime . . . ," *Blues and Soul and Disco Music Review*, 2–15 June 1981, 12–13, 31.

2. In general, the best source for information about Gaye's departure from Motown is David Ritz, *Divided Soul: The Life of Marvin Gaye* (New York: Da Capo, 1991). Berry Gordy recalls his version of the story in his autobiography *To Be Loved: The Music, the Magic, the Memories of Motown* (New York: Warner, 1994), 373–77.

3. Quoted in Ritz, *Divided Soul*, 280–81.

4. Several of the examples in this chapter include transcriptions for an abbreviated group of instruments. Most important for my argument are the lead melody, lyrics, and chord changes (including the actual bass), which are always included. However, in other instances I found that it was important also to include a representation of the background vocals and the drum kit.

5. The lyrics provided in example 4.1 are only approximate because of the inexact pronunciation in Gaye's performance. Furthermore, the lyrics printed in the liner notes accompanying the 1994 compact disc version of *In Our Lifetime* reflect the difficult process of transcribing Gaye's mumbled performance in this song. Although there is a literal copy of the opening material used after the bridge, the printed lyrics have notable differences. (This has been corrected in the more recent Expanded Love Man edition.) "Far Cry" also lacks the layered backing vocals that were a hallmark of Gaye's sound in the 1970s (see my subsequent discussion).

6. The first cut is at 2:37, and the paste begins at 3:07. The extended version is available on the *In Our Lifetime (Expanded Love Man Edition)*.

7. To be sure, this nonlinear process is at the foundation of many of the most important post–World War II genres of popular music that rely heavily on the studio environment. Electronic dance music (EDM), the rock music of U2, and mashups are only a few of the musical forms recently documented by music researchers that rely heavily on creative methods that allow the composer(s) to assemble actual recorded parts and compose in a simultaneous or alternating fashion. For EDM, see Mark J. Butler, *Unlocking the Groove: Rhythm, Meter, and Musical Design in Electronic Dance Music* (Bloomington: Indiana University Press, 2006). For U2, see Paul Harris, "U2's Creative Process: Sketching in Sound," PhD diss., University of North Carolina at Chapel Hill, 2006. Scholars such as Mark Katz

and Wayne Marshall have presented widely on modern composition that uses extensive digital editing.

Among the many other studies of music and technology, some noteworthy works include Joseph Auner, "'Sing It for Me': Posthuman Ventriloquism in Recent Popular Music," *Journal of the Royal Music Association* 128 (2003): 98–122; Mark Katz, *Capturing Sound: How Technology Has Changed Music* (Berkeley: University of California Press, 2004); Louise Meintjes, *Sound of Africa! Making Music Zulu in a South African Studio* (Durham: Duke University Press, 2003); Timothy Warner, *Pop Music: Technology and Creativity—Trevor Horn and the Digital Revolution* (Aldershot and Burlington: Ashgate, 2003); and Albin Zak, *The Poetics of Rock: Cutting Tracks, Making Records* (Berkeley: University of California Press, 2001).

8. Scholarly research on Motown includes Gerald Early, *One Nation under a Groove* (Ann Arbor: University of Michigan Press, 2004); Ben Edmonds, *What's Going On: Marvin Gaye and the Last Days of the Motown Sound* (Edinburgh: Mojo, 2001); Jon Fitzgerald, "Motown Crossover Hits, 1963–1966, and the Creative Process," *Popular Music* 14 (1995): 1–11; Jonathan Andrew Flory, "I Hear a Symphony: Making Music at Motown, 1959–1979," PhD diss., University of North Carolina at Chapel Hill, 2006; Nelson George, *Where Did Our Love Go? The Rise and Fall of the Motown Sound* (New York: St. Martin's, 1985); Suzanne E. Smith, *Dancing in the Street: Motown and the Cultural Politics of Detroit* (Cambridge: Harvard University Press, 1999); and Jacqueline Warwick, "I Got All My Sisters and Me: Girl Culture, Girl Identity, and Girl Group Music," PhD diss., University of California, Los Angeles, 2002.

9. Motown is both the name of the company and the name of the company's most popular label. (The bulk of Motown's most popular material of the 1960s and 1970s was released on four labels: Motown, Tamla, Gordy, and Soul.) Although these two entities share the same name, they should not be confused with one another.

10. Many other companies used "assembly line" methods to create popular music during the 1960s. The Brill Building, the entire Nashville-based country music industry, and many other R & B companies (including Vee-Jay, Stax, Chess, and King) all similarly used large creative teams with dedicated functions to create music in an assembly line fashion at this time. Motown's assembly line, however, is arguably the most famous. Although more frequently cited in the popular press, academic treatments of this process at Motown include Fitzgerald, "Motown Crossover Hits"; Ian Inglis, "Some Kind of Wonderful: The Creative Legacy of the Brill Building," *American Music* 21 (2003): 214–35; and Smith, *Dancing in the Street*, 94–138. For a more thorough treatment of the popular music recording process outside of Motown, see Zak, *The Poetics of Rock*.

11. In the nineteen years between his first single to hit the charts, "Stubborn Kind of Fellow" (1962), and "Heavy Love Affair" (1981), his last Motown single, Gaye placed nearly sixty songs on the pop and R & B charts (this includes duets and one group release), more than any other Motown artist during these two decades. Twelve of these singles reached number 1 on the R & B charts, and three crossed over to number 1 on the pop charts.

There has been considerable controversy surrounding the use of record chart data as a marker of popularity because it is unclear exactly how magazines such as *Cashbox* and *Billboard* derived the information included in their charts. In the case of Motown, however, it is clear that chart position was an acknowledged benchmark for a song and thus affected decision making at the company. For a more detailed discussion of the use of charts in research and the temporary discontinuation of the *Billboard* rhythm and blues chart in 1964, see David Brackett, "What a Difference a Name Makes: Two Instances of African-American Popular Music," in *The Cultural Study of Music: A Critical Introduction,* ed. Martin Clayton, Trevor Herbert, and Richard Middleton (New York: Routledge, 2003), 238–50.

12. Ritz, *Divided Soul,* 63. A common anecdote cites Gaye as the drummer on the Marvelettes' "Please Mr. Postman," which became the first number 1 pop hit for Motown in late 1961. According to Motown archivist Harry Weinger, however, there is no documented instance of Gaye having performed as drummer on a Motown record (e-mail correspondence with the author, 4 January 2008). This is because there is little available documentation of the performers on *any* Motown backing session from the 1960s.

13. The songs included in the appendixes represent the released recordings of Gaye-penned songs. In fact, Gaye is credited with writing many more songs in the printed Jobete Catalog dated January 1959 to 31 March 1967. Furthermore, songwriting credit is not always a true marker of actual writing. Frequent deals were made between the people who had actually written the songs and those who had sufficient influence at Motown to get them recorded and released. Crucial to a later argument of this chapter, producers (and influential artists such as Gaye) could receive songwriting credit for simple editorial suggestions or changes made during a recording session.

14. Producer and cowriter Norman Whitfield made several recordings of "I Heard It Through the Grapevine" before the Marvin Gaye version became so popular. The first version of the song, produced by Whitfield in 1966, was performed by Smokey Robinson and the Miracles and not released to the public until 1998. This version is available commercially on the collection *Motown Sings Motown Treasures.* Gaye performed on the next recording of "Grapevine" in the spring of 1967, but it was not released as a single in favor of the song "Your Unchanging Love" in June 1967. Distraught by his failure to get the song to the public, Whitfield revamped "Grapevine" and recorded it for a third time in the summer of 1967 with Gladys Knight and the Pips. The Gladys Knight version was the first to be released to the public, on 14 September 1967; by December of the same year, this recording had reached the number 2 position on the pop chart and the top slot of the R & B chart. The success of Gaye's "Grapevine" escalated dramatically after the song appeared as filler on his *In the Groove* album, released in August 1968. As Berry Gordy remembers, "The DJs played it so much off the album that we had to release it as a single" (Gordy, *To Be Loved,* 275). This is supported by the 16 November 1968 "Top 10" listing in the *Michigan Chronicle,* which showed Gaye's version at number 3 despite the fact that it would not be released officially as a single until two weeks later.

15. Gaye's first production credit was for Chris Clark's "I Love You," a B-side from 1967 (see appendix 2).

16. Since 1963, Gaye had been married to Berry Gordy's older sister Anna,

but even with his family ties to Gordy, Gaye did not have ready access to the producer's chair at this point in his career. (This date is surmised from Ritz, *Divided Soul*, 82–83.)

17. Ben Edmonds has carefully traced the path Gaye took to the producer's chair beginning in June 1968 (Edmonds, *What's Going On,* 53–75).

18. The August 1968 version of "The Bells" is included in the collection *Motown Sings Motown Treasures.*

19. Quality Control was the formal name for weekly production meetings during which a team of Motown employees voted to determine which singles to release. As Berry Gordy remembers it, "The Friday morning product evaluation meetings were my meetings. They were exciting, the lifeblood of our operation. That was when we picked the records we would release. Careers depended on the choices we made those Friday mornings. Everybody wanted to be there" (Gordy, *To Be Loved,* 151). Edmonds writes that Gordy knew the real production history of these recordings, and, just as he did with his sister Anna, he communicated with Gaye indirectly through Morris (Edmonds, *What's Going On,* 56–57).

20. The reversal of the process was not unheard of at Motown and is reminiscent of the process used by Holland, Dozier, and Holland to write lyrics and melodies during their most creative period.

21. "Baby I'm For Real" was released as an album track in July 1969. However, Edmonds reveals that Motown's original strategy was to release a song called "Green Grows the Lilacs" as the Originals' single from this set. Only after this song failed to achieve success did the company release "Baby, I'm For Real" (Edmonds, *What's Going On,* 68–72). A recording of "Baby, I'm For Real" that allows the listener to separate the lead vocal from the background track appears on the *Motown Classics: Dancing in the Street* karaoke collection.

22. The song "The Bells" that was edited to become "Baby, I'm For Real" should not be confused with the song "The Bells" released as a single in January 1970. These are two different pieces of music in terms of recording history, yet the 1969 version contains many musical similarities to the released version that Gaye produced with Richard Morris: the verse section is in F major and follows the exact harmonic progression of the verse for "The Bells" (1968) and "Baby, I'm For Real." Unlike Gaye's first two versions of "The Bells," this recording was officially released by Motown and entered the charts during winter 1970, peaking at number 12 pop and number 4 R & B.

23. Although different members of the Originals sing lead throughout the song, Freddy Gorman performs lead on the first verse. See Bill Dahl, *Motown the Golden Years* (Iola, WI: Kraus, 2001), 287. This "rhythmic fluidity" is the result of a level of stratification between vocal line and backing track that pervades the music of the Originals just as it does the solo music of Marvin Gaye. It becomes apparent through transcription the ways in which Gaye's writing style often includes hemiola and other types of intricate cross rhythms at both the beat and measure levels and sometimes even across bar lines. The transcription of "Let's Get It On" (example 4.5) offers a good example of this kind of localized rhythmic disjuncture in Gaye's solo work.

24. These two mixes are included on the *What's Going On (Deluxe Edition).*

25. Zak, *The Poetics of Rock;* Katz, *Capturing Sound;* Walter Everett, *The Beatles as Musicians:* Revolver *through the* Anthology (New York: Oxford University Press, 1999); Joseph G. Schloss, *Making Beats: The Art of Sample-Based Hip-Hop* (Middletown, CT: Wesleyan University Press, 2004).

26. Zak, *The Poetics of Rock*, 46.

27. Samuel A. Floyd, *The Power of Black Music: Interpreting Its History from Africa to the United States* (New York: Oxford University Press, 1991), 232. This is one of the main themes of Floyd's study. He writes, "For in Signifyin(g), the emphasis is on the signifier, not the signified. In African-American music, musical figures signify by commenting on other musical figures, on themselves, on performances of other music, on performances of the same piece, and on completely new works of music" (95). He later clarifies that "this is why, in contrast to the European musical orientation, the *how* of a performance is more important than the *what*. Certainly, African Americans have their favorite tunes, but it is what is done with and inside those tunes that the listeners look forward to, not the mere playing of them" (96–97, emphasis in original).

28. Travis Jackson, "What's Going On: Authorship, Accidents, and the Concept Album," paper presented at Cornell University, Ithaca, NY, 25 October 2004.

29. This argument is reflected in the documentary *Standing in the Shadows of Motown* (dir. Paul Justman, Artisan Home Entertainment, 2002), which advocates for greater public recognition of the behind-the-scenes stable of backing musicians at Motown, who nicknamed themselves the Funk Brothers.

30. Gaye's self-production debut, *What's Going On,* was most indebted to the assistance of arranger David van de Pitte; Gaye's major collaborator for both *Let's Get It On* and *Here, My Dear* was songwriter and engineer Ed Townsend; and the disco-infused *I Want You* was the brainchild of Leon Ware. In addition, the Bobby Scott sessions were greatly influenced by engineer Art Stewart, who worked on several other Gaye projects in this decade.

31. One concrete instance of this is Obie Benson's claim concerning Gaye's contribution to "What's Going On." Benson and Al Cleveland wrote the song and brought it to Gaye to record during his self-imposed performing hiatus; Gaye, however, still received partial songwriting credit. Initially, this credit came from Benson himself, who agreed to give Gaye a portion of the royalties for simply recording the piece. Yet, Benson claims that in the end Gaye participated in the compositional process: "He definitely put the finishing touches on it. . . . He added lyrics, and he added some spice to the melody. He fine-tuned the tune, in other words. He added different colors to it. He added some things that were more ghetto, more natural, which made it seem more like a story than a song. He made it visual. He absorbed himself to the extent that when you heard the song you could see the people and feel the hurt and pain. We measured him for the suit and he tailored the hell out of it" (quoted in Edmonds, *What's Going On,* 97–98).

32. Gaye recorded many long-playing records of conservative cabaret material throughout the 1960s, none of which appeared on the album charts. After *The Soulful Moods of Marvin Gaye* (1961), there were the albums *When I'm Alone I Cry* (1964), *Hello Broadway* (1964), and *A Tribute to the Great Nat King Cole* (1965).

33. The modern compilation of performances from these shows, *Marvin Gaye at the Copa,* focuses on the favorable reviews of these concerts, although Gaye himself once confessed that the Copacabana run "didn't go well" (quoted in Ritz, *Divided Soul,* 108). This album was originally scheduled for release in January 1967 but was eventually withdrawn.

34. Gaye stated, "[W]hen Bobby played me his charts, I had to put away my own work. His arrangements were absolute genius. There were four ballads and two jazzy big-band numbers, and never before had I been so excited about music. Strange, though, because when I went in to record, I couldn't pull it off. It was as though the arrangements were too deep for me. Maybe I froze up thinking that the ballads would flop like all the ballads I'd sung before. Later I learned that it wasn't really a block. I couldn't sing the songs because I wasn't old enough. I didn't know enough. I had more suffering to do before I could get to the feelings" (quoted in Ritz, *Divided Soul,* 136). See also David Ritz, liner notes accompanying Marvin Gaye's *Vulnerable.*

35. During this interpretive process, Gaye treated the background tracks much like a jazz performer would use a set of standard chord changes, improvising new melodies, groups of layered vocal parts, and backing vocals that only partially accounted for the original tune. Though similar, this technique should not be equated wholly with the jazz tradition due to the important difference in the method of musical communication that resulted from Gaye improvising over a fixed performance. Whereas jazz improvisation is often based on the communal exchange of ideas between the musical support mechanism and the soloist, Gaye's performances were created against a fixed background, and he therefore could not rely on the backing musicians' reaction to his ideas. Representative studies that discuss the importance of communication and exchange among jazz musicians include Ingrid Monson, *Saying Something: Jazz Improvisation and Interaction* (Chicago: University of Chicago Press, 1996); and Travis Jackson, "Performance and Musical Meaning: Analyzing 'Jazz' on the New York Scene," PhD diss., Columbia University, 1998.

36. Due to the nature of Gaye's approach to the Scott ballads, exact dates for these sessions are very difficult to determine. It is clear, however, that Gaye began serious work on the ballads during the late 1970s with engineer Art Stewart. When asked about specific dates, Motown archivist Harry Weinger revealed only that "a timeline for what became *Vulnerable* would be a massive research project" (Harry Weinger, e-mail correspondence with the author, 7 June 2006).

37. Three earlier performances of different Scott ballads, which include the original 1960s vocal takes, appear on the album *Romantically Yours.* The 1960s vocals for "I Wish I Didn't Love You So," however, have not been released. Although *Vulnerable* is now out of print, one of the versions included on this album is now available on the album *Love Songs: Bedroom Ballads.* At the present time, based on the released material, it is impossible to know exactly how much of the Scott ballad material exists in the Motown vaults. The various "strains" I will consider represent only those available to the record-buying public.

38. Frank Loesser, *The Frank Loesser Songbook* (Milwaukee: Hal Leonard, 1994), 75–77.

39. I have elected to transcribe the meter as 12/8 in example 4.4, which al-

lows for a 1:1 ratio between the measures of both the original and the Scott arrangement (quarter = dotted quarter).

40. An argument could certainly be made for a voice transfer to complete the octave. Yet, as will become clearer later, these performances are not necessarily wedded to one another, and without both included in the final mix the span of the melody would only reach the interval of a fifth or fourth (depending on which voice was present).

41. This is particularly important in the version of the song on *The Marvin Gaye Collection*, which includes only the higher voice of the duet.

42. Early, *One Nation under a Groove*, 10.

43. Bill Schnee, who mixed *Vulnerable*, says that the final choices for the performances to include on this album were taken from a cassette prepared by Gaye and engineer Art Stewart in the late 1970s. He also confirms that the two strains included in example 4.4 were the only existing interpretive strains on the raw twenty-four-track master tape. Schnee noted, however, that there were multiple performances of each strain. This is apparent in the slight differences between the performances included on the *Vulnerable* and *Marvin Gaye Collection* versions. The most important lesson from the source material is that even though these performances seem extemporaneous Gaye meticulously crafted them. This was so much the case that he was able to reproduce each performance in a nearly identical manner during the recording sessions (Bill Schnee, telephone interview with the author, 1 August 2006).

44. Information about the recording of *Let's Get It On* can be found in the annotations and session research accompanying the *Let's Get It On (Deluxe Edition)* written by Harry Weinger and Andrew Skurow. See also Blair Jackson, "Marvin Gaye's *Let's Get It On*," *Mix* (1 January 2002), http://mixonline.com/recording/interviews/audio_marvin_gayes_lets/.

45. Basic tracks and demo vocals were recorded the same day for two other songs as well: "If I Should Die Tonight" and "Keep Gettin' It On" (the title track reprise).

46. There is a contrasting bridge (from 1:34) that slows the harmonic motion by resting on the subdominant chord with flatted seventh (A♭7) for two whole measures and then moving through a tonicized V as a retransition to the core progression.

47. See producer Ed Townsend's foreword to the *Let's Get It On (Deluxe Edition)*.

48. This particular vocal performance is littered with audible pops and clicks, which provide evidence of the way Gaye pieced it together by "punching in" phrases. The naked vocal track is included on the Singing Machine karaoke disc of *Let's Get It On*.

49. Michael Eric Dyson, *Mercy, Mercy Me: The Art, Loves, and Demons of Marvin Gaye* (New York: Basic Civitas Books, 2004), 101, 108. The term *hyper-sexualized soul* comes from Mark Anthony Neal, "The Tortured Soul of Marvin Gaye and R. Kelly," in *The Best Music Writing 2004* (New York: Da Capo, 2004), 222–29. We may also view Gaye's sonic acknowledgment of the black body as akin to what Guthrie Ramsey finds in his analysis of the Four Jumps of Jive's "It's Just the Blues" from 1945. Ramsey writes, "If one of the legacies of nineteenth-century

minstrelsy involved the public degradation of the black body in the American entertainment sphere, then one hundred years after minstrelsy's emergence, African Americans used this same signifier to upset a racist social order and to affirm in the public entertainment and the private spheres their culture and humanity." Guthrie P. Ramsey Jr., *Race Music: Black Cultures from Bebop to Hip-Hop* (Berkeley: University of California Press, 2003), 51.

Gaye played a huge role in the transformation of the coded hokum blues of the 1940s and 1950s to the explicit, overtly romanticized rhythm and blues of the 1970s and 1980s. He was a leading force in this movement, which also included contemporaries such as Al Green, Isaac Hayes, and Barry White and followers such as Teddy Pendergrass, Keith Sweat, and R. Kelly. See Orea Jones, "The Theology of Sexual Healing," in *Black Sacred Music: A Journal of TheoMusicology* (Durham: Duke University Press, 1989), 68–74.

50. Quoted in Ritz, *Divided Soul,* 178.

51. Gaye's unofficial last Motown album was the unfinished *In Our Lifetime,* which was (as discussed earlier) released without his approval.

52. The studio was closed for years after Gaye's financial troubles in the late 1970s, but it has since been reopened under the name Marvin's Room.

53. Unlike the previous examples in this chapter, Gaye actually used different takes (performances) of the original template in this case. Another example from *Here, My Dear* that uses this sort of cut-and-paste technique to create a song is "Funky Space Reincarnation" (working title "Song #2 [Breakdown]"), which grew out of a breakdown section of "Anger" (working title "Song #2").

54. The connection between these songs is evident in their working titles, "I Got Love" ("Everybody Needs Love") and "I Got Love II" ("Here, My Dear").

55. See Ritz, *Divided Soul,* 233–38. Although it is not certain when this agreement took place, it is more than likely the case that Gaye was already at work on what would become *Here, My Dear* when he learned of this financial arrangement. According to Weinger, Gaye began work on these sessions as early as April 1976.

56. Ritz, *Divided Soul,* 234.

57. The bass and drum set parts are shown in example 4.6 as in "Here, My Dear." There are slight differences in both parts in "Everybody Needs Love" (e.g., in the second half of measure four, the bass guitar in "Here, My Dear" plays B♭–A♮–A♭ as shown, while in the corresponding place in "Everybody Needs Love," the bass guitar plays the pitches C–B♭–A♭ in tandem with the backing bass vocal part). The differences in the backing tracks for "Here, My Dear" and "Everybody Needs Love" do not necessarily preclude them from having used the same multitrack master. Nevertheless, their tempi are markedly different and there is no noticeable difference in pitch. I would guess that the two tracks are from different takes of the same tracking session or different sections of a larger jam used to produce the master background after editing.

58. The bass guitar is muted from the mix during this segment, and as it fades in the vocal bass actually disappears.

59. Gaye was murdered by his father in Los Angeles on 1 April 1984, the day before his forty-fifth birthday.

60. Gaye had a strong connection to the doo-wop style of the 1950s. After

dropping out of high school and a brief stint in the Air Force, he moved to Chicago in 1959 to perform in the doo-wop group Harvey and the Moonglows. The Moonglows had formed in the early 1950s in Cleveland and, after signing with Chess records in the mid-1950s, the group scored several hits between 1955 and 1958 with songs such as "Sincerely," "Most Of All," "We Go Together," "When I'm With You," "Please Send Me Someone To Love," and "Ten Commandments Of Love." (Although Harvey Fuqua was the main songwriter and head of the group, Bobby Lester often sang lead.) When Gaye joined the group, the original members had recently disbanded, leaving only Harvey Fuqua to carry on as leader. Gaye only sang lead on one single—"Mama Loochie"—for the newly formed Harvey and the Moonglows. This new configuration was not very successful, and Fuqua moved to Detroit in 1960. There he founded several small record labels—including Harvey Records and Tri-Phi—to which he signed the young Gaye (although no Gaye records were ever released under these labels). Fuqua's most notable involvement with the Gordy family at this time was with sister Gwen Gordy (Berry's older sister), who became his business partner and love interest. Later that year Berry Gordy bought the entire Harvey Records roster, effectively adding Gaye to the growing stable of young artists that would eventually record for the Motown Corporation's group of labels.

61. David Ritz, e-mail communication with the author, 8 June 2006. In this communication Ritz also confirmed that the process used to create "Sexual Healing" (which he cowrote with Gaye) began with a completed set of backing tracks with chord changes, after which Ritz wrote a set of lyrics and Gaye used these words (altering them slightly) to write the melody of the song. Ritz is an acknowledged expert on the day-to-day lives and working methods of a variety of rhythm and blues artists. He has written collaborative autobiographies with Ray Charles, Smokey Robinson, Etta James, B. B. King, Aretha Franklin, and the Neville Brothers and written songs with Gaye, Janet Jackson, and Cyril Neville.

FIVE   §   A Study of Maximally Smooth Voice Leading in the Mid-1970s Music of Genesis

KEVIN HOLM-HUDSON

FOR MANY ROCK HISTORIANS, and certainly for many listeners, it would seem that there were two bands named Genesis: the darkly theatrical, at times surreal progressive rock band fronted by Peter Gabriel; and the altogether more accessible (and commercially successful) group fronted by Phil Collins. The latter "radio-ready" Genesis, responsible for such hit albums as *Abacab* (1981), *Genesis* (1983), and *Invisible Touch* (1986), would appear on the surface to have very little in common with its earlier incarnation. Gabriel's reemergence as a major solo artist with the success of *So* (1986) and soul-inflected hits such as "Sledgehammer" and "Steam" (1992) similarly belies little of his early Genesis style. In fact, many fans of Peter Gabriel and Phil Collins in the 1980s were unaware that they had come from the same band.

Yet the first incarnation of Genesis created a body of music that was unique among its progressive-rock contemporaries. From the beginning, this was a different band in part due to the upper-class backgrounds of its founding members. Genesis came together among Peter Gabriel, keyboardist Tony Banks, guitarist Anthony Phillips, and guitarist/bassist Michael Rutherford as a kind of "songwriting club" at Charterhouse, an exclusive English secondary school. Their privileged background initially "didn't assist their acceptance in a rock culture which prefers its heroes, if not genuinely working class, at least superficially so."[1] Indeed, Genesis gained its first major following not in England but in Italy, where audiences apparently appreciated the connections between the group's dramatic music (and Gabriel's theatrical performing style) and their country's own rich operatic tradition.

The absence of "superficial" working-class connotations in Genesis is readily apparent when one compares their music with that of many of their progressive-rock contemporaries, particularly regarding the "white rock man's burden," namely, the influence of the blues.[2] Unlike Yes, Emerson, Lake & Palmer (ELP), Jethro Tull, and King Crimson, to name a few, Genesis's music (with the notable exception of the 1972 track "Twilight Alehouse") avoids overt blues models.[3] Like their sometime label mates Van der Graaf Generator, Genesis's music has other roots; whereas Van der Graaf Generator's style owes much to Stravinsky and jazz, Genesis's harmonic style draws on intricate—and often unpredictable—chromatic passages reminiscent of late-nineteenth-century romanticism. This aspect of their harmonic style makes Genesis's music notably more romantic—in an authentic sense—than that of such contemporaries as Yes or ELP.[4]

Mark Spicer, in his analysis of Genesis's multisectional suite "Supper's Ready" (1972), asserts that the group "possessed an uncanny natural ability to mimic and assimilate musical styles from outside of the pop-rock domain and transform them into something fresh and unique."[5] Spicer's analysis focuses on the large-scale compositional structure of "Supper's Ready" and also on its stylistic mediations between nineteenth- and early-twentieth-century art music and rock, with his analysis of the group's harmony limited to examples chosen to support his intertextual reading of the song. Such stylistic borrowings are not unique to Genesis, of course, for references to various aspects of art music practice alongside rock and jazz passages are characteristic of progressive rock in general, as John Covach has noted.[6]

It is the kind of chromatic harmony so often employed by Tony Banks that makes Genesis's music distinctive. More specifically, Banks's chord voicings often progress chromatically from one to the next, a technique that I will refer to in this chapter as *maximally smooth chromatic voice leading*.[7] For example, moving from a C major (or C+) chord to an E major (or E+) chord in the smoothest possible manner at the keyboard involves subtle contrary motions of individual tones as C moves to B and G moves to G-sharp: $\{C, E, G\} \rightarrow \{B, E, G\sharp\}$.[8] This type of chord progression is sometimes referred to as a *chromatic mediant* progression because the chord roots—C and E—are a third (mediant) apart from each other and yet, unlike a diatonic mediant progression, the second chord has been chromatically altered from E minor to E major. Such progressions, so intuitive at the keyboard, were a hallmark of the chromatic harmonic language of Franz Schubert, Richard Wagner, Franz Liszt, César Franck, and other nineteenth-century composers. In guitar-based rock music, however, chromatic mediant progressions came from a different source and without necessarily the same concern for smooth voice leading, as the construction of the guitar facilitated parallel chord movement by shifting one's hand position on the neck and rock musicians more readily experimented with modal mixture. Consider, among myriad examples in 1960s rock, the <C+, A+> introduction of Creedence Clearwater Revival's "Proud Mary" (1969), the <G+, B♭+> progression (resulting in a Lydian mixture) in the refrain of the Beatles' "Yesterday" (1965), and the <A+, C+> progression in the Rolling Stones' response to the Beatles, "As Tears Go By" (1965).

In analyzing chromatic mediant progressions in music of the Western concert tradition, a number of scholars, including Richard Cohn, the late David Lewin, and John Roeder, have recently revived and expanded on the harmonic theories of the nineteenth-century theorist and pedagogue Hugo Riemann.[9] Although these writers have confined their study to examples of maximally smooth chromatic voice leading in art music from the late-nineteenth- and early-twentieth-century repertoire, the analytical approaches of neo-Riemannian theory can also be applied profitably to much pop and rock music, as Guy Capuzzo has demonstrated.[10] Genesis's harmonic language, also, often exhibits the very transformational characteristics that Cohn, Lewin, and Roeder have found in their studies of late romantic and postromantic music.

Isolated examples of such progressions in the music of Genesis may be found as early as their first album, *From Genesis to Revelation* (1969), and they occurred with increasing frequency as the band's songs became more intricately structured. Banks's propensity for chromatic voice leading culminated in two albums—*A Trick of the Tail* and *Wind and Wuthering* (both 1976)—that marked the transition between Gabriel's departure from the group in 1975 and their ascendancy as one of the most successful pop-rock groups of the 1980s.[11] This chapter addresses the evolution of such progressions in Genesis's music from the group's debut album to 1980's *Duke*.[12]

As Banks himself has confirmed in several interviews, his style is intuitive and eclectic. Some songs employ the "conventional" harmonic syntax of early- to mid-nineteenth-century European classical music, whereas others employ progressions that would have been deemed functionally aberrant (e.g., V → III). Occasionally Banks employs sonorities that are not strictly tertian or that juxtapose triads against foreign bass notes. Accordingly, in this chapter I employ several analytical methodologies. Some progressions are analyzed drawing on the neo-Riemannian concepts explored in articles by Hyer and by Cohn.[13] Other progressions that are not strictly triadic will be analyzed following the taxonomies of chromatic voice leading given by Roeder and Lewin.[14] Where harmonic examples are best described using conventional Roman numerals and inversion symbols, those symbols are also used.

Technique

Tony Banks's classical training was rather limited. He took lessons in violin and piano as a boy (encouraged by his mother, who was an accomplished amateur pianist) and continued to study the piano while at Charterhouse, but he admits that he always found playing by ear much more attractive than reading pieces from notation. Banks is a self-taught composer.[15] Among his art music influences he has acknowledged Ravel,[16] as well as Rachmaninoff and other "crossed-hand type things."[17] As his casual reference to Rachmaninoff perhaps implies, his approach to harmony is intuitive and tactile rather than based on any explicit modeling: "I think a lot of it is done by how it feels on the keyboard. Some things just feel lovely to play."[18] He elaborates:

> The idea is that you come up with interesting changes when you change chords simply by changing the bass notes. It's difficult to explain, but when I'm at the piano it's almost like I'm creating music by making mistakes. When you come up with something nice, you stick to it, and you come up with some really unlikely things that sound good. Like in the introductory bit to "The Eleventh Earl of Mar." . . . One of the chords in that is basically a G minor chord with an A-flat in the bass. That sounds unlikely, but it sounds great in context. A lot of this comes out of improvising—doing things that you originally didn't intend to do and finding that it sounds nice.[19]

Banks's remarks, given their rather offhand nature, are in fact not entirely accurate. The type of "wrong-note bass" motion he describes in this passage is more applicable to the so-called slash-chord harmonies characteristic of a number of 1970s pop artists, especially Steely Dan, Marvin Gaye, and Todd Rundgren.[20] Banks's harmonic effects typically result instead from half- or whole-step motion, often contrary, in *inner* voices as well as the bass. Example 5.1 contains two such harmonic progressions placed at the beginning and end [0:26–0:40 and 7:07–7:39] of "Eleventh Earl of Mar,"[21] the opening track on *Wind and Wuthering*. The progressions are linked to one another by identical instrumentation (organ, Mellotron, bass synthesizer pedal, rolled cymbals, and a repeated electric-guitar glissando from D_4 to D_5) and dynamic contour (a crescendo accompanying the chord changes). The second progression (labeled B in the example) begins with a root-position version of the second chord from the opening progression (labeled A in the example), implying that the second progression is a continuation of the first. The chord marked with an asterisk in each example—which, depending on its inversion, might be described as an E-flat major-seventh chord with no third and added ninth (in the first instance) or as a B-flat major chord with added eleventh (in the second instance)—acts as a linear chord in both progressions, the result of individual voice leading. It is also significant that nearly all of the voices in these progressions exhibit the same kind of "complementary chromatic voice leading" that John Roeder discusses in his study of atonal voice leading, and thus the mo-

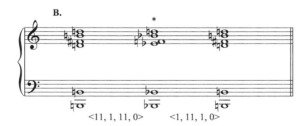

Example 5.1. "Eleventh Earl of Mar" (1976), (A) opening progression [0:26–0:40], (B) closing progression [7:07–7:39]. Numbers in angle brackets represent voice-leading intervals after Roeder in his 1994 article "Voice Leading as Transformation," in Raphael Atlas and Michael Cherlin, eds., *Musical Transformation and Musical Intuition: Eleven Essays in Honor of David Lewin* (Delham, MA: Ovenbird, 1994), 41–58.

tion of individual chord voices may be analyzed using Roeder's voice-leading vectors (VLVs), the technical details of which I will explain later.

Many of Banks's most striking harmonic progressions are triadic in nature and may be profitably analyzed in neo-Riemannian terms. Example 5.2 provides a summary of the neo-Riemannian progression types to which I will refer throughout this chapter. In this regard, Carol Krumhansl's research regarding perception of neo-Riemannian progressions provides an interesting empirical confirmation of Banks's compositional process: "[N]on-musicians are especially sensitive to pitch proximity, the principle underlying the neo-Riemannian transformations, measured in both actual and abstract pitch-class distances."[22] As Cohn

Example 5.2. Summary of neo-Riemannian triadic progression types

has summarized her findings, "[C]ommon-tone relations are more likely to guide the judgments of subjects without musical training."[23] Although Banks is by no means a nonmusician, he does by his own admission "create music by making mistakes" or through intuitive trial and error.

Banks as a Composer

In spite of his limited formal training, Banks has always thought of his music as a fixed compositional entity rather than a fluid improvisational process; as he puts it, "I'm more interested in the compositional aspect of music than I am in actual performance."[24] Even though he generally does not use notation, his songs—and even his extended keyboard solos in songs such as "Supper's Ready"—are extensively worked out and played identically from night to night. "For me, the solo is as much a part of the song as the melody line," he has said. "You could vary from it, but it's kind of difficult, because either you've got to change it completely because of the way the bass and the drums work with it, or you've got to leave it alone. Playing the same thing has never really worried me. I see it as part of the composition."[25]

This interest in the compositional aspects of his music no doubt contributes to the chromatic boldness of his harmonic progressions. One of his earliest examples occurs in the song "In the Wilderness" from Genesis's pop-oriented debut album *From Genesis to Revelation* (example 5.3). The opening line is similar to the first half of a Romanesca progression (familiar to many listeners as the harmonic progression for Johann Pachelbel's famous Canon in D Major), ending instead on a chromatically altered III chord (A+). In the context of the song's F major tonality, we would expect this chord to tonicize vi (D–), but instead the chord resolves back to F major. Using transformational procedures, we may interpret the movement <A+, F+> as a PL progression.[26] This progression, although it occurs early in Banks's compositional output, is typical of his voice-leading style in that it exhibits what Guy Capuzzo has called *p parsimony*, where one or two pitches are shared between triads (as opposed to *pitch classes*, which would constitute *pc parsimony*).[27] Banks's use of a 4–3 suspension (D to C♯) in the uppermost voice of the A major triad further marks the chromaticism of this passage.

Lest the chromatic alteration of the expected iii chord be thought of as mere surface detail, the A major chord also plays an important structural role by pointing toward the D major tonality of the song's chorus, a move that offers early evidence of Banks's interest in chromatic mediant

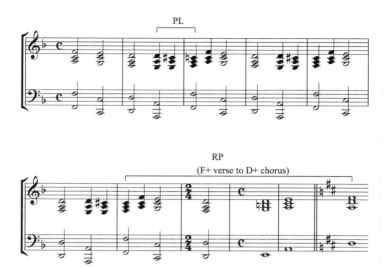

Example 5.3. "In the Wilderness" (1969), verse, textural reduction

key relationships; the movement from the F major key of the verse into the D major key of the chorus is a large-scale RP progression, as I have shown in example 5.3. The transition to the chorus is achieved by substituting an E minor seventh (ii[7] of D) at the point [0:28] where the listener expects to hear an A major triad for a fourth time. The harmonic rhythm is then augmented twofold for the ii[7] and fourfold for the minor v that follows [0:30], building tension that is finally released with the arrival of D major at the chorus [0:35]. (Substituting minor v for the expected major V also brings balance to the original substitution of A+ [III] for the expected minor iii of F, A–, in the verse.) "In the Wilderness" is unique among the songs on *From Genesis to Revelation* in having this sort of parsimonious progression, but it hints at the later direction the group would take.

By the time of the group's third album, *Nursery Cryme* (1971), Genesis's style had considerably matured; songs became longer and more formally complex, and harmonies became more experimental by rock standards. Example 5.4a shows a simplified transcription of the introduction to the song "Seven Stones," which opens the second side of the album. The organ line in descending thirds seems to imply the key of G major, but just before the entry of the vocal ("I heard the old man tell his tale") the V chord retrogresses to IV, setting off a temporary tonicization that suggests a modulation to C major. The last four chords of example 5.4a, however, again steer the listener off course in preparation for the verse, which is in B-flat major. Transformational analysis demonstrates that PR transforms the D+ chord to F+, and the C+ chord to E♭+. The second progression is a nearly exact sequence of the first but for the addition of a major seventh above the E-flat triad. The voice-leading maps for these progressions are shown below; doubled tones are assigned according to the "law of the shortest way," and tonal shifts in semitones are expressed as positive numbers whether ascending or descending.

D	→	F	=	3
D	→	C	=	2
A	→	A	=	0
F♯	→	F	=	1

Net voice-leading change: 6

E	→	D	=	2
C	→	B♭	=	2
G	→	G	=	0
E	→	E♭	=	1

Net voice-leading change: 5

Example 5.4b shows the progression of the second chorus as it leads into the song's extended coda, the end of which is shown as example 5.4c. In example 5.4b, a modulation from C– to F♯– is achieved by means of what Lewin has called a "SLIDE" (S) in which two triads of opposite qualities are inverted about a common third.[28] This is the first instance of an S progression in Genesis's output, and it was to become a favorite transitional device. Framing the S are two R' progressions (inversions around the Riemannian dual fifth).[29] Example 5.4c also shows an LP progression from G♯– to E– (because the B of the triad is doubled by the Mellotron, I hear the C♯ in the organ as an added sixth over E–).

Example 5.4c concludes with the elegant protracted chromatic descent that ends the song, a seeming homage to Chopin's famous Piano Prelude in E Minor, op. 28, no. 4.[30] As in the Chopin, the chords here function in more of a linear fashion than as a sequence of functional vertical sonorities. Unlike the Chopin, however, some chords are incomplete, leaving the listener to infer the missing tones. Example 5.5 accordingly provides a harmonic reduction of the last six measures; note that, with the exception of the first two and last two chords, the net voice-leading change is 1 semitone throughout, with the chromatic movement

a) Introduction [0:00–0:16]

G+: ii   V   IV I IV⁶ V⁶ B♭+: V V⁷/V IV⁷

b) Transition from second chorus to coda [3:43–4:00]

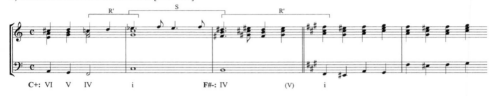

C+: VI V IV   i   F#-: IV   (V)   i

c) Coda (conclusion) [4:17–5:08]

(mellotron)

(organ)

F+: I ♭VI   B+: vi⁶₁₄   iv (added 6th)

g#-: IV   i iv i vii°⁴₃ i⁶₁₄

I

(I prolonged to end via linear chords)

Example 5.4. "Seven Stones" (1971)

Total voice-
leading change: 3   1   1   1   1   1   1   5

Voice-leading
vectors, after
Roeder
(1994):   <11, 0, 10> <11, 0, 0> <11, 0, 0> <0, 11, 0> <11, 0, 0> <0, 11, 0> <11, 0, 0> <10, 2, 11, 0>

Example 5.5. Harmonic reduction of the last six measures of "Seven Stones"

alternating between the lowest and middle voices after the second progression.

"Seven Stones" recounts three stories—concerning a tinker, sailors,
and a farmer—through their common connection to an old man whose
"guide is chance." Journalist Chris Welch comments that the song is
based on the philosophical notion that "the secret of success and good
fortune is based purely on random events and chance."[31] Perhaps it is to
underscore the apparent randomness of this philosophical construct
that the chord progressions in "Seven Stones" meander rather unpre-
dictably.

The next three examples show similar progressions from Genesis's
songs, only one of which—"Robbery, Assault and Battery" (example
5.6)—is explicitly credited to Banks. Before *A Trick of the Tail,* all songs
were credited to the group as a whole, reflecting their practice of assembling songs from ideas brought into rehearsals by individual members.
Banks's role on the early recordings was often to provide effective transitions between sections. Reflecting on his early musical training, he has
said, "I suppose that training was useful in some ways. . . . I think techni-
cally it has helped me a great deal in that I have quite a good knowledge
of chords and scales and if we're ever trying to find a bridge between two
passages which are in different keys, I can usually come up with a chord
or sequence of chords that glides one into the other without too much
difficulty."[32] Example 5.6 shows how Banks creates a succession of chords
that "glide" into one another by means of a network of interlocking de-
scents. The first bracketed set of progressions alternates chromatic de-
scents in the upper two voices with voice-leading vectors <0, 0, 0, 11> and

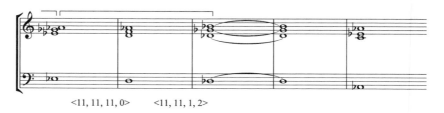

VLV: <0, 0, 0, 11>   <0, 0, 11, 0>   <0, 0, 0, 11>   <10, 0, 10, 0>   <0,10, 0, 0>   <0, 0, 0,10>

<11, 11, 11, 0>   <11, 11, 1, 2>

Example 5.6. "Robbery, Assault and Battery" (1976), harmonic reduction with voice-leading vectors [3:18–3:32]

<0, 0, 11, 0>. The next bracketed set of progressions changes the half-step descents to whole steps and subjects each voice in turn to the step-wise motion. Eventually the progression comes to rest (for two measures) on a second-inversion G♭+ triad (suggesting a cadential six-four chord), but the expected resolution to D♭+ (V of G♭) is instead deflected by a motion to A♭+, the tonality of the ensuing passage.

Even in their earlier "group" compositions, some sections with a high degree of chromaticism have been traced to Banks in various interviews. Example 5.7a shows the opening of "Supper's Ready" (from 1972's *Foxtrot*), the chord sequence of which Banks claims to have written on the guitar.[33] Mark Spicer has analyzed this progression in some detail,[34] so for our purposes it will suffice to show the downward chromatic slippage (and some pertinent neo-Riemannian progressions). The progression shown in Example 5.7b, from the "Guaranteed Eternal Sanctuary Man" section of "Supper's Ready," is interpreted by Spicer as having its origins in rock as opposed to art music practice because of the overt parallel fifths in the voice leading. Genesis biographer Armando Gallo relates that Banks composed this progression using barre chords on the guitar.[35] However, rock songs do not tend to employ SLIDE or S progressions such as that from C♯– to C+; moreover, the fingering of these two chords

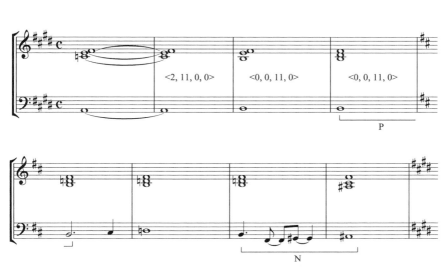

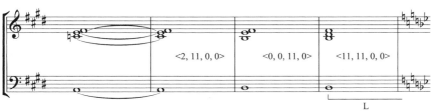

Example 5.7a. "Supper's Ready" (1972), opening progression

Example 5.7b. Excerpt from the "Guaranteed Eternal Sanctuary Man" section of "Supper's Ready"

in sequence on the guitar would require a fair degree of hand contortion (it is, in fact, much easier on the keyboard).[36] This implies a certain degree of intentionality on Banks's part and may even imply that his "keyboard thinking" extends to other instruments. Banks told another interviewer, "I do some of my writing from guitar, but I find it a bit restrictive chord-wise so I generally prefer the piano."[37]

Banks's harmonic style is also consistent enough that one may infer his contributions to other songs. Example 5.8 shows a section not specifically credited to Banks that most likely comes from his hand, from "The Fountain of Salmacis," another song from *Nursery Cryme*. The song recounts the myth of the first hermaphrodite, as found in Ovid's *Metamorphosis*. The passage shown here makes its first appearance on the lyric "unearthly calm descended from the sky" as the hunter and nymph are fused into "one flesh." In its inexorable chromatic descent, it is similar to the "Robbery, Assault and Battery" progression of four years later; it also employs the SLIDE progression found in the "Guaranteed Eternal Sanctuary Man" section of "Supper's Ready."

On the *A Trick of the Tail, Wind and Wuthering, . . . And Then There Were Three . . .* (1978), and *Duke* albums, all of the songs with parsimonious chromatic voice leading are credited or cocredited to Banks. Moreover,

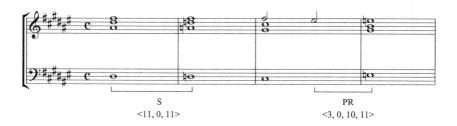

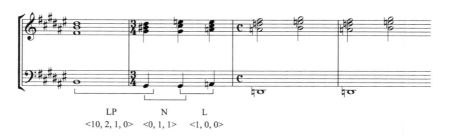

Example 5.8. "The Fountain of Salmacis" (1971) [4:34–4:58]

the more ambitious songs from these albums exhibit chromatic third relationships not only on the foreground level of chord-to-chord progression but also in middleground key relationships. "Mad Man Moon,"
from *A Trick of the Tail*, is one such song and one of Banks's finest compositions. It is also a song on which Banks played virtually all of the parts:
"A song like 'Mad Man Moon' only has one guitar phrase on it. That's all.
All the rest was done on keyboards."[38]

"Mad Man Moon" hints at a more directly narrative style of songwriting for Genesis, as it recounts the fate of someone who leaves a loved one
to "search beyond the final crest" into the desert. The second verse contains a number of references to mirages and illusions: the protagonist
"pretended to have wings for my arms / and took off in the air," en-
countering "a thousand mirages, the shepherds of lies" before concluding that "I would welcome a horse's kick to send me back / If I could find
a horse not made of sand." In the final verse of the song, the protagonist
concludes that "Forever caught in desert lands one has to learn / To dis-
believe the sea." These ephemeral images are enhanced by the harmonic

Example 5.9a. "Mad Man Moon" (1976), introduction

progressions, which evade predictable resolutions from as early as the song's introduction, a reduction of which is shown in example 5.9a. The opening two-bar progression suggests ii–V in G major, but, while the melody is sequenced down by step in measures 3–4, the accompanying harmonies do not comply. Instead of I–IV in G major (a diatonic sequence of the opening two-bar progression), Banks substitutes a iii chord (B–) for the expected tonic (G+), which has the effect of veering toward the relative key of E minor, the key of the ensuing verse.

Example 5.9b provides a harmonic reduction for the first section of the song. Like the haze of rising heat off desert sand, triads are consistently obscured by added tones, and deceptive cadences occur at the ends of phrases (measures 13–14 [0:33–0:38] and 22–23 [1:00–1:07]). Moreover, the auspicious fully diminished seventh chord at measure 20, accompanying a melodic high point, promises a move to C major but is instead dragged back down to E minor. Susan McClary has described the submediant key area in minor as conveying "false hope" in Schubert's *C Minor Impromptu* (op. 90, no. 1);[39] if that signification applies here, the false hope is indeed illusory for it is barely hinted at. The chorus (measures 25–34 [2:01–2:27]), which begins in the parallel E major, contains a number of progressions involving complementary chromatic voice leading. Throughout the chorus, any sense of forward momentum (in the traditional functional-harmony sense) is continually thwarted. Only with the transition to the middle section of the song, in the chromatic submediant key of C-sharp major (an RP transformation away from E major), are we released from the grip of E minor.

After a lengthy instrumental section [2:38–4:49], the middle section proper kicks off with the first appearance of a character other than the protagonist—in this case the "sandman," who may in any case be a mere hallucination. The steady 4/4 meter of the opening section is replaced here by a lively additive meter (3 + 2 + 2), and the harmonic language changes as well; entire phrases serve as prolongations of the tonic triad, and modulations are achieved mostly by sequence rather than chromatic slippage. The transition back to the opening section, however, provides perhaps Banks's most breathtaking moment (example 5.9c). On the words "sun and sand," an F♯/E "slash chord" is followed by a {D♯, G♯, A♯, C♯} linear sonority, which to the ears would most likely suggest a D-sharp dominant seventh with a suspended fourth awaiting resolution. Instead, as the G♯ moves down to F× (enharmonically G), the other voices move chromatically as well (and a fifth voice, F♯, is added), landing on a Gmaj7/D sonority, which signals a reprise of the original verse progression.

Example 5.9b. "Mad Man Moon," opening section [0:17–2:38], harmonic reduction

C♯	→	D	=	1
A♯	→	B	=	1
G♯	→	G	=	1
D♯	→	D	=	1

Net voice-leading change: 4

Interestingly, this chord progression involves not only complementary chromatic voice leading but textural symmetry (expressed through the

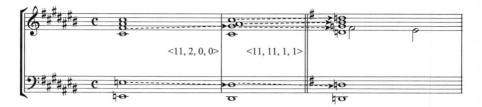

Example 5.9c. "Mad Man Moon," transition from the middle section to reprise of the opening section [5:16–5:28]

voice-leading vector <11, 11, 1, 1>). Most striking is the chromatic contrary motion in the outer voices, which is highly evocative of an augmented-sixth resolution in classical tonality. Banks has described this moment as "one of my favorite chord changes of all time" and "an uplifting sort of change."[40]

The *A Trick of the Tail* and *Wind and Wuthering* albums represent the peak of Genesis's neoromantic chromatic style. After *Wind and Wuthering*, Genesis began to have their first commercial successes in the United States. The success of the song "Follow You Follow Me" (from . . . *And Then There Were Three* . . .), their first U.S. top-forty single, apparently encouraged the group to adopt a more direct pop style. As a result, the distinctive chromatic progressions of vintage Genesis begin to diminish in the albums after *Wind and Wuthering*, but Banks's first solo album, *A Curious Feeling* (1979), continues in his lavish chromatic style, evidently an outlet for a harmonic style that was increasingly circumscribed within his band. Example 5.10 depicts the progression that introduces the album's opening instrumental, "From the Undertow."[41]

Genesis's 1980 album *Duke* contains the group's first sizable U.S. hit, "Misunderstanding" (which peaked at number 14), written by Phil Collins. (The following year, Collins would enjoy the first of his many solo successes with *Face Value* [U.K. number 1, U.S. number 7], which contained the iconic hit "In the Air Tonight.") Compared to previous Genesis albums, the keyboard work on *Duke*—especially on songs such as "Misunderstanding" and "Turn It On Again"—often takes on a strictly utilitarian quality. Moreover, the lyrics to Banks's composition "Guide Vocal" seem to declare his abdication as the group's behind-the-scenes musical leader. In studio parlance a guide vocal or scratch vocal is a preliminary vocal track not intended for the final mix that acts as a guide in fleshing out the arrangement of a song. Here, however, Banks's lyric be-

Example 5.10. Tony Banks, "From the Undertow" (1979), opening [0:00–0:58]

gins "I am the one who guided you this far." The guide's role had to this point been behind the scenes and anonymous ("Nobody must know my name / For nobody would understand") and yet now seems to have outlived its usefulness with the arrival of success ("There was a choice but now it's gone / I said you wouldn't understand / Take what's yours and be damned"). Nevertheless, traces of Banks's chromaticism can be found even in Genesis's more streamlined pop style. The introduction and main riff for the hit single "Turn It On Again," for example, features the sequence of an <E+, B+, F♯+> progression (IV–I–V in B major) up a minor third to <G+, D+, A+> (IV–I–V in D major), over a B pedal. The background progression <B+, D+>, then, is a PR transformation.

The pedal point in "Turn It On Again" warrants discussion as another Genesis trademark. Spicer notes that textures dominated by pedal points can be traced to 1960s acid rock and were fixtures of commercial rock styles by the late 1970s and early 1980s. Still, "Genesis remain . . . the masters of the 'pedal-point groove.' What experienced listener can forget, for example, the giant crescendo that precedes the entrance of the vocal in 'Watcher of the Skies' (1972), or the sheer power of the booming bass pedals in 'Back in NYC' (1974)?"[42] With this insight, Spicer illuminates an important facet of Genesis's style that can be found as far back as "Stagnation" (from 1971's *Trespass*). In Genesis's "classic" progressive period, the years between the arrival of Phil Collins and Steve Hackett and the departure of Peter Gabriel, such pedal points are sometimes grafted onto elaborately dexterous rhythmic patterns epitomized by songs such as "Watcher of the Skies" and "Riding the Scree" (1974), the latter of which Spicer notes is in 9/8 time subdivided as 2 + 2 + 2 + 3.[43] In later Genesis songs such as "Turn It On Again," the pedal point is articulated in eighth notes, helping to emphasize the meter and propel the momentum of the introduction. This type of pedal point is much more consistent with contemporary "stadium rock" examples—such as Van Halen's "Jump" (1984)—and generally more in keeping with rock stylistic practice. Thus, as "Turn It On Again" demonstrates, earlier markers of Genesis's progressive style—such as chromatic mediant progressions and the dramatic use of pedal points—have been sublimated into more conventional song structures and commercial pop-rock styles.

Outtakes from this period—issued on the *Genesis Archive #2, 1976–1992* CD boxed set—reveal that the group continued to experiment with chromatic harmony even if these tracks never made it to the final song selection. Among the *Abacab* outtakes from 1981, the song "Naminanu" features a <D+, F+> vamp—a PR transformation—over a pedal G. Another track, the instrumental "Submarine" (which sounds like a Banks composition even though it is credited to all three group members), uses chromatic mediant relationships at two key transitional points in the progression. An E-flat minor-seventh chord resolves to B– (with D in the bass), an LP transformation, and an E+ chord resolves to a D-flat major-seventh chord, an RP transformation.[44]

Conclusion

By common consensus, *Duke* marked a turning point in Genesis's commercial fortunes. The aforementioned Phil Collins composition "Misunderstanding" (which Collins later said "was meant to be a song that anyone could listen to—girl meets boy") became their first major American hit and broadened the group's appeal to a mainstream pop audience.[45] At the time of Peter Gabriel's departure, the members of Genesis were 150,000 pounds in debt to their record company;[46] the success of *Duke* enabled them to invest in their own studio, which in turn changed their songwriting approach:

> [W]e didn't play each other anything we'd had before. And the songs just kind of evolved. We started putting things down on tape as soon as they took any kind of shape. It was an exciting way to work. You can get more spontaneity that way. Sometimes, when you get a song be-forehand and go into rehearsals with it, develop parts of it, and end up changing it, you overwork it.[47]

Duke accordingly represents a turning point in Genesis's musical style. "Turn It On Again" notwithstanding, the radio friendly songs of Phil Collins coexist somewhat uneasily with such Banks contributions as "Guide Vocal" and "Cul-de-Sac" (a fleeting progression from which is shown in example 5.11). With the exception of the album's closing in-strumental, "Duke's Travels/Duke's End," gone are the lengthy solos and intricate song structures. In their place is the sound of a band capitaliz-ing on its first mainstream successes in the United States, then the world's largest pop music market. Indeed, Genesis's new emphasis on

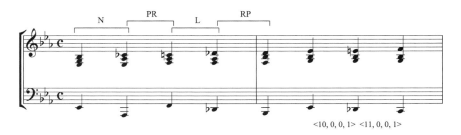

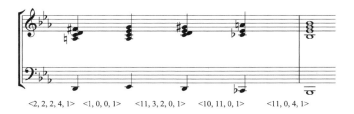

Example 5.11. "Cul-de-Sac" (1980), excerpt [4:29–4:36]

simplicity paralleled a wave of simplification in rock music: progressive rock gave way to punk and then new wave; Paul Simon's lush chromatic pop of the 1970s gave way to the three-chord South African grooves of 1986's *Graceland*;[48] and Steely Dan went into hiding for two decades after 1980's *Gaucho*. The changes in pop music's microcosm are analogous to the sweeping changes in musical style as the baroque gave way to the classical era.

Until his surprise departure from Genesis in 1996, Phil Collins was to lead the group on to ever greater commercial successes, peaking with 1986's *Invisible Touch* (which yielded five U.S. Top 5 singles) and 1991's *We Can't Dance,* but also arguably to some of their least distinctive music.[49] During their 1970s heyday, however, Tony Banks's intuitive slips of the fingers and secondhand knowledge of romantic and impressionist works led the band into a musical style that, for all its surface similarities to the music of their progressive rock contemporaries, was quite different. The experimental impulse embodied in their best work from this period may be taken as emblematic of a time in post–*Sgt. Pepper* culture when the worlds of "art" and "popular entertainment" were briefly intermingled.

NOTES

An earlier version of this chapter was presented at the annual meeting of the Society for Music Theory in Columbus, Ohio, 31 October 2002.

1. Nick Logan and Bob Woffinden, *The Illustrated Encyclopedia of Rock* (New York: Harmony, 1977), 91.

2. I discuss progressive rock's treatment of twelve-bar blues form in Kevin Holm-Hudson, ed., *Progressive Rock Reconsidered* (New York: Routledge, 2002), 9.

3. "Twilight Alehouse," an outtake from the *Foxtrot* sessions, originally appeared as the B-side to the "I Know What I Like" single in 1973, although it had previously been a staple of the group's live performances. It did not appear on a full-length Genesis album until the 1998 release of the *Genesis Archive, 1967–75* CD boxed set (Atlantic 82858-2).

4. Even beneath the high-classical veneer of these other groups, there always lurked blues-rock roots, sometimes at the same time as explicit classical quotations (as in Keith Emerson's 1971 "blues variation" on "The Old Castle" from Mussorgsky's *Pictures at an Exhibition*).

5. Mark Spicer, "Large-Scale Strategy and Compositional Design in the Early Music of Genesis," in *Expression in Pop-Rock Music: Critical and Analytical Essays,* 2nd ed., ed. Walter Everett (New York: Routledge, 2008), 323.

6. John Covach, "Progressive Rock, 'Close to the Edge,' and the Boundaries of Style," in *Understanding Rock: Essays in Musical Analysis,* ed. John Covach and Graeme M. Boone (New York: Oxford University Press, 1997), 8.

7. David Lewin defines "maximally close voice leading" as a function V that maps each member x of pcset X to a member y of pcset Y [$Y = V(x)$ of Y], such that each voice of pcset X is led to the closest possible pitch of pcset Y. This is the definition that I adopt in describing "maximally smooth" voice leading. See David Lewin, "Some Ideas about Voice Leading between PCSets," *Journal of Music Theory* 42, no. 1 (spring 1998): 15–72, especially 15–17.

8. Throughout this chapter, I shall use the neo-Riemannian symbols of a plus sign for major chords and a minus sign for minor ones. Progressions from one chord to another will be designated with angle brackets, so that the progression from C major to E major, for example, would be written as <C+, E+>. Chords—or unordered collections of pitches—will be designated by pitch names within curly brackets. C major, then, would be written as {C, E, G}.

9. For studies of "parsimonious" harmonic progressions in late romantic music, see Richard Cohn, "Maximally Smooth Cycles, Hexatonic Systems, and the Analysis of Late-Romantic Triadic Progressions," *Music Analysis* 15, no. 1 (1996): 9–40; and his "Neo-Riemannian Operations, Parsimonious Trichords, and their *Tonnetz* Representations," *Journal of Music Theory* 41, no. 1 (1997): 1–66. Lewin's aforementioned article, "Some Ideas about Voice Leading between PCSets," offers a generalized taxonomy of voice leading applicable in both tonal and posttonal contexts. Finally, John Roeder's study of transformational voice leading describes how the consistent use of "complementary contrary voice leading" connects otherwise unrelated sonorities in music by Arnold Schoenberg and Elliott Carter; see his "Voice Leading as Transformation," in *Musical Transformation and Musical Intuition: Eleven Essays in Honor of David Lewin,* ed. Raphael Atlas and Michael Cherlin (Delham, MA: Ovenbird, 1994), 41–58.

A good survey of neo-Riemannian concepts and progressions may be found in Miguel Roig-Francolí, *Harmony in Context* (New York: McGraw-Hill, 2002), 863–71. For a streamlined and modernized version of Hugo Riemann's *Tonnetz,* or "table of triadic relations," see Brian Hyer, "Reimag(in)ing Riemann," *Journal of Music Theory* 39, no. 1 (1995): 101–38. A special issue of the *Journal of Music Theory* devoted entirely to neo-Riemannian theory (42, no. 2 [1998]) contains a number of important foundational articles on the topic.

10. See Guy Capuzzo, "Neo-Riemannian Theory and the Analysis of Pop-Rock Music," *Music Theory Spectrum* 26, no. 2 (2004): 177–99.

11. In fact, Tony Banks has since referred to *Wind and Wuthering* as "the most musically complex of our albums. You had to hear it several times before you could fully appreciate it." See the booklet accompanying the *Genesis Archive #2, 1976–1992* CD boxed set (Atlantic 83410-2, 2000), 17.

12. Fans of Genesis's vintage era output will note the absence of examples from the group's final album with Peter Gabriel, *The Lamb Lies Down on Broadway.* This album largely forgoes Banks's distinctive chromatic harmonic style, however, a fact I attribute to the story's American setting and "earthy" protagonist. For a detailed study of the album, see Kevin Holm-Hudson, *Genesis and* The Lamb Lies Down on Broadway (Aldershot and Burlington: Ashgate, 2008).

13. Hyer, "Reimag(in)ing Riemann"; Cohn, "Maximally Smooth Cycles"; Cohn, "Maximally Smooth Cycles"; Cohn, "Neo-Riemannian Operations."

14. Roeder, "Voice Leading as Transformation"; Lewin, "Some Ideas about Voice Leading."

15. Armando Gallo, *Genesis: I Know What I Like* (Los Angeles: DIY, 1980), 123–25. See also Banks's recollections of his childhood music lessons in Philip Dodd, ed., *Genesis: Chapter and Verse* (New York: Thomas Dunne, 2007), 13–14.

16. Dominic Milano, "Tony Banks and the Evolution of Genesis" (interview), *Keyboard* 10 (November 1984): 46.

17. Dominic Milano, "Tony Banks" (interview), *Contemporary Keyboard* 2 (September–October 1976): 38.

18. Milano, "Tony Banks and the Evolution of Genesis," 46.

19. Ibid.

20. For a detailed study of Steely Dan's rich, jazz-infused harmonic language, including their use of "slash chords," see Walter Everett, "A Royal Scam: The Abstruse and Ironic Bop-Rock Harmony of Steely Dan," *Music Theory Spectrum* 26, no. 2 (2004): 201–35, especially 206. For examples of Marvin Gaye's fondness for slash-chord constructions, see Andrew Flory's essay in chapter 4 of this volume.

21. Timings within square brackets in this article refer to chronological points on the CD recordings for ease in consultation.

22. Carol Krumhansl, "Perceived Triad Distance: Evidence Supporting the Psychological Reality of Neo-Riemannian Transformations," *Journal of Music Theory* 42, no. 2 (1998): 279.

23. Richard Cohn, "Introduction to Neo-Riemannian Theory: A Survey and Historical Perspective," *Journal of Music Theory* 42, no. 2 (1998): 178.

24. Milano (1976), "Tony Banks," 38.

25. Milano, "Tony Banks and the Evolution of Genesis," 40, 45.

26. For a thorough treatment of neo-Riemannian transformation in triadic music, see Cohn, "Neo-Riemannian Operations, Parsimonious Trichords, and their *Tonnetz* Representations."

27. See Capuzzo, "Neo-Riemannian Theory and the Analysis of Pop-Rock Music," especially 181–82.

28. David Lewin, *Generalized Musical Intervals and Transformations* (New Haven: Yale University Press, 1987), 178. Robert Morris refers to this progression as P prime (P'); see his article "Voice-Leading Spaces," *Music Theory Spectrum* 20, no. 2 (fall 1998): 175–208.

29. This terminology is also Morris's ("Voice-Leading Spaces").

30. Banks would most likely have known this famous piece from his childhood, having noted that he "grew up listening to [his mother] playing Chopin on the piano" (Dodd, *Genesis: Chapter and Verse,* 13).

31. Chris Welch, *The Complete Guide to the Music of Genesis* (London: Omnibus, 1995), 18.

32. "Genesis's Banks: A Current Account," *Beat Instrumental,* April 1976.

33. Ibid.

34. Spicer, "Large-Scale Strategy and Compositional Design in the Early Music of Genesis," 320–23.

35. Gallo, *Genesis: I Know What I Like,* 15–16.

36. It is possible that Banks simply left out the third of each chord—result-

ing in bare fifth "power chord" voicings—when he originally composed this progression on the guitar.

37. Lorna Read, "Genesis: All Set to Crack America," *Beat Instrumental*, February 1977.

38. Dominic Milano, "Tony Banks" (interview), *Contemporary Keyboard* 4 (July 1978): 23.

39. Susan McClary, "Pitches, Expression, Ideology: An Exercise in Mediation," *Enclitic* 7, no. 1 (spring 1983): 76–86.

40. Milano, "Tony Banks and the Evolution of Genesis," 46.

41. This composition is loosely based on the Banks song "Undertow," found on . . . *And Then There Were Three.* . . . The earlier Genesis song is much more straightforward harmonically, although it does contain a surprise cadential modulation from E major to C-sharp major—again, a typically Banksian chromatic third key relationship—at the end of the chorus.

42. Spicer, "Large-Scale Strategy and Compositional Design in the Early Music of Genesis," 324.

43. For more on the use of "pedal-point grooves" in Genesis's classic period, see Mark Spicer, "Genesis's *Foxtrot*," in *Composition and Experimentation in British Rock, 1966–1976,* a special issue of *Philomusica Online* (2007).

44. The <E♭–7, B–> progression is heard at [1:11–1:18], [2:26–2:33], [3:37–3:43], and [4:48–4:55]. The <E+, D♭+7> progression is heard at [1:40–1:51], [2:54–3:03], and [4:04–4:14].

45. Booklet accompanying *Genesis Archive #2, 1976–1992,* 30.

46. Ibid.

47. Milano, "Tony Banks and the Evolution of Genesis," 38.

48. For a study of Paul Simon's "chromatic period," see Walter Everett, "Swallowed by a Song: Paul Simon's Crisis of Chromaticism," in *Understanding Rock: Essays in Musical Analysis,* ed. John Covach and Graeme M. Boone (New York: Oxford University Press, 1997), 113–53.

49. Collins would reunite with Rutherford and Banks in 2007 for the "Turn It On Again" world tour, but as of this writing (2008), the members of Genesis have not announced plans to compose or record any new material.

SIX ❀ "Reggatta de Blanc"

Analyzing Style in the Music of the Police

MARK SPICER

THE ISSUE OF STYLE in popular music analysis remains a thorny one. For some artists, it might seem that identifying their style is quite straightforward (Nirvana was the consummate "grunge" band, for example), yet for many artists (the Beatles being probably the most obvious example) it is impossible to categorize them within the boundaries of one particular style; indeed, stylistic *eclecticism* becomes the defining feature of their music.

My intent in this chapter is to confront this very issue of stylistic eclecticism by focusing on a body of work that offers a particularly interesting case study in this regard, namely, the music of the Police. This groundbreaking trio—consisting of drummer Stewart Copeland, bassist, lead vocalist, and main composer Sting (born Gordon Sumner), and guitarist Andy Summers—was formed in London in 1977, an especially turbulent year in the history of British pop. On the one hand, punk, led by bands such as the Sex Pistols and the Clash, was at the height of its popularity; on the other hand, disco, imported mainly from the United States and fueled by the massive transatlantic success of the movie *Saturday Night Fever* and its accompanying soundtrack album, was all the rage for those (slightly older) young adults who did not relish the idea of dyeing and spiking their hair or piercing their cheeks with safety pins.[1]

Table 6.1 shows a chronology of the five studio albums released by the Police over the course of their relatively brief career together, from their 1978 debut *Outlandos d'Amour* through their 1983 swan song *Syn-*

TABLE 6.1.   Chronology of Police Studio Albums

Album Title	Release Date	Peak Chart Position
Outlandos d'Amour	October 1978 [February 1979]	U.K. #6, U.S. #23
Reggatta de Blanc	October 1979	U.K. #1, U.S. #25
Zenyatta Mondatta	October 1980	U.K. #1, U.S. #5
Ghost in the Machine	October 1981	U.K. #1, U.S. #2
Synchronicity	June 1983	U.K. #1, U.S. #1

(*Note:* The month of U.S. release is given if it is different from that of the original U.K. album.)

chronicity, by which point the trio had risen to become the most successful pop group in the world.[2] With the title of their second album, *Reggatta de Blanc*, the Police endorsed a label that the music press was already using to describe their style: literally, "white reggae."[3] Spearheaded by the crossover success of Bob Marley and the Wailers (a Jamaican group that was cleverly marketed like a rock band to international audiences), reggae had at last shed its novelty status and become a real fixture on the mainstream pop charts in Britain at exactly the same time punk and disco were at their respective heights.[4] The "white reggae" moniker certainly then seemed an apt one for the Police: it was, after all, quite unusual in 1978 to see and hear reggae performed so well by a group of three bleached-blond white guys.[5] Yet, as I hope to demonstrate in this chapter, there is much more to the Police's music than reggae alone.

Before we proceed with our analysis of the Police's music, let us pause for a moment to consider more broadly the notion of style, particularly as it pertains to popular music of the past fifty years or so. As Allan Moore has neatly put it, the word *style* "refers to the manner of articulation of musical gestures, and . . . operates at various hierarchical levels, from the global to the most local."[6] This top-to-bottom conception of musical style is useful to a certain degree; for example, within the global style of "rock" we can identify myriad subsidiary styles, such as heavy metal and punk, into which we can better situate the music of specific bands such as, in the case of heavy metal, Black Sabbath and Iron Maiden. Following Richard Middleton, Moore prefers the more pointed term *idiolect* when referring to style characteristics that identify an individual band; for example, as Moore would say, the idiolects of Black Sabbath and Iron Maiden each "carve out spaces" within the style known as heavy metal.[7]

How, then, do we account for those many artists in the post-Beatles era, like the Police, whose idiolects seem to resist such classification and carve out spaces within a number of different styles?[8] As a metaphorical starting point for my analysis, I have mapped out in figure 6.1 a provisional "Universe of Style" for the Police's music (provisional in that I make no claims to it being comprehensive). At the center of this universe we find planet Reggae and its neighboring planet Punk, the two musical worlds where, at least initially, the Police most often resided. As we shall see, sometimes the Police chose to leave these planets behind in order to visit neighboring musical worlds such as jazz, prog, and synth pop. More often than not, however, the Police remained firmly rooted on planet Reggae while allowing visitors from these neighboring worlds, and, indeed, from musical worlds that are even further removed, such as baroque lament and music hall, to interact with them and create unique stylistic hybrids. Identifying the Police's idiolect, then, will largely be a matter of our navigating this Universe of Style and, in turn, unraveling the various stylistic threads that fed into their music.

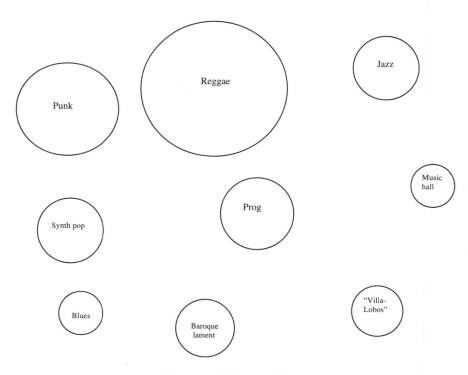

Figure 6.1. A Universe of Style

Some readers will no doubt recognize the similarity between my notion of a Universe of Style and the so-called Universe of Topic that Kofi Agawu maps out for the classical music of Mozart, Haydn, and Beethoven in his book *Playing with Signs.*[9] Following Leonard Ratner, Agawu identifies in his universe a number of specific musical signs, or "topics" (topoi), that an informed late-eighteenth-century listener would have immediately recognized as being characteristic of a particular style or affect. He then demonstrates through elegant analyses how a classical piece can be thought of as a kind of "drama of styles" in which an array of style topics are introduced by the composer—perhaps in rapid succession or at times even simultaneously—much as individual characters are made to interact with one another in a novel or play. Although the universe of available topics in pop and rock is quite different from what we might expect of a Mozart opera or Beethoven piano sonata, I would argue (as does Rebecca Leydon in chapter 8 of this volume) that many of the most interesting and stylistically eclectic pop songs forge their musical meaning in much the same way. For our purposes here, however, I would like to make a clearer distinction than Agawu does between what constitutes a "style" and what constitutes a "topic" (since some of the topics listed by Agawu in his universe are actually styles such as "fantasia style" and "learned style"). I prefer instead to think of a style as a musical world that is defined by a family of specific musical devices; in other words, a style can be thought of as a *collection* of topics. This is an important distinction, because sometimes just one little topic can be enough to evoke the essence of a style as a whole.

As with many significant moments in rock history, the Police's discovery of their "white reggae" formula was largely accidental, but first, to place this story in context, let us look back again to the summer of 1977. Since their formation in January of that year, the original Police lineup—consisting of Stewart Copeland, Sting, and the Corsican guitarist Henri Padovani—had been trying hard to make it on the London scene as a punk band. The group's first single, "Fall Out/Nothing Achieving"—two Stewart Copeland-penned numbers squarely in the punk style, released in May 1977 on Copeland's own independent label, Illegal Records— had gone nowhere. Around this same time, Copeland and Sting also became involved with a side project called Strontium 90, a group put together by Mike Howlett (former bass player for the progressive rock band Gong) and featuring none other than Andy Summers on guitar.[10]
Born in 1942, Summers was almost a decade older than his two new

bandmates, a detail that is important only because it helps us to situate historically the range of musical expertise that he would soon bring with him into the Police. In his recent autobiography *One Train Later*, Summers recalls fondly the day he received his first guitar, a gift from his uncle, at the age of thirteen:

> Scratched and dented with a string missing, it isn't much of an instrument, but I love it instantly and sit at the edge of the bed with it cradled in my arms, holding it in the position that I have seen used by guitarists on TV. I study it and gaze at its dents and scratches, its evidence of a long life, and wonder how many songs have been played on it, where it's been. It is an immediate bond, and possibly in that moment there is a shift in the universe because this is the moment from which my life unfolds.[11]

Like countless other aspiring young guitarists growing up in England in the mid-to-late 1950s (including a certain group of lads in Liverpool), Summers first learned how to play by memorizing simple chords by rote and imitating the early rock and roll and rockabilly records of the day, most of which, of course, were imported from the United States (not surprisingly, young Andy's first band, formed in Bournemouth with four of his school friends, was a skiffle outfit that called themselves the Midnighters). But Summers soon was captivated by American jazz—Thelonius Monk, Miles Davis, Sonny Rollins, and especially guitar greats such as Wes Montgomery and Kenny Burrell—and sought to expand his technical and harmonic vocabulary by playing along with records and transcribing solos note by note.

By the time he moved to London in the mid-1960s, Summers was an accomplished musician, fluent in a wide range of styles. He quickly made a name for himself as a sought-after session guitarist within the burgeoning electric blues and progressive scenes in London, performing and recording with the likes of Zoot Money and the Big Roll Band and the Soft Machine, as well as his own psychedelic group Dantalian's Chariot. In 1968, after he was let go by the Softs right in the middle of their first U.S. tour (as the supporting act for the Jimi Hendrix Experience), Summers was invited to join Eric Burdon and the Animals, the veteran U.K. electric blues band now based in Los Angeles. His stint with the "West Coast" Animals also proved to be short-lived, however, since Burdon broke up the band in early 1969, leaving Summers far from home and without a steady gig. But he decided to take a chance and stay in California, eking out a living teaching guitar at a local music shop and ultimately enrolling at the University of California, Los Angeles, where he studied composition and classical guitar for a few years. After moving back to London in late 1973, Summers soon resumed his career as a musical journeyman, playing in progressive bands led by bassists Kevin Ayers (formerly of the Soft Machine) and Kevin Coyne, touring briefly as a sideman for Neil Sedaka, and even subbing for Mike Oldfield in a November 1976 performance of *Tubular Bells* with the Newcastle Symphony Orchestra.

It would have been difficult in 1977 to find a guitarist with a wider range of experience than Summers, making him perhaps the unlikeliest of candidates for membership in an up-and-coming punk group. Punk was, after all, a back-to-basics style that essentially celebrated rank amateurism and was viewed by its practitioners and fans as a deliberate reaction against the sheer virtuosity (and pretentiousness) of progressive rock.[12] Truth be told, however, Summers's new bandmates were only masquerading as punks. The idea of forming a punk trio and calling it the Police was the brainchild of Stewart Copeland, yet Copeland himself had just spent almost two years as the drummer for the "long-hair group" Curved Air (as Copeland described it),[13] and Sting, prior to moving to London and joining the Police, was a Newcastle schoolteacher who moonlighted as bassist and vocalist for a jazz-rock fusion group called Last Exit (a band that Mike Howlett described as "sounding a bit like Weather Report with vocals").[14] Within the original Police lineup, then, only Henri Padovani—who had been playing guitar for just a few months when he joined the band—actually jibed with punk's amateur aesthetic.

Sting, especially, was becoming increasingly dissatisfied with the all-punk direction in which the Police had been moving. An aspiring songwriter, he had already composed several songs before joining the band, songs whose lyrics and harmonic complexities were simply a mismatch for the three-chord outrage typical of most punk rock. In the end, it did not take much for Sting to convince Copeland that the Police had the potential to go much farther musically with a "real" guitarist onboard, and so by August 1977 Summers was in and Padovani was out and the trio began searching for the signature sound that would set them apart from the other punk groups.

As the story goes, at the end of 1977 the band took a break from their rehearsals, during which Summers and his wife Kate went to the United States to visit Kate's parents for the holidays. While Andy was away, and as Paul McCartney's Wings song "Mull of Kintyre" sat firmly atop the U.K.

singles charts, Sting decided to throw a party for which Copeland loaned him a stack of records that included some albums by Bob Marley and the Wailers. Sting apparently had not paid much serious attention to reggae up to that point, and yet now, with Stewart's Bob Marley records as his primary tutor, he quickly became fascinated with the style. In a 1979 interview with *Melody Maker,* Sting explained:

> I'd always wanted to make a connection between the energetic music of punk and more sophisticated musical forms. There was this amazingly aggressive music full of energy on the one hand, and I wanted to take it and bridge a gap between interesting chords and harmonic variations and this wild energy. And what eventually allowed me to do it was listening to reggae. Bob Marley especially. I saw a rhythmic connection between the fast bass of punk and the holes in reggae. I got interested in writing songs that combined these apparently diverse styles.[15]

The Police resumed rehearsing after the holidays and immediately began fusing elements of the reggae style into their sound, honing the songs that they would soon record for their debut album. Another key piece of the sonic puzzle around this time was Summers's acquisition of an Echoplex, an analog tape-delay device that allows a player to control echo at varying speeds during a live performance, creating, as he put it, "a guitar sound that becomes huge and prismatic, like a rainbow arching over the band."[16] Vividly recalling this experimental period in the band's development, Summers offered the following capsule description of the Police's newfound idiolect:

> Under the influence of Bob Marley and the groove of reggae, the bass parts move away from the thumping eighth-note pattern into a sexy, loping line that is as much about notes not played as those struck. Over the top of these patterns I begin playing high, cloudy chords that are colored by echo and delay, and Stewart counters this with back-to-front patterns on the hi-hat and snare. From a dense in-your-face assault, the songs now become filled with air and light . . . to bring about a sound that no trio in rock has possessed before. . . . [W]e can take almost any song and, as we say, "policify" it—even a piece of material by Noël Coward or a folk song from the Scottish Isles. From an instinctive and self-conscious journey, we discover a

sound for which there is no previous formula, a space jam meets reggae meets Bartók collage with blue-eyed soul vocals.[17]

I will now begin putting Summers's description of the Police's idiolect to the test through analysis of representative tracks, starting with an
identification of those specific musical devices (or topics, if you will) that
characterize "the groove of reggae."[18] Sting's composition "The Bed's
Too Big Without You" from *Reggatta de Blanc* is one of the few Police
songs to remain exclusively in the reggae style throughout, and it will
therefore serve well as our model example (I have transcribed the vamp
that underscores the verses to this song in example 6.1).[19] First of all, the
harmonic language of reggae, like much modal rock harmony, tends to
favor plain triads rather than seventh chords or larger, and its grooves
are often built around short, circular progressions of two or three chords

a) Verse groove "normalized"

b) Actual verse groove

Example 6.1. "The Bed's Too Big Without You" (Sting)

(in the verse vamp from "The Bed's Too Big," for example, the progression is a simple E Aeolian i–iv–v). The chords are played by the guitar and/or keyboard in an offbeat staccato pattern known in reggae parlance as the "skank." The basic skank pattern emphasizes the second half, or "and," of each beat in 4/4 time; at faster tempi, two notated 4/4 measures can sometimes represent one "real" measure, in which case the chords of the skank will fall on beats 2 and 4. While this skank pattern tends to be pretty formulaic from one reggae song to the next, the bass line in reggae is usually very distinctive and memorable, what I like to describe as a "rolling" bass. A rolling bass follows the chord progression of the skank very strictly, often oscillating between the root and third or root and fifth of the chord and at times arpeggiating through the whole triad. The rhythmic pattern of a rolling bass is typically very active, employing subdivision of the beat at the sixteenth-note level, and often includes long rests, creating "holes" in the texture that allow other elements of the groove to shine through (we recall Summers's observation that a reggae bass "is as much about notes not played as those struck"). The rolling bass in the verse vamp of "The Bed's Too Big" provides a good example of this; notice that the bass riff arpeggiates through the tonic chord in the first measure but drops out entirely during the second measure as the chords move through iv and v.

Probably the key element in defining a reggae groove, however, is its drum pattern. In a 1981 interview with Jools Holland, Stewart Copeland sheds light on the essential differences between rock and reggae drumming styles:

JH: Why is your drumming different from another drummer?

SC: Longer arms? I play with my feet? I suppose it's because I've stolen all my licks from different sources. You see, all the licks get passed back and forth, most of them, and the trick is to find new ones, turn them around a bit, camouflage them a bit. . . . My source of licks has been South America, and, of course, the West Indies.

JH: A lot of people say it's white man's reggae.

SC: Let's examine this word *reggae*. In the main rock and roll stuff that everything's based on, even since the jazz days . . . there's always a backbeat . . . on two and four. Now reggae turns the whole thing upside down . . . and invented something really different. . . . [T]he bass drum and the snare drum both land on the same place, [three].[20]

Copeland then proceeds to illustrate for Holland two contrasting grooves at the drum kit, moving back and forth between a stereotypical rock pattern with big snare accents on beats 2 and 4 and a stereotypical reggae pattern with a single snare accent on the third beat of each bar. This latter pattern, known as the "one drop" (immortalized in the 1979 Bob Marley song of the same name), is actually one of several possible drum grooves in reggae. It is also common in reggae drumming to eliminate the big snare hits altogether, instead moving the accents on 2 and 4 to the bass drum, as we see in "The Bed's Too Big" (hence turning the rock backbeat "upside down," as Copeland would say). Another favorite reggae pattern, known as "steppers," features bass drum hits on all four beats of the bar ("four on the floor"), typically complemented by interlocking syncopated rim-shot figures and hi-hat splashes.[21]

Although Copeland freely admits his allegiance to reggae as a crucial factor in shaping his highly idiosyncratic drumming style, he was rarely if ever content with adopting drum licks wholesale; as he says, he would "turn them around a bit, camouflage them a bit." In light of this, let us look again more carefully at the groove to "The Bed's Too Big." Although it is composed of otherwise standard reggae devices, what makes this particular groove special is the metric conflict created by the bass and drums against the guitar skank. If we were to listen to the bass riff alone without the other instruments, we naturally would expect that the riff begins each time on the downbeat. As the notated example shows, however, the bass riff actually begins on the *second* beat of the measure; the rim shots, likewise, seem to have been displaced by one quarter note compared to the corresponding rhythmic figure in the guitar, an exemplar of Copeland's "back-to-front patterns . . . on snare" that Summers described. I have illustrated this in example 6.1 by aligning a "normalized" version of the verse vamp above the vamp as it actually occurs in the song. The resulting sensation is one of ever-conflicting downbeats that paint vividly in musical terms the restlessness felt by the protagonist of the song, who tosses and turns nightly in a bed that is "too big" now that his lover has left him.

It turns out that such rhythmic displacement is quite typical of the Police's unique appropriation of the reggae style and therefore a crucial defining feature of the band's idiolect. Let us consider another example taken from their breakthrough hit "Roxanne." In his autobiography *Broken Music*, Sting describes how the groove for what would become the Police's trademark song first came together:

While originally written as a jazz-tinged bossa nova, the song will evolve into a hybrid tango through the trial-and-error of the band process. It is Stewart who suggests stressing the second beat of each bar on the bass and bass drum, giving the song its lopsided Argentinian gait.[22]

Andy Summers, however, has a slightly different take on the evolution of the "Roxanne" groove:

At the moment, it's a bossa nova. . . . So, how should we play it? We have to heavy it up and give it an edge. We decide to try it with a reggae rhythm, at which point Stewart starts to play a sort of backward hi-hat and tells Sting where to put the bass hits. Once the bass and drums are in place, the right counterpoint for me to play is the four in the bar rhythm part.[23]

So is the groove for "Roxanne" a "hybrid tango," as Sting describes it, or in a "reggae rhythm," as Summers asserts? I would argue that the groove underscoring the verses of "Roxanne" (see example 6.2a) is most definitely reggae in style, but it is by no means a typical reggae rhythm. For one thing, the guitar is playing staccato chords that fall *on* rather than off the beat, effectively displacing the typical skank pattern by one eighth note.[24] Second, there is no rolling bass. Instead the bass plays a jabbing repeated-note riff that accents the second beat of the bar, in tandem with the bass drum, effectively displacing the typical "one-drop" accent on beat 3 by one quarter note. Above all this (not shown in the example), Sting's soaring and angular "blue-eyed soul" tenor implores his beloved Roxanne to abandon her career in the world's oldest profession. The apex of Sting's vocal line is the top D♭ he sings on the word "sell" in measure seven: this is the flattened-fifth scale degree, a fitting melodic nod to the blues that seems entirely appropriate for the subject matter at hand.

The composite texture created by the guitar and bass here is very clever, evoking the style of a so-called bubble organ—another stereotypical reggae topic—without having to use a keyboard. In example 6.2b, I have written out a hypothetical bubble organ accompaniment for the opening measures of the verse. In a typical bubble pattern, the left hand plays staccato chords in the low register on the "and" of every beat in "fast" skank fashion, while the right hand plays "slow" skank chords in the middle register on beats 2 and 4; the two parts combine to produce

a) Verse groove

b) Hypothetical "bubble" organ accompaniment for the opening measures of the verse

c) Chorus (truncated), bass only

Example 6.2. "Roxanne" (Sting)

the characteristic "oom-chacka" bubble rhythm, as illustrated in parentheses below the staff.[25] Similarly, I have illustrated in parentheses below the actual verse groove in example 6.2a the composite rhythm suggested by the interaction between the guitar and bass, showing the bubble rhythm to be pushed forward by one eighth note (one has to imagine the bass riff sounding also in the second half of each measure, but I think the groove is strongly implied).

In the chorus, the plea to Roxanne becomes more urgent: the modality abruptly shifts to the relative major, and Sting's high tenor repeats the lyric "put on the red light" again and again, set to a variant of the vocal motive that had ended the verse (with the top D♭ adjusted to become D♮); joining in the plea are two background vocals in close harmony, picking up the syncopated guitar and bass rhythmic figure that ends the verse as a vehicle for chanting Roxanne's name over and over. But what is most striking about the chorus is the abrupt shift in style: the Police have left planet Reggae behind and entered the neighboring musical world of punk.

What identifies the punk style most strongly is a topic that I have whimsically labeled in example 6.2c as the "safety-pin" riff: a driving accompaniment figure played by the bass (and essentially doubled by the guitar, not shown in the example), consisting of constant eighth notes grouped in fours with three repeated pitches preceded each time by their chromatic lower neighbor. This stock accompaniment figure is, of course, a throwback to early rock and roll and was adopted by the punk rockers as something of a cliché, no doubt because it sounds best when played loud and fast and, perhaps most important, because it is *easy* to play (one listen to the Sex Pistols' iconic 1977 album *Never Mind the Bollocks . . .* will testify to the prevalence of the safety-pin riff in punk). In "Roxanne," the abrupt shift from reggae in the verses to punk in the choruses is masterful and entirely appropriate, serving only to intensify the song's message by adding an increased sense of urgency to the lyric. Needless to say, this juxtaposition of reggae and punk would become a hallmark of the Police sound on their early hit singles, ensuring that the group was just punk enough for punk fans to like them. (The Police would follow this same basic formal template of reggae verses starkly juxtaposed against punk choruses on their two other singles from *Outlandos d'Amour,* "So Lonely" and "Can't Stand Losing You.")

With respect to harmonic vocabulary, the verse and chorus of "Roxanne" are also markedly different from one another. The punk chorus, as we might expect, features only plain triads and thirdless power-chord voicings, while the reggae verse is peppered with seventh and "sus" chords.[26] I mentioned earlier that the harmonic style of reggae tends to favor simple triads over a more extended chord vocabulary, and yet we recall Sting's comment that he saw reggae as a means of "bridg[ing] a gap between interesting chords and harmonic variations" and the "wild energy" of punk. Indeed, it is in the realm of harmony that the Police's jazz and progressive-rock pedigrees can be felt most strongly. In a recent interview for *Guitar Player* magazine, Andy Summers elaborates:

> I wanted to exploit the openness of the band's arrangements, so I couldn't play Steve Jones-style, punk power chords. . . . I'd seldom play full chords that had a major or minor third in them—which I considered old-fashioned harmony. Instead, I explored a much cooler, sort of disinterested chord style that utilized stacked fifths or an added ninth to get the harmony moving without the obvious sentimental association of major and minor thirds.[27]

As the Police's primary songwriter, Sting's working method was quite typical of the era with regard to the way in which he would introduce songs to his fellow band members. By 1979 the Police were touring almost constantly, and so Sting reportedly wrote most of his new songs during snatches of downtime as the band traveled from gig to gig, aided by a four-track Sony tape recorder with a built-in drum machine (which he nicknamed "Dennis").[28] He would build up a song section by section, recording all of the parts himself, until he had a demo four-track version of the song to present to Stewart and Andy, at which point the full band would begin the process of working out their distinctive "policified" arrangement. While Sting received sole songwriting credit for the majority of the Police's songs, the contributions of Copeland and Summers to the finished arrangements can hardly be overstated.[29]

With this in mind, let us take a close look now at two of the signature guitar riffs from the *Reggatta de Blanc* album. The first of these is the opening guitar riff to "Message in a Bottle" (example 6.3a), which became the group's first U.K. number 1 single in September 1979. As I have shown in parentheses below the staff, this arpeggiated riff is based on a simple C-sharp Aeolian progression, i–VI–VII–iv, yet its distinctive "open" sound results from the third being omitted entirely from the first three chords and replaced with an added ninth in the topmost voice. I had long thought that Andy Summers must have come up with this very special riff himself during the full-band arranging process, especially in

a) "Message in a Bottle" (Sting)

b) "Bring on the Night" (Sting)

Example 6.3. Two signature riffs from *Reggatta de Blanc*

light of his comments about favoring chord voicings with missing thirds or built in stacked fifths (both criteria of which apply here). Sting, however, has confirmed that the guitar riff for "Message in a Bottle" was fully intact when he first presented the song to the band and, in fact, was the seed from which the rest of the song developed.[30]

Example 6.3b shows the signature guitar riff that repeats throughout the verses of the Sting composition "Bring on the Night." The basic underlying chord progression here is a tried-and-true rock harmonic formula, an Aeolian VI–VII–i, yet Summers plays above this an elaborate series of rolling sixteenth-note arpeggios in a classical *pim* fingering pattern that seems worlds removed from rock, evoking strongly the style of a Villa-Lobos étude.[31] It would take a serious student of the classical guitar to master such a fingering pattern, and so, in the absence of any evidence to the contrary, I'm convinced—unlike "Message in a Bottle"—that it was Summers and not Sting who came up with the design of this special riff. The chorus for "Bring on the Night" moves into a bouncy reggae groove in which the classical arpeggios are replaced with a more stereotypical guitar skank, yet we should not overlook the reggae influence on the verses as well, for underneath the guitar arpeggios the offbeat skank pattern is played instead by the bass.

Example 6.4 shows a transcription of the opening groove from the Police's second U.K. number 1 hit, "Walking on the Moon," a track that has been aptly described by more than one critic as "space reggae."[32]

Here the signature guitar riff is actually a single chord, a ringing D minor eleventh chord dredged in echo by way of Andy Summers's Echoplex. In fact, all of the instruments here are soaked in reverb, an effect that is particularly noticeable, for example, in the interlocking "one-drop" rim shots that Stewart Copeland introduces on the third repetition of the four-bar pattern.[33] This brings us to an extremely important aspect of the reggae style that so far has gone unmentioned in this chapter, namely, *dub*. The aesthetics of dub evolved among Jamaican producers and recording engineers in the earlier 1970s and was reflected in their practice of reinventing a preexisting reggae song as a "dub mix" in which the original vocal and instrumental tracks could be freely layered in and out of the texture and treated to any number of studio effects, hence "shattering" the songs, as Michael Veal puts it in the title of his illuminating recent book on the subject.[34] While dub was originally a studio-based practice, allowing, as Veal notes, for "real-time improvisation performed by engineers on the multitrack mixing console," reggae musicians soon began to incorporate elements of the dub aesthetic into live performances.[35] The Police embraced this practice in their live shows almost from the very beginning, often extending certain songs through improvised "dub-style" instrumental passages where the texture might be reduced down, say, to just the bass drum, rim shots, and fragments of the bass line, colored by splashes of guitar harmonics and all dripping with echo and reverb.[36] One can also hear extended dub-style passages featured on several tracks from the studio albums, such as the aforementioned "The Bed's Too Big Without You" (3:03–3:44, leading into the final chorus) and the coda to "Voices Inside My Head" from *Zenyatta Mondatta*.[37]

Just prior to the recording sessions for the 1980 *Zenyatta* album, Andy Summers added a formidable new gadget to his arsenal of effects—a Roland GR-330 guitar synthesizer—a device that allowed him to create a

Example 6.4. "Walking on the Moon" (Sting), opening groove

broader range of timbres with his guitar than ever before. Example 6.5 shows the incessant four-bar repeated guitar and bass groove that sounds throughout the verses and choruses of "When the World Is Running Down, You Make the Best of What's Still Around," one of the several tracks on *Zenyatta* to feature the Roland.[38] The basic underlying progression, clearly marked by Sting's bass, is another Aeolian VI–VII–i, but above this Summers has chosen to play huge ringing jazz chords, omitting the thirds and spicing up the harmony again with his trademark added ninths and elevenths. (In the transcribed example, I have notated the echo effect as triplet quarter notes, representing the rhythm of the echoing chords as they actually sound, yet Summers simply strikes each chord on the downbeat.) Underneath all of this, and somewhat surprisingly, Stewart Copeland chooses to lay down what amounts essentially to a meat-and-potatoes rock drum pattern, with heavy snare on the backbeat. From a rhythmic standpoint, there is really nothing about this groove that is overtly reggae in style, and yet the dub aesthetic looms large on this track both in the heavy use of effects on all the parts and, especially, in the use of a "drum and bass" breakdown section (1:51–2:20) to provide sonic relief from the otherwise incessant ringing guitar chords.

So far we have seen how one small topic—such as a distinctive riff, a rhythmic pattern, a chord, or even an effect—can be enough to evoke the essence of a style as a whole. The stylistic references in "Spirits in the Material World," the opening track from 1981's *Ghost in the Machine*, reach even farther outward in our Universe of Style (the repeating two-bar vamp that underscores the verses is shown in example 6.6a). The tempo here (quarter note = 140) is considerably faster than what is typical for the reggae grooves on the Police's earlier albums, perhaps in response to the massive rise in popularity of ska—reggae's "faster" precursor style—which had occurred in Britain during 1979–80.[39] Also noteworthy is the prominence of the synthesizer, about which I'll have

Example 6.5. "When the World Is Running Down, You Make the Best of What's Still Around" (Sting)

a) Verse vamp

b) Hypothetical "baroque" normalization of verse vamp

c) Chorus

Example 6.6. "Spirits in the Material World" (Sting)

more to say later.[40] Nevertheless, we should by now immediately recognize two of the standard reggae topics at work here: a syncopated skank and a rolling bass.

If we examine the voice-leading and harmonic design of this verse vamp more closely, we find that what rests as the basis for this passage is the model progression shown in example 6.6b. This ostinato progression is grounded on a descending bass tetrachord pointing from the tonic to the dominant in minor, a topic that served as an emblem of lament in countless compositions from the baroque era (the chain of suspensions in the inner voices further marks the "baroqueness" of this progression).[41] Admittedly, the progression as it actually occurs in the song is quite distorted from this normalized version: the harmonic move

to VI is missing, not to mention the raised leading tone. Also, given the
stylistic constraints of the era, what baroque composer would have allowed for such overt parallel fifths between the outer voices? (I should,
however, point out that outer-voice parallel fifths such as these are not
only quite typical of mode-based rock but also serve here as an important
unifying motive throughout the track; witness, for example, the Debuss-
ian melodic planing that characterizes the harmonic texture of the chorus [example 6.6c].)[42] Yet it is precisely these distortions that make "Spirits in the Material World" so unique. What we have here is a bona fide
stylistic hybrid: a baroque style—the lament—has been passed through
the filter of rock harmony and cloaked in the rhythmic conventions of
reggae. Again I would contend that the stylistic reference to the lament
is not arbitrary here but rather serves to amplify the underlying message
of the song, in which Sting is lamenting nothing less than the decay of society itself.

   In all of the Police tracks we have examined thus far, elements of the
reggae style have proved to be important in some way, either overtly
(through full-blown reggae grooves) or more subtly (through just one or
two distinctive reggae topics). But let us now consider a song in which
the Police leave behind planet Reggae entirely. "Invisible Sun" was the
first single from *Ghost in the Machine* to be released in the United Kingdom, where it peaked at number 2 in October 1981 (the song did not
chart in the United States). This had long struck me as an unusual decision on the Police's part. To be sure, "Invisible Sun" is a great track, but
given that this album also contains several more immediately catchy or
danceable songs, such as the later singles "Every Little Thing She Does Is
Magic" (U.K. number 1, U.S. number 3) and "Spirits in the Material
World" (U.K. number 12, U.S. number 11), a bleak song about the
conflict in Northern Ireland seemed an unlikely choice for the leadoff
single. In hindsight, however, I can see that the Police were cleverly responding to the prevailing stylistic trends in British pop at the time. By
1980, punk was all but dead in Britain, and synth pop was surfacing as
the next important style. Like punk, synth pop (with a few notable exceptions) was a style largely performed by novices who could barely play
their instruments, relying instead on the new wave of affordable synthesizers, sequencers, and drum machines to play much of their parts for
them.[43] This resulted in a style of music that was essentially minimalist;
synth-pop grooves were typically woven together from simple, repeated
riffs, often with no real harmonic "progression" to speak of.[44]

   The introduction to "Invisible Sun" (example 6.7a) has a classic synth-pop texture. After the initial fade-in, the bass oscillates back and forth between E♭ and C, doubled by a droning synthesizer at the fifth above and, in the second measure, at the fifth and ninth above.[45] The guitar plays a repeated riff that similarly transposes back and forth between E♭ and C; there are no drums save for a relentless tom-tom on the backbeat. Given such limited harmonic materials, it is difficult to pinpoint which of the two bass pitches, E♭ or C, should be heard as the tonic (I tend to hear C as the tonic, although I think it is intentionally left ambiguous). During the first three repetitions of this two-bar pattern, a robotic voice (not shown in the example) counts from one to six on the downbeat of each measure. On the fourth repetition, a unison chant enters ("oh-oh-oh / oh-oh-oh"), reminiscent of the style of chant sung by the fans at U.K. football games.[46] Example 6.7b shows how the E♭/C harmonic stasis is ultimately relieved at the end of the verse: following a chromatic walkdown (B♭–A♮–A♭), the bass settles on G, and the texture gives way to a repeated angular G Mixolydian riff, doubled in octaves by

a) Introduction

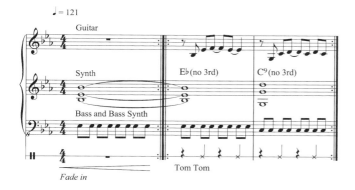

b) End of verse, leading into the chorus

Example 6.7. "Invisible Sun" (Sting)

the bass and guitar, which serves as the undercurrent for the chorus. (This chorus riff reminds me very much of the type of ostinato figures one finds all over the place in classic progressive rock.)

With *Ghost in the Machine,* and even more so with *Synchronicity,* Stewart and Andy found Sting wanting to assert greater control over the band's arrangements of his compositions. Copeland recalled, "Sting doesn't bring in half-finished songs anymore. His ideas are brilliant, but more and more we're stuck with them, and he's liking it less and less when we mess with them."[47] While *Synchronicity* is often viewed as the Police's crowning achievement, in retrospect one cannot help but think of this album as essentially a Sting solo project (especially side 2), with Summers and Copeland serving as mere sidemen.[48] With the notable exception of three tracks ("Wrapped Around Your Finger," "Tea in the Sahara," and, albeit more subtly, "King of Pain"), the "white reggae" that had been so important in defining the Police's idiolect seems to be largely absent on *Synchronicity,* and yet the record still sounds like no one but the Police.[49]

For our final example, and to conclude this study of style in the Police's music, I wish to look briefly at the leadoff single from *Synchronicity,* the worldwide number 1 smash "Every Breath You Take."[50] Admittedly, it is difficult for me to be objective about this iconic song or, indeed, the *Synchronicity* album in general since I was among the legions of young Police fans that purchased the album on the very first day of its release in June 1983 (the same month I graduated from high school), and the record therefore holds a very special place in my heart. Putting aside the fan mentality for a moment, I have transcribed Andy Summers's signature guitar riff for "Every Breath You Take" in example 6.8.

Unlike his other songs on *Synchronicity,* Sting's original demo version for "Every Breath You Take" apparently sounded very different in style from how it ended up sounding on the finished album (Summers recalls that Sting's demo "sound[ed] not unlike the group Yes with a huge rolling synthesizer part").[51] The song's main groove is built, as Summers rightly notes, around a "classic pop song chord sequence," the old doo-wop formula of I–vi–IV–V–(I). After tinkering with the arrangement in the studio for a couple of weeks, Sting reportedly was unable to come up with a chording part that did not sound like a cliché. Having reached a creative impasse, and with the bass, drums, and vocal tracks already in place, Sting invited Summers to give the song its final, golden touch. I will let Summers continue the story:

Example 6.8. "Every Breath You Take" (Sting), Andy Summers's signature riff

> It's a simple chord sequence and shouldn't prove a problem. . . . What
> are the criteria? It should sound like the Police—big, brutal barre
> chords won't do, too vulgar; it has to be something that says Police but
> doesn't get in the way of the vocals; it should exist as music in its own
> right, universal but with just a hint of irony, be recognized the world
> over, possibly be picked up by a rapper as the guitar lick to hang a
> thirty-million-copy song on. . . . The track rolls and I play a sequence
> of intervals that makes it sound like the Police, root, fifth, second,
> third, up and down through each chord. It is clean, succinct, imme-
> diately identifiable. . . . I play it straight through in one take. There is
> a brief silence, and then everyone in the control room stands up and
> cheers. . . . With this lick I realize a dream that maybe I have cherished
> since first picking up the guitar as a teenager—to at least once in my
> life make something that would go around the world, create a lick
> that guitarists everywhere would play[.][52]

Like so many important bands in rock history, the Police as a unit were
always greater than the sum of their individual parts. The signature riff
that Summers came up with—apparently on the spot—for "Every Breath
You Take" was in the end almost identical in harmonic design to the signature riff that Sting himself had composed for his beloved "Message in
a Bottle" almost four years earlier (compare example 6.8 with example

6.3a). Perhaps, then, Sting's perspective was already clouded with visions of his impending solo superstardom, and it took his trusty bandmate to remind him just what had made the Police's style so unique in the first place.

NOTES

An earlier version of this chapter was presented at the annual meeting of the Society for Music Theory in Toronto, November 2000. I am most grateful to Jay Summach for sharing with me his 2007 unpublished essay on "white reggae" in the Police, which alerted me to some key sources that proved very helpful during my final stages of revision.

1. While the disparate styles of punk and disco were certainly prevalent on British pop radio in 1977, a quick glance at the U.K. singles charts for that year reveals a much broader palette of styles among those songs that reached the Top 20. *Music Week's* chart of the Top 10 singles for the week of 6 August 1977, for example, included the Sex Pistols' punk anthem "Pretty Vacant" at number 8 and Donna Summer's electro-disco smash "I Feel Love" at number 1 but also "You Got What It Takes," a cover of Marv Johnson's 1960 early Motown hit from the doo-wop nostalgia group Showaddywaddy at number 9, "We're All Alone" from country-pop songstress Rita Coolidge at number 6, "Fanfare for the Common Man," Aaron Copland's beloved World War II era symphonic fanfare reinvented as a rock instrumental by perennial British progressive rockers Emerson, Lake & Palmer (a track that could well be considered the very antithesis of punk) at number 5, and "Angelo," the latest hit from 1976 Eurovision Song Contest winners (and "Abba clones") Brotherhood of Man at number 2. Interestingly, Bob Marley and the Wailers' reggae single "Exodus"—the group's first U.K. single to crack the Top 20—was bubbling just outside the Top 10 at number 19 that same week, having peaked at number 14 the week before.

2. *Outlandos d'Amour* went largely unnoticed in the United Kingdom on its initial release in October 1978, but sales of the album were revived in April 1979, sparked by the breakthrough success of the single "Roxanne," which peaked at number 12 in May (I offer a close analysis of "Roxanne" in example 6.2). The peak chart positions for the five Police albums listed in table 6.1 show that the band's ascent to megastar status in the United States came about a year later than it had in the United Kingdom, with the 1980 album *Zenyatta Mondatta* and its two U.S. Top 10 singles, "De Do Do Do, De Da Da Da" and "Don't Stand So Close to Me."

3. Evolving from the earlier 1960s Jamaican styles known as "ska" and "rock steady," the term *reggae* has been used widely since the late 1960s as a kind of catchall for describing Jamaican pop generically. The precise origins of the word remain unclear, but its first documented use on a Jamaican recording was Toots and the Maytals' "Do the Reggay," produced by Leslie Kong and released on his Beverley's label in 1968. As Steve Barrow and Peter Dalton have rightly noted, "It's fitting that the word 'reggae' has endured as the favored label for all Ja-

maican popular music, because reggae began in a period of extraordinary experimentation, in which almost all later styles were prefigured and all previous styles absorbed" (Steve Barrow and Peter Dalton, *Reggae: The Rough Guide* [London: Rough Guides, 1997], 83).

Of course, the Police were not the first white pop and rock musicians to experiment with the reggae style. Some noteworthy earlier examples include the Beatles' "Ob-La-Di, Ob-La-Da" (from the "White Album," 1968), a cover version of which the Scottish group Marmalade took to the top of the U.K. singles charts in January 1969; Paul Simon's 1972 U.K. and U.S. Top 5 single "Mother and Child Reunion" (his first solo hit following the breakup of Simon and Garfunkel), a track produced by Leslie Kong and recorded at Kingston's Dynamic studio with Jamaican backing musicians; Paul McCartney and Wings' 1973 hit "Live and Let Die" (U.K. number 9, U.S. number 2) from the soundtrack of the James Bond movie of the same name (much of which, not coincidentally, is set in Jamaica), a track that features a decidedly reggae-tinged groove for its bridge; Eric Clapton's cover of the Bob Marley and the Wailers song "I Shot the Sheriff," a number 1 U.S. hit in September 1974; "Watching the Detectives," the first U.K. Top 20 hit for a young Elvis Costello in December 1977; and 10cc's "Dreadlock Holiday," a number 1 U.K. hit in September 1978. All of these early examples of "white reggae," however (with the exception of Costello's), represent one-off "novelty" hits within the overall output of that particular artist. What distinguished the Police (and also, though to a lesser extent, the Clash) from these earlier acts was that they were really the first white musicians to adopt the musical elements of reggae as a *consistent* and defining feature of their style.

4. Success outside of their native Jamaica eluded the Wailers until they were signed to Chris Blackwell's U.K. label Island Records in 1972. For an illuminating study of the group's subsequent rise to international stardom, see Jason Toynbee, "Authorship Meets Downpression: Translating the Wailers into Rock," in *This Is Pop: In Search of the Elusive at Experience Music Project* (Cambridge: Harvard University Press, 2004), 173–86.

5. In a recent scholarly article devoted to the subject of white reggae, Mike Alleyne harshly criticizes the whole phenomenon—and the Police in particular—as woefully "inauthentic." See his "White Reggae: Cultural Dilution in the Record Industry," *Popular Music and Society* 24, no. 1 (2000): 15–30. As Alleyne puts it, "[P]seudoreggae songs by white pop artists have utilized fragments of the music's syntax while simultaneously divorcing it from the political polemics of Rastafari, and reggae culture in general" (15). This is certainly a valid point, although, as I will argue in this chapter, the Police never sought to be an authentic reggae band; rather, they sought to sound like no one but themselves.

6. Allan F. Moore, "Categorical Conventions in Music Discourse: Style and Genre," *Music and Letters* 82, no. 3 (2001): 441–42.

7. See Allan F. Moore, "Gentle Giant's *Octopus*," in *Composition and Experimentation in British Rock, 1966–1976*, a special issue of *Philomusica Online* (2007). For further discussion of this hierarchy of style and idiolect, and its semiological implications, see Richard Middleton, *Studying Popular Music* (Milton Keynes: Open University Press, 1990), 172–246; David Brackett, *Interpreting Popular Music* (New York: Cambridge University Press, 1995; rpt., Berkeley: University of

California Press, 2000), 9–14; and Allan F. Moore and Anwar Ibrahim, "'Sounds Like Teen Spirit': Identifying Radiohead's Idiolect," in *The Music and Art of Radiohead,* ed. Joseph Tate (Aldershot and Burlington: Ashgate, 2005), 139–58.

8. For Allan Moore, this is precisely the defining characteristic shared by the many so-called progressive bands that arose in the United Kingdom during the late 1960s and early 1970s. He notes that "what defines the progressive 'moment' musically is that it marks, chronologically, the moment within the history of modern Anglophone popular music which actualizes the insubordination of idiolect to style" (Moore, "Gentle Giant's *Octopus*"). While I would not go so far as to describe the Police as a full-blown progressive rock band (in the same camp as, say, Genesis or Yes), they most definitely shared progressive rock's experimental impulse and penchant for stylistic eclecticism and virtuosity, the "hippie aesthetic," as John Covach has coined it; see his *What's That Sound? An Introduction to Rock and Its History,* 2nd ed. (New York: Norton, 2009), 310–11. Had the Police emerged on the London scene a couple of years earlier, prior to the punk explosion, I imagine their music would have sounded very different.

9. Kofi Agawu, *Playing with Signs: A Semiotic Interpretation of Classic Music* (Princeton: Princeton University Press, 1991), 30.

10. Although the Strontium 90 project with Mike Howlett quickly fizzled out once Summers officially joined the Police, the group did manage to record a few songs, both live and in the studio, which were eventually released two decades later as the compact disc *Strontium 90: Police Academy* (Pangæa Records, 1997). In addition to being an invaluable document of the first recordings of Copeland, Sting, and Summers playing together, this CD also includes an early (autumn 1976) four-track demo version of Sting performing his then brand new song "Every Little Thing She Does Is Magic," recorded at Mike Howlett's home studio in Acton (a song that would later be reworked for the Police's 1981 album *Ghost in the Machine*), as well as two other Sting compositions, "Visions of the Night" (later re-recorded as the B-side for the 1979 "Walking on the Moon" single) and "3 O'Clock Shot" (the main groove of which Sting would soon recycle for "Be My Girl—Sally" on *Outlandos d'Amour* and whose lyrics he would revive several years later—set to entirely different music—as the first verse and refrain for "Oh My God" on *Synchronicity*).

Howlett would go on to enjoy a highly successful career as a producer in the 1980s, working with several important new wave acts such as Blancmange, China Crisis, A Flock of Seagulls, Orchestral Manoeuvres in the Dark (OMD), Tears for Fears, and the Thompson Twins.

11. Andy Summers, *One Train Later* (New York: St. Martin's, 2006), 19–20.

12. Looking back on the conditions surrounding the rise of punk in 1976 among disenfranchised British youths, pop impresario and former Sex Pistols manager Malcolm McLaren observed, "They played three chords and it was good enough. It didn't matter. Everybody was playing the same Chuck Berry chords, putting the *new poetry* on top" (transcribed from a McLaren interview in "Punk," episode 9 of the Time-Life documentary series *The History of Rock 'n' Roll* [Warner Home Video, 1995]).

Facing high rates of unemployment and seeing few prospects for their future, many young British punk fans at the time strongly identified with reggae's message of protest and rebellion, and it is therefore not surprising that the two styles ended up largely fueling one another. The complex social and cultural factors that led to this cross-fertilization of punk and reggae in the late 1970s have been well documented by several researchers, beginning with Dick Hebdige's watershed study of youth subcultures in postwar Britain, *Subculture: The Meaning of Style* (London: Methuen, 1979).

13. Narrating his own recent documentary film *Everyone Stares: The Police Inside Out* (Crotale, 2006), Stewart Copeland recalled, "The cognoscenti are onto us. They know that we're just carpetbaggers. I have a dark past with the long-hair group Curved Air, and Andy Summers has consorted for years with the enemy generation." Copeland also enjoyed modest success outside of the Police in 1978 as his disguised alter ego Klark Kent, singing and playing all the instruments on the two quirky Klark Kent singles, "Don't Care" (which narrowly missed the U.K. Top 40, peaking at number 48) and "Too Kool to Kalypso."

14. Mike Howlett, liner notes to *Strontium 90: Police Academy*, 3.

15. Allan Jones, "Sting: Can't Stand Losing," *Melody Maker*, 22 September 1979, 42.

16. Summers, *One Train Later*, 191. Invented by Mike Battle in 1959, the Echoplex, as Summers himself describes it, is "basically a device to create echo by using a piece of quarter-inch tape that revolves in a spool around two tape heads [one play head, one record/erase head]. You can speed up or slow down the number of repeats by sliding a little metal arrow up and down the length of a metal bar that runs along the top of the spool."

17. Ibid., 190–92.

18. In an attempt to formalize the term for purposes of music analysis, I have elsewhere defined *groove* as "the tapestry of riffs—usually played by the drums, bass, rhythm guitar and/or keyboard in some combination—that work together to create the distinctive rhythmic/harmonic backdrop which identifies a song." See my "(Ac)cumulative Form in Pop-Rock Music," *twentieth-century music* 1, no. 1 (2004): 30.

19. The musical examples in this chapter represent my transcriptions of various textures from the original Police studio albums, ranging from individual riffs to complete grooves. (Due to copyright restrictions, excerpts of the actual vocal melody and lyrics are not included in any of the notated examples.) While it is customary for guitarists and bassists automatically to transpose their parts down by octave when reading from notation, I have chosen instead to notate all the guitar and bass parts in the register in which they actually sound, using the transposing treble and bass clefs only when necessary to avoid awkward multiple ledger lines.

20. The Copeland interview is transcribed from the 1981 promotional film *Police in Montserrat* (shot on location during the recording sessions for *Ghost in the Machine*), available as "bonus material" on *The Police: Every Breath You Take—the DVD* (A&M Records, 2003).

21. As a means of illustrating the difference between the one-drop and steppers drum patterns, I invite the reader to listen to Bob Marley and the Wailers' iconic 1977 album *Exodus* (U.K. number 8, U.S. number 20), which surely was among those Marley records that Copeland reportedly loaned to Sting at the end

of that year. Of the ten tracks on *Exodus*, seven are built on a one drop ("Natural Mystic," "So Much Things to Say," "Guiltiness," "Waiting in Vain," "Three Little Birds," "The Heathen," and "One Love/People get Ready"), and two on a steppers (the title track and "Jamming"). Curiously, the remaining track, "Turn Your Lights Down Low," features a decidedly "nonreggae" snare backbeat on beats 2 and 4, which, along with the lush extended harmonies, marks this song as a real stylistic anomaly among the other tracks on the album (to my ears, "Turn Your Lights Down Low" sounds more like a Philadelphia soul number than it does a reggae song).

In its 31 December 1999 issue, *Time* magazine named *Exodus* the "best album of the twentieth century."

22. Sting, *Broken Music* (New York: Dial Press, 2003), 295. Elsewhere in his autobiography, Sting reveals how his original inspiration for "Roxanne" came from seeing an old poster for *Cyrano de Bergerac* in the foyer of a Paris hotel where the Police were staying in October 1977. "That night," he wrote, "I will go to my room and write a song about a girl. I will call her Roxanne. I will conjure her unpaid from the street below the hotel and cloak her in the romance and sadness of Rostand's play, and her creation will change my life" (286).

23. Summers, *One Train Later*, 189.

24. Only the upper three voices of the guitar skank are shown in example 6.2a (octave doublings in the lower voices have been omitted for the sake of notational clarity).

25. For examples of reggae songs that feature a bubble organ, I again refer the reader to the *Exodus* album. The bubble is especially prominent in "Jamming" and "Waiting in Vain."

26. A so-called suspended chord in jazz and rock parlance is a close-position voicing in which the fourth (most commonly) or second above the chord root substitutes for the third. Unlike suspensions in classical harmony, the dissonant fourths and seconds need not resolve, and two or more "sus" chords may be found in succession (as we can see, for example, in the cadential figure that ends the first phrase of the verse in "Roxanne").

27. Michael Molenda, "Harmo-Melodic Spaceman," *Guitar Player*, June 2007, 88.

28. Sting explained his working method—and offered a live demonstration of Dennis in action—in his interview with Jools Holland for the 1981 documentary *Police in Montserrat*.

29. Sting receives sole songwriting credit for thirty-seven of the fifty-four tracks on the Police's five studio albums, while Copeland and Summers typically receive sole or joint credit for one or two tracks each per album. The notable exception to this is *Reggatta de Blanc*, on which Sting receives the sole credit for only five of the eleven songs (although two of these—"Message in a Bottle" and "Walking on the Moon"—were the album's hit singles). We recall that Stewart Copeland penned both of the songs for the Police's ill-fated first single, "Fall Out/Nothing Achieving." Copeland's contribution as a songwriter was most prominent on *Reggatta*, where he receives sole credit for three of the six tracks on side 2 ("On Any Other Day," "Contact," and the music-hall-tinged "Does Everyone Stare") and joint credit with Sting for "It's Alright For You" on side 1. Two of

the tracks on *Reggatta* (the title track and "Deathwish") originated from group improvisations during their early live performances (see note 36) and remain the only songs among the Police's recorded output to be credited to the full band.

30. Sting discusses the origins of the "Message" riff in his 1981 interview with Jools Holland for *Police in Montserrat.* When asked by Holland to name his favorite song that he'd written so far, Sting replied, "Probably 'Message in a Bottle.' Both lyrically and musically, I think it's the most unified piece I've ever written." Interestingly, "Message" reverses the "reggae/punk" formal template of the three singles from *Outlandos d'Amour,* featuring instead a hard-driving rock style for the verse (underscored by the signature riff) and prechorus and shifting abruptly to a more subdued reggae groove for the chorus.

31. In the acronym *pim, p* stands for the thumb, *i* for the index finger, and *m* for the middle finger. Summers discusses the "Bring on the Night" riff in his June 2007 interview with Michael Molenda for *Guitar Player* ("Harmo-Melodic Spaceman," 95).

32. See, for example, Martin C. Strong, *The Great Rock Discography,* 1st U.S. ed. (New York: Times Books, 1998), 634.

33. Stewart Copeland's reverb-soaked hi-hat part—which fades in alone to open the track—is surely one of the most memorable components of the "Walking on the Moon" groove. I have simplified the hi-hat part in example 6.4 into a constant pattern of alternating dotted-eighth and sixteenth notes in "shuffle" rhythm, showing its essential rhythmic strata within the groove, but Copeland actually improvises freely around this rhythm (particularly at the opening of the track and during the instrumental breaks), spicing up the basic pattern with random flourishes of repeated thirty-second notes. Copeland's virtuoso hi-hat playing quickly became legendary and would remain a signature feature of his highly idiosyncratic drumming style. For example, shortly after the Police broke up, Peter Gabriel hired Copeland to play the special hi-hat part spotlighted at the beginning of "Red Rain," the track that opens side 1 of Gabriel's 1986 hit album *So* (U.K. number 1, U.S. number 2).

34. Michael E. Veal, *Dub: Soundscapes and Shattered Songs in Jamaican Reggae* (Middletown, CT: Wesleyan University Press, 2007). Recalling with excitement the first time he heard imported dub remixes from Jamaica played in the punk clubs of London, the late Joe Strummer of the Clash remarked, "Completely destroy the track, and double and triple echo . . . that was dub" (transcribed from a Strummer interview in "Punk," episode 9 of the Time-Life documentary series *The History of Rock 'n' Roll*).

35. Veal, *Dub,* 77.

36. For example, a dub-style instrumental jam provided a nifty way for the Police to extend "Can't Stand Losing You" during live performances, and the resulting improvisation was ultimately reworked and recorded separately as the title track for the *Reggatta de Blanc* album. The "Can't Stand Losing You/Reggatta de Blanc" medley would become a favorite closer for their live shows. (On the 1995 CD *The Police Live!* one can hear two largely similar versions of the medley from different stages in the band's career, the first recorded at the Orpheum in Boston in November 1979 and the second recorded at the Omni in Atlanta in

November 1983; indeed, it came as no surprise to me to hear the Police resurrect the medley as one of the closing numbers on the set list for their long-awaited 2007–8 reunion tour.)

37. For a detailed analysis of "Voices Inside My Head," see my "(Ac)cumulative Form in Pop-Rock Music," 42–44.

38. The Roland guitar synthesizer is featured most prominently on "Don't Stand So Close to Me," where Summers uses the device to create those trademark swelling eleventh chords during the dub-style instrumental bridge (2:48–3:15). The Roland also reigns supreme on Summers's own composition, "Behind My Camel," a "haunted Middle Eastern theme," which Sting reportedly hated so much that he refused to play on the track but which garnered Summers a Grammy award for Best Rock Instrumental in 1981 (see Summers, *One Train Later,* 259). Summers would go on to explore the potential of the Roland guitar synthesizer more fully on his two collaborative albums with King Crimson's Robert Fripp, *I Advance Masked* (1982) and *Bewitched* (1984).

39. I am, of course, referring to bands such as the Specials, the [English] Beat, and Madness, all of which took ska grooves into the U.K. Top 10 in 1979 and 1980. For a useful assessment of the U.K. ska revival written when the style was still fresh, see Simon Frith's 1980 essay "The Coventry Sound: The Specials," in his *Music for Pleasure: Essays in the Sociology of Pop* (New York: Routledge, 1988), 77–80. The Police had actually first experimented with a noticeably faster ska groove on two of the tracks from 1980's *Zenyatta Mondatta,* "Canary in a Coalmine" and "Man in a Suitcase."

40. The marked sonic shift of *Ghost in the Machine* compared to the previous three Police albums can be attributed to a number of factors. For one thing, like its 1983 follow-up, *Synchronicity,* this album (with the exception of one track, "Every Little Thing She Does Is Magic") was recorded at George Martin's Associated Independent Recording (AIR) studios on the remote Caribbean island of Montserrat. Also, the Police parted ways with their coproducer Nigel Gray and replaced him with Hugh Padgham, an up-and-coming young sound engineer who had recently scored back-to-back successes with his work on Peter Gabriel's 1980 self-titled third album and Phil Collins's 1981 debut solo album *Face Value* (on which Padgham is credited for capturing Collins's trademark massive, reverberant drum sound on songs such as "In the Air Tonight"). In general, the arrangements on *Ghost in the Machine* became much denser, with several of the tracks featuring layers of synthesizers played by keyboardist Jean Roussel (marking the first time a musician from outside the group had been brought in for a Police record). Andy Summers, especially, did not see this as a step forward, telling one interviewer, "All those layers were there because it was a group head trip we went through that wasn't exactly welcomed by me. I would say, 'F**k the keyboard part—I can play it all on guitar.' But these things happened anyway. I'd just try to blend with the synths and keep the guitar part strong" ("Harmo-Melodic Spaceman," 91).

41. See Ellen Rosand, "The Descending Tetrachord: An Emblem of Lament," *Musical Quarterly* 65, no. 3 (1979): 346–53.

42. The contrasting grooves for the verse and chorus in "Spirits" are further marked by Stewart Copeland's drums, where, in trademark Copeland fashion, he

limits his reggae drum pattern during the verses to just the bass drum and hi-hat and saves the big rock snare hits on the backbeat for the choruses.

43. To be fair, it did require considerable skill to program the synthesizers and sequencers, as evinced, for example, by the pioneering work of Yaz[oo]'s Vince Clarke.

44. See, for example, Allan Moore's analysis of the Human League's "Seconds" from *Dare* (1981) in his *Rock: The Primary Text,* 2nd ed. (Aldershot and Burlington: Ashgate, 2001), 153–54. Moore refers to the synth-pop style as "synthesizer rock."

45. In his interview with Jools Holland for *Police in Montserrat,* Sting demonstrates a working version of "Invisible Sun" (which, interestingly, he had already singled out as one his favorite songs for the new album), showing how he created the four-track demo with the aid of bass synthesizer pedals set to a patch that automatically doubled each bass pitch a fifth higher. I cannot be certain, since the texture on the finished recording is much thicker, but it sounds to me like these bass synth pedals were also played by Sting in tandem with his electric bass on the final studio version of "Invisible Sun."

46. Such textless chanting was another hallmark of the Police sound, one that I have yet to mention in this chapter. Compare, for example, the textless vocal melody featured on the earlier track "Reggatta de Blanc."

47. Stewart Copeland, transcribed from the narration to his documentary film *Everyone Stares.*

48. Summers and Copeland contributed one song each to the *Synchronicity* album as sole composers: Summers with his 7/8 bizarro rock of "Mother," and Copeland with his bouncy world pop of "Miss Gradenko" (a song that, clocking in at exactly two minutes, stands as the shortest track on any of the Police albums). The two non-Sting tracks are positioned back-to-back in the middle of side 1. (Summers receives cowriting credit with Sting for "Murder by Numbers," on which he composed the jazz-styled music and Sting wrote the lyrics. This track was omitted from the original LP version of *Synchronicity,* so fans in 1983 who wanted a copy of it had to buy the chromium dioxide audiophile cassette.)

49. In his review of *Synchronicity* for *Rolling Stone,* Stephen Holden made the following astute observation: "Though the Police started out as straightforward pop-reggae enthusiasts, they have by now so thoroughly assimilated the latter that all that remains are different varieties of reggae-style syncopation" (*Rolling Stone,* 23 June 1983, 54).

50. I will focus my discussion here on the song's signature riff. For a complete formal analysis of "Every Breath You Take," see John Covach, "Form in Rock Music: A Primer," in *Engaging Music: Essays in Music Analysis,* ed. Deborah Stein (New York: Oxford University Press, 2005), 75. On the song's form, Covach asserts that "a clear thirty-two-bar AABA form frames a central bridge section . . . making the overall form a compound ABA."

51. Summers, *One Train Later,* 323.

52. Ibid., 323–24.

SEVEN ✼ Vocal Authority and Listener Engagement

Musical and Narrative Expressive Strategies in the Songs of Female Pop-Rock Artists, 1993–95

LORI BURNS

The myth of confessional music or poetry as the truth, pure and unmediated, is, of course, just that: myth. Confession is narrative, even in our most private journals, we interpret, select, frame our lives like a painting.

VOCAL STYLES SEEMED TO FLOURISH in the music of female pop-rock artists of the 1990s. There is an abundance of vocal creativity and expressive power in the albums released during 1993–95 by artists such as Tori Amos, Björk, Ani DiFranco, PJ Harvey, Sarah McLachlan, Alanis Morissette, Sinead O'Connor, Liz Phair, and Jane Siberry. Individually, each artist contributed her unique vocal style to a developing musical genre; collectively, these artists can be recognized for setting a new standard of vocal expression that has profoundly influenced subsequent artists.

These female artists of the 1990s tended to write lyrics that explore and grapple with social identities, developing themes of gender, sexuality, desire, power, and resistance within the flow of narratives that feature an intensely personal style of vocal address. The musical elements of this brand of vocal delivery are integrally bound to the narrative perspective and social meaning of the lyrics. The expressive integration of words and music in this style has such a striking impact on the reception and interpretation of an individual artist's musical work that sometimes the artist is considered to be indistinguishable from her art. It is all too easy—and often vastly oversimplifying—to approach the music as merely a reflection of the artist's personal experience, an interpretive move that has a tendency not only to pass over crucial but perhaps subtle aspects of the song's aesthetic effect but also to reduce the impact of the artist's expression and ultimately to dismiss the power of her narrative authority.

Dismissive assessments of "personal" expression can be found even in feminist writings on female artists. For instance, Bonnie Gordon, in attempting to situate Kate Bush as a creative female voice in the rock industry, implicitly suggests that the use of the personal voice in the female singer-songwriter tradition has led to that music having less of a creative impact than it otherwise might have had:

> [Kate Bush] does not fall into the tradition of Joni Mitchell, Suzanne Vega, or Tori Amos, whose music works by creating the illusion of the performer sharing her personal experience with an empathetic listener. This is not to say that Bush's music does not draw on personal experience at all. But instead of telling a story about herself, Bush takes inspiration from feelings, gestures, and preexistent stories that provide molds for articulating her experience.[1]

While some critics and fans thus entangle the artist's identity with the artistic message, other scholars in the field of popular music studies are busy debating the role of the author and questioning the concept of authorship. While the former group perhaps gives the artist too much credit, the latter group may at times risk not giving the artist enough credit. This latter approach, however, has helped make popular-music scholars aware that there are often more creative personalities in play than are immediately apparent on any given recording. Due to the complex nature of song production, with producers, engineers, and supporting musicians involved in the process, the role of the author is being seriously scrutinized.[2]

Devoting special consideration to the multiple layers of authorship, musical artist, and musical persona, this chapter develops an interpretive framework for the integration of musical strategies with lyrical narrative perspectives in female pop-rock expression. Responding to current literature, this research incorporates theories of narrative authority[3] into a framework of popular music analysis that engages vocal expression, melodic and harmonic idioms, instrumental strategies and recording techniques.[4] Of course, a full examination of these issues would extend far beyond the scope of a single chapter. My critical objective is to explore female vocal authority by examining strategies of narrative voice and vocal musical expression in four selected songs. The analyses will demonstrate how these strategies contribute to the sociomusical communication from artist to listener. But before undertaking the analyses, it will be helpful to consider the theoretical elements of my analytical approach since the four case studies follow this theoretical framework very closely.

Narrative Voice and Authority

First and foremost, it is important to acknowledge that *authority* is something that is ascribed. Narrative theorist Susan Sniader Lanser defines *discursive authority* as the "intellectual credibility, ideological validity, and aesthetic value claimed by or conferred upon a work, author, narrator, character, or textual practice."[5] In order to address such values (intellectual, ideological, and aesthetic) in the writings of female authors, she explores different modes of narrative voice and their attributes of authority. For Sniader Lanser, the interpretation of narrative voice and authority requires a consideration of the modes of contact between narrator and narratee, as well as the narrative stance as it reveals the explicit or implicit ideologies that shape a lyrical narrative. These modes of narrative are meaningful for the interpretation of female pop-rock artists in combination with other interpretive elements of narrative structure as identified by literary theorists.[6] My analysis of lyrical content in the pop-rock singer-songwriter genre will consider not only the stories and social messages that are conveyed but also how these are communicated through narrative (storytelling) strategies. This analysis of narrative voice is offered with a view to exploring the larger question of female vocal authority. Through the careful examination of an artist's musical expression of narrative voice, the music analyst can interpret the ideologies, values, and authority of the multiple agents within the narrative structure. Thus, the author/artist is disentangled from her musical persona, permitting her to engage fully in contemporary commentary and *ascribing* to her the full authority to convey her sociocritical message.

Musical Persona and Agency

In song, the singer is a mediator, an agent, the voice of the song narrative. In most cases of popular music listening, the listener is familiar with the singer, that is, familiar with the popular persona of that recording artist and possibly with the artist's political and social views. The listener or fan might have formed an impression of the artist's values from the artist's recordings and videos, as well as from media coverage. It is sometimes quite difficult to separate the artist from the musical product, and it is all too easy to interpret the music as a realistic reflection of the artist's worldview.

In *The Sex Revolts,* Simon Reynolds and Joy Press categorize popular music artists based on aspects of the personal life of the artist intermingled with the artistic product. The following remarks illustrate their approach to the interpretation of an artist's work:

> For Jones, Siberry, Chandra and the rest, these "voices" or external forces seem to be a useful way to conceptualize the creative process, which otherwise might seem overwhelming. It allows them partially to disown their own dark emotions. . . . But there's a slightly disturbing division between interior life and public self, an inability to connect the inner turmoil with everyday, practical existence.[7]

Popular music artists must negotiate the question of personal versus professional identity on an ongoing basis. When asked directly if her songs are about firsthand personal experience, PJ Harvey remarked, "I'm just growing to realize that it's not you when you see your picture in the paper. I can now see that it's something completely removed from what I am."[8] Harvey thus assesses the product as having layers of mediation between her self and her public musical image.

Tori Amos also reflects on the presence of the self in her music, admitting to the personal elements of her songs but then also bringing society into the equation when she states, "We're not actors. I think songwriters are the consciousness or the unconscious of the time. . . . I'm only a mirror. . . . 50 percent of it is me and 50 percent of it is them."[9] Here Amos points to the potential for multiple layers of meaning and social mediation in her writing.

Song lyrics are a very important part of the social communication of song. As Holly Kruse writes, "Not only do lyrics provide the 'narrative' for a song, but lyrics help determine how artists are perceived by audiences, what they seem to 'stand for.' Lyrics are meaningful because they appear to give listeners insights into an artist's thoughts and feelings, and they allow listeners the pleasure of textual interpretation, of trying to determine the ever-elusive, ever-shifting 'true meaning' of a song."[10] A postmodern sensibility would lead one to value the social elements that impact the production of art, including the individual artist's personal and social contexts. This sensitivity to context, however, paradoxically opens up the problem of the confusion between author and artistic persona. In order not to equate author with persona, one must tease apart the expressive layers of the lyrical message from that of the individual experience (author) and social engagement present in the performance (persona). In advocating this approach, I do not mean to disengage the artist entirely from her musical expression but rather to allow the artist to explore more voices than merely her own.

Toward this end, Simon Frith accounts for the following "voices" in a popular song text:

> There is, first of all, the character presented as the protagonist of the song, its singer and narrator, the implied person controlling the plot, with an attitude and tone of voice; but there may also be a "quoted" character, the person whom the song is about (and singers . . . have their own mannered ways of indicating quote marks). On top of this there is the character of the singer as a star, what we know about them, or are led to believe about them through their packaging and publicity, and then, further, an understanding of the singer as a person, what we like to imagine they are really like, what is revealed, in the end, by their voice.[11]

Frith captures here the multivoiced nature of the popular song text. The analytic model to be presented in this chapter also distinguishes between and among the subjective layers of protagonist, character, and artist, defining these roles within narrative theory and demonstrating how important they are to the expressive strategies of a female singer-songwriter.

Female Singer-Songwriters: Genre and Gender

A popular music listener has expectations for vocal expression that are dependent on the genre, as well as the gender of the artist. Female songwriters gained recognition during the 1970s with artists such as Carole King and Joni Mitchell (their work was often referred to as "women's music"), with a second wave or a coming of age in the early to mid-1990s. For these artists, the gender of the voice cannot be set aside or bracketed. The vocal expression spans the range from intimate and reflective to harsh and angry.[12] The themes that are explored are gender-specific stories that examine a female protagonist's situation in relation to her social world. The vocal address communicates and develops a relationship with the listener, and the narrative content explores specific experiences of women in society in a wide range of themes and social positions. But one aspect of the address is sustained fairly consistently across the genre: the narrative voice most commonly invoked is the first-person narrator. One could cite historical reasons why female songwriters would more naturally adopt the personal voice in presenting stories of female experiences, but my intent here is not to ask why the personal voice is adopted but rather to question and explore its potential for musical-narrative authority.

As I work to place this genre in its appropriate contexts, I return to Sniader Lanser's definition of discursive authority as the "intellectual credibility, ideological validity, and aesthetic value claimed by or conferred upon a work, author, narrator, character, or textual practice." Further, in response to the question of ideological validity she explains that "one major constituent of narrative authority . . . is the extent to which a narrator's status conforms to [the] dominant social power." It is also important to note that the production of authority must be "characterized with respect to specific receiving communities."[13] To put this into the context of the genre of pop-rock singer-songwriters, we know that genres and subgenres are received by specific social groups that share common values and ideologies and that a genre might be well received by one group but misunderstood or undervalued by another. Specifically in the case of female artists, that undervaluation could take the form of a negative response to the presentation of private details in the narrative or to resistant or oppositional strategies. The following remarks reveal one reviewer's need to distance himself or from that aspect of Alanis Morissette's music. Stephen Thomas Erlewine writes, "It's remarkable that Alanis Morissette's *Jagged Little Pill* struck a sympathetic chord with millions of listeners, because it's so doggedly, determinedly insular. . . . She never disguises her outright rage and disgust. . . . Morissette unflinchingly explores emotions so common, most people would be ashamed to articulate them." He also reveals his cynicism concerning Morissette's adoption of the style, saying that "this is clearly an attempt to embrace the 'women in rock' movement in alterna-rock."[14]

We can read in these comments the reviewer's discomfort with Morissette's mode of address, as well as his delineation of the boundaries that have been crossed. Sniader Lanser identifies this discomfort when she asserts that "the female voice is a site of ideological tension made visible in textual practices"[15] She examines that tension, choosing female fiction authors for her study of narrative voice and making a positive claim about their impact on the world of literature, writing, "The texts I explore construct narrative voices that seek to write themselves into Literature without leaving Literature the same."[16] As I select singular musical artists for study here, I shall explore how these musicians write themselves into music without leaving music the same.

A Narrative-Theoretical Framework for the Interpretation of Voice

My interpretive framework for the critical distinction of narrative voice in the analysis of pop-rock song considers the following perspectives: (1) *narrative agency;* (2) *narrative voice;* (3) the *modes of contact* between narrator and narratee; and (4) the *engagement* of the listener.[17]

1. Narrative Agency: Author–Implied Author–Narrator

Narrative theorists distinguish the author from the multiple voices that might emerge within a narrative. Seymour Chatman represents this framework in a schema (reproduced here as fig. 7.1) that represents the author and reader as external elements that frame the internal fictional elements of implied author, narrator, narratee, and implied reader. In figure 7.2, I have annotated this schema to include the aspects of narrative that I have culled from my readings in narrative theory. My annotations illustrate the important terms that I will use in the interpretive framework. As with any theoretical borrowing, I have developed the apparatus to suit a music-analytical perspective. The discussion that immediately follows explains the critical terms featured in figure 7.2.

The schema begins with the *author,* to be distinguished from the *implied author.* This distinction immediately cautions the interpreter to be sensitive to the function of *agency* in narrative.

> **Sensibility, Values, Ideologies.** Chatman explains that the implied author establishes the norms of the narrative and is reconstructed by the reader based on what is offered by the narrative.[18] Wayne Booth identifies the distance between the narrator and the implied author and characters, a distance that might be emotional, moral, or intellectual.[19] As Mieke Bal, in *Narratology,* receives the concept of the implied author, the reader understands or infers the implied author's

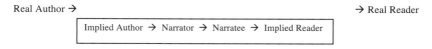

Figure 7.1. Seymour Chatman's model of narrative communication. (From Chatman, *Story and Discourse*, 151.)

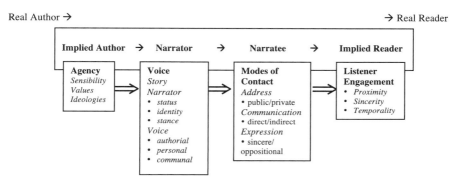

Figure 7.2. Lori Burns, critical terms for interpretation of voice

values and ideologies through the function and content of the narrative and consequently develops a better understanding of the meaning of the text. As defined by Abbott, the implied author is "that sensibility (that combination of feeling, intelligence, knowledge, and opinion) that accounts for the narrative."[20] Through the consideration of how an author negotiates the narrative, the reader forms an interpretation of the narrative voice, as well as the ideologies, values, and authority of the persona that guides the narrator, that is, the implied author. While the implied author's values may in fact shed light on the real author, the real author retains the privilege of invention. As Sniader Lanser explains, the real author has the power to create new master plots, change literature (the work does not leave literature the same), and expose the "fictions" of authority.[21]

This distinction of different agents within a narrative scheme is valuable for the interpretation of the popular music artist who engages the "personal" voice. An ongoing awareness of the author–implied author–narrator schema reminds the interpreter to be alert to questions of agency even when the lines become blurred. The ability to interpret a variety of narrator strategies is critical to a clear reception and appreciation of such agency.

2. Narrative Voice: Narrator–Character–Persona

While the author and implied author are agents whose authority and values are inferred through a critical apparatus, it is the narrator with whom the reader (or listener) is "actually" engaged. And it is the narrator who serves as mediator, agent, or voice of the story. Thus, it is for the narrator that literary theorists have developed the most detailed interpretive approach. In the genre of pop-rock singer-songwriters, the voice of the story is central to the network of meanings that an artist constructs.

> **Narrator Status, Identity, Stance.** As a reader immediately enters a story, he or she will evaluate whose story is being told and by whom. Is the narrator of the story a character (possibly the protagonist) or is the narrator uninvolved in the events? By what claim does the narrator have access to the story? Narrative theorists refer to this construct as *narrator status*. As part of the determination of the narrator's status in the story, the reader forms an understanding of the *identity* of the narrator. Is the narrator reliable, honest, and sincere in the telling of the story? A related term, *narrative stance,* is traditionally defined as point of view, but for this element Sniader Lanser focuses her attention on the concept of ideological stance, on "the relationship between the narrator's personality and values and . . . a set of social and cultural norms against which literary discourse is traditionally read."[22]
>
> **Voice.** Borrowing from Gérard Genette's categories of narrative perspective, Sniader Lanser develops three modes of narrative voice.[23]
>
> *Authorial* voice accounts for narratives that are heterodiegetic (third person) and public, the omniscient narrator addressing a narratee who is analogous to a reading audience. Sniader Lanser recognizes that this mode of voice is typically granted the greatest degree of "authority" because the narrator (and narratee) both exist outside of the fiction and are not "humanized" by the events.[24]
>
> *Personal* voice is used to refer to autodiegetic (first-person) narrators who are self-consciously telling their own histories. In this case, the

authority ascribed to the personal voice is contingent in a way that the authorial voice is not; the protagonist narrator does not carry the omniscient privileges that attach to authorial voice. Sniader Lanser asserts that this makes the "personal voice less formidable for women than authorial voice, since an authorial narrator claims broad powers of knowledge and judgment, while a personal narrator claims only the validity of one person's right to interpret her experience."[25] She does address the question of the potential confusion between real author and narrator when she states that "the creator retains the liberty to invent." She also suspects that "the more frequently a writer uses first-person narration—the greater number and variety of I-narrators he or she creates—the smaller the likelihood that autobiographical connections will continue to be presumed."[26]

Communal voice is a narrative mode named by Sniader Lanser as a collective voice or a collective of voices that share narrative authority, a practice in which narrative authority is invested in a definable community and is textually inscribed either through multiple, mutually authorizing voices or through the voice of a single individual who is manifestly authorized by a community. This mode might be expressed through a plural "we" or might allow for individuals to speak sequentially.[27]

Sniader Lanser's sensitivity to the contingencies and agencies evident in narrative voice are invaluable to this study of pop-rock singer-songwriters, especially to my effort to distinguish the social value of an apparently personal or private story. In the analyses to be offered, these three modes (authorial, personal, and communal) will be illustrated.

3. Modes of Contact: Narrator–Narratee

The songs I am concerned with here convey intensely personal stories of speaking subjects. The subject is often addressing a specific person, and the contact between the narrator-subject and the narratee is an important aspect of the song scenario. Narrative theory provides a framework for critical questions about the narrator's communication to the narratee. Is the *address* public (aimed at a broader readership) or private (aimed at a specific character inside the narrative)? Is the *communication* from the narrator to the narratee direct and active or indirect and passive? Is the *expression* (position or perspective) of the narrator sincere—

one might ask, authentic—to that narrator/character or does the narrator adopt other positions and/or roles through the strategies of irony or character focalization? These questions invite reflection on the power relationship between narrator and narratee, as well as on the larger conception of authorship. For instance, the way in which a narrator might address a narratee can reveal a great deal about the implied author's values and message.

> **Address: Public versus Private Voice.** The narrator might adopt a form of public address, through which a broad readership (historical reader) is understood to be the narratee. A private address would suggest that the narrator is communicating to a specific individual inside the narrative. The conception of public voice versus private voice is important to feminist theory because of the nature of the stories that a woman might wish to tell.[28] Although stories of sexual inequality might appear to have only individual value, the feminist tenet that the personal is political holds that private stories develop from institutionalized distributions of power and authority.

> **Communication: Direct versus Indirect.** The narrator can very directly address the narratee with an "I/you" communication or indirectly through a narrative account of actions, events, and feelings that are not directly offered to a narratee.[29] This direct communication can be self-conscious such that we are very aware of both the "I" and the "you" in the narrative or it can be unconscious such that the presence of the narratee is not constructed within the text.

> **Expression: Sincere versus Oppositional.** Ironic expression can suggest an oppositional position toward the narratee. The critical assessment that an expression is ironic requires attention to a number of discursive details. Sincerity and irony are sometimes judged by the content of the expression, especially if the content is intensely personal and private. In a musical expression, irony can be conveyed using a number of strategies, including tone of voice, style of delivery, and musical support.

4. Listener Engagement: Artist–Reader/Listener

Female songwriters create narratives that strongly engage the listener. When a first-person narrator uses the personal pronoun "I" and directly addresses a narratee ("you"), the listener is drawn in and might even have the sense that he or she is the "you" in question. Andrea Schwenke Wyile's concept of *engaging narration* allows us to focus our interpretive attention on moments when the reader would be persuaded "inside" the story. Her interpretation of engaging narration is based on elements in the narrative that develop the relationships between and among the characters (including the narrator and narratee).

> **Proximity.** The term *proximity* might be useful to suggest that an en-gaged narrator is so close to the character that we conflate narrator and protagonist. In first-person narration, Schwenke Wyile explains that the "narrator and character blend into one another in many readers' minds despite the fact that one can make a technical distinc-tion between the 'I' who narrates and the 'I' who experienced the events."[30]

> **Sincerity.** Schwenke Wyile also considers the *sincerity* of the narrator's expression, claiming that engaging narration develops from "an earnest telling of events in which the narrator is entirely devoted to relating the character's experiences." The sincerity of the narrator is assessed by the listener as that character's position is defined through the telling of events and the establishment of feelings. If the narrator is engaged as a consonant single voice, then the listener receives what seems to be an unmediated expression; as Schwenke Wyile puts it, an *engaging narrator* offers a "single voice that is so highly confident that it is ultimately unassailable within the text."[31] If the narrator offers a shift in the engagement or perspective, then the listener is witness to the critical presentation of the narrator/character's situation with op-positional viewpoints. Mikhail Bakhtin's conception of the double-voiced discourse is important here as a discourse that is infused with the author's and speaker's intentions at the same time. Bakhtin also developed the concept of the dialogic discourse in which a narrative might present two or more competing voices.

> **Temporality.** Temporality is another important element in the process of developing an engaged reader. The literary theorist Dorrit Cohn identifies a narration as *consonant* when there is no temporal inter-ruption between the events and their telling and as *dissonant* when techniques such as retrospection and critique are used.[32] Schwenke Wyile's engaging narration is similar to consonant narration and is clearly contrasted with dissonant narration. When the narrator in the first person is looking back on a younger self (dissonant narration),

the reader is more aware of a critical process and thus is also able to distance himself or herself from the narrative. This results in the reader being less "engaged." Strategies of dissonant narration allow for fragmentation and shifts in perspective, including irony and double-voiced discourse.

Musical Expression and Interpretation

For a singer-songwriter who adopts these narrative strategies, how might the narrative elements be developed in the musical realm? For this study, I will focus my music-analytic attention on the details of vocal expression that are bound to the narrative elements just outlined (agency, voice, contact, and engagement). The musical elements of vocal expression that I will consider for interpretation include *vocal quality* (aspects of the expression that derive from the physical limitations of range, resonance, and vibrato, as well as performed aspects of quality such as volume, intensity, and inflection), *vocal space* (aspects of the melodic phrasing and ornamentation), *vocal articulation* (elements of rhythm and meter, as well as diction and textual utterance), *texture* (considering the role of the voice as part of the instrumental texture and the interactions among the musicians in the ensemble), and *recording techniques* (how the voice is recorded, mixed, and processed). For each of these musical layers, the listener interprets the extramusical connotations of musical gesture within the context of style and genre.

Interpretive responses to vocal quality, vocal space, and vocal articulation (three of the categories mentioned) are evident in critical writings on the artists in question. For instance, let us examine the following remarks:

> But what sets these women [PJ Harvey, Björk, and Tori Amos] apart from the mainstream soft soul of Mariah Carey and Dina Caroll is their extraordinary singing voices. Björk's is a heavenly hiccuping thing that almost defies terrestrial description; Polly's [PJ's] is as if an opera diva had eaten a drum kit, swooping and percussive, and Tori's is a finely tutored instrument that manages to simultaneously preach, purr and plead.[33]

In very imaginative terms, this critic has captured the distinctiveness of Björk's *articulation,* Harvey's *vocal quality* and movement within *vocal space,* and Amos's expressive strategies, which rely on her control of *vocal quality, articulation,* and *space.* It is evident that these aspects of a singer's artistic persona are integral to the critical reception of her music. In the evaluative terms that are implicit in this type of critical review, the versatility of vocal expression is valued for its contribution to the artist's meaning and message.

To illustrate the interpretive framework I have outlined, I will work with a gathering of musical examples that offers a variety of expressive strategies. My analytic path through each song will follow the same steps, addressing questions of narrative agency and authorship, narrative voice, modes of contact from narrator to narratee, listener engagement, and musical expression. These are not meant to be fully integrated close readings of the chosen songs but rather illustrations of the potential array of strategies developed by these unique artists.

Four Analyses

1. Tori Amos: "Bells for Her," Under the Pink *(WEA International CD82567, 1994)*

VERSE 1

And through the life force and there goes her friend
On her nishiki it's out of time
And through the portal they can make amends
Hey would you say whatever we're blanket friends

CHORUS

Can't stop what's coming
Can't stop what is on its way

VERSE 2

And through the walls they made their mudpies
I've got your mind I said
She said I've got your voice
I said you don't need my voice girl
You have your own
But you never thought it was enough of

VERSE 3

So they went years and years
Like sisters blanket girls

Always there through that and this
There's nothing we cannot ever fix I said

CHORUS

Can't stop what's coming
Can't stop what is on its way

VERSE 4

Bells and footfalls and soldiers and dolls
Brothers and lovers she and I were
Now she seems to be sand under his shoes
There's nothing I can do

CHORUS

Can't stop what's coming
Can't stop what is on its way

VERSE 5

And now I speak to you are you in there
You have her face and her eyes
But you are not her
And we go at each other like blankettes
Who can't find their thread and their bare

CHORUS

Can't stop loving
Can't stop what is on its way
And I see it coming
And it's on its way

Agency: "Bells for Her"

Tori Amos claims that her 1994 album *Under the Pink* explores the "emotional violence between women, rather than between the sexes," critically identifying a personal (emotional violence) level, as well as a broader social (gender relations) one, for her thematic content. As one critic describes the song "Bells for Her," "Girlhood friends face the adult games of love, war and death with a strange, existential hope."[34] The situation is thus at once intimate (personal friendship) and socialized (the games of love and war). Amos identifies the autobiographical nature of the song's content when she offers this context for the song: "[T]he main thing about Bells is that there is no resolve. . . . I would have bet that I could have worked anything out with this person. I would have bet my hand I could have worked anything out. I'd be missing a hand right now. It'd be the one-armed Tori tour."[35]

As an *author*, Tori Amos proclaims her personal connection to the story, suggesting an autobiographical foundation for the song. However, if we consider also the concept of the *implied author*, we open up a critical awareness of the broader social message and its ideological source. We infer that the implied author of this story is someone who recognizes the social threats to the construct of female friendship. The author laments the loss of a personal friend, but the implied author warns the listener about the negative impact of particular social issues. As narrative theorists claim, the listener infers the implied author's values through consideration of the narrative strategies employed.

Narrative Voice: "Bells for Her"

The *story* of "Bells for Her" is an account of a relationship between two girls from childhood to adulthood. The story is told in momentary reminiscences of the past ("they made their mudpies") interwoven with expressions of concern for the present and future ("There's nothing I can do"). The narrator is at times a third person ("there goes her friend") and sometimes the first person ("And now I speak to you"). This shifting of narrative stance destabilizes the narrative voice so that we are not certain if it is a protagonist or an observing narrator speaking. The moments of first-person expression could be interpreted as moments of character focalization where we can gain a better understanding of the emotional position of the protagonist in relation to the friend. It is interesting that whenever the subjective "I" is invoked it is concomitant with the presence of the friend, for instance, in "I've got your mind I said / she said I've got your voice." The shifting of stance affects the overall narrative mode; the presence of the personal (first-person) voice disturbs the momentary efforts to assert an impersonal and authorial (third-person) voice. I would speculate that Amos plays quite deliberately with these narrative shifts.

Modes of Contact: "Bells for Her"

The narrative is constructed to tell the history of this friendship, moving from the farthest point back in time to the present. For the most part, the narrative *address* is public. The moments of private address are recounted or imagined, as in verse 5 ("And now I speak to you are you in there"). The contact between the subject/narrator and the narratee is mediated by the factors of time, as well as social distance. The sense of time travel is made evident through the early reference to the "portal." Despite the passage of time, the protagonist does not let go of her feelings of friendship, although it is evident that the friendship has been affected by social factors that have led to an estrangement. Verse 4 expresses her frustration with the interference of another relationship that the subject sees as damaging to her friend ("Now she seems to be sand under his shoes").

Listener Engagement: "Bells for Her"

The listener is certainly engaged in this story, drawn in through the sincere lament for a friendship. However, the shifts from first to third person and the shifts in time create an unstable perspective inside the narrative that encourages the listener to develop a critical distance. The opaque poetic style of the narrative also distances the listener; for example, the line "And through the walls they made their mudpies" causes the reader/listener to pause and reflect on the meaning, this critical distance creating a sense of remove from the personal voice. This poetic style is the hallmark of Tori Amos's lyrics and has led to much debate over meaning in her songs.

Musical Elements: "Bells for Her"

"Bells for Her" is musically notable for its unique recording of a prepared piano (the "bells"), for its lush yet meticulous capturing of Amos's voice, for her subtly nuanced and expressive delivery of the words, and for her compelling melodic and rhythmic phrase structure. These four musical elements complement and advance the narrative strategies I have described in the lyrics.

The prepared piano has a close-mic immediacy, although it is soft and muted. The immediacy of such details as the clacking of the piano mechanism (yet without an edgy quality) brings the instrument very close, while a dark reverberation (emphasizing the lower end of the harmonic spectrum) creates a warm and round wrapping for her voice.

Amos's voice is in counterpoint with the piano in the stereo spectrum, the voice oriented to the left and the piano to the right. The vocals are compressed and given a gentle reverb that suggests small-venue immediacy for the listener. The compression imparts a whispery thickness to her voice. The lower harmonics are present, but there remains clarity and detail in the upper frequency.

These recording factors combine to bring the performance very close to the listener. The stereo distinction of piano and voice creates an interesting counterpoint that draws the listener into this very particular musical world. The recording strategies for piano and voice reinforce features that I have described in the narrative conception of the song. The distinctive effect of the prepared piano suggests the passage of time and provides the "bells" that toll for the subject's friend ("Bells for Her"). The vocal intimacy contributes to the personal engagement of the narrator, and even when the narrator becomes more distant with third-person expression, the act of telling the story is made intimate through the consistently close presentation of the voice.

Amos is well known for her nuance of vocal gesture. In her articulation, she plays with consonances and vowels to create distinctive sound shapes, and she uses a variety of vocal qualities and colors to reflect the emotional content of her songs. In the opening verse, for instance, she creates an unusual emphasis on the final word of each phrase ("friend," "time," "amends," "friends") by drawing out the last consonant of each. During the last word of the first phrase ("friend"), she pauses between the *n* and the *d* and then pronounces *d* with its own tongue articulation (*deh*) rather than linking the *d* with the preceding *n*. The second phrase closes with the word "time," the final consonant of which is developed through a melodic ornament on the *m* sound. "Amends" and "friends" close lines 3 and 4 with a similar exaggeration of closing consonants. The consequence of this distinctive musical pronunciation is that the listener hears musical and lyrical time slowing down for the production of a single word. Musical time appears to stand still while the lyrical thought is completed.

Another important dimension of performance in Amos's song is the variety of qualities and timbres that she exploits in her voice. She uses a breathy quality at times and also an occasional raspy or growly quality. Her vibrato changes when she wishes to create different timbres and sometimes different levels of intensity. The placement of her voice can change from a forward "natural" placement to a back placement with a lowered palate. This quality can be used to create a sound that we associate with crying and thus can be used for moments of emotional intensity. The breathiness and vibrato or any of these qualities are not merely colors but can be used dynamically to create emphasis or tension in the performance expression. Another means of creating markedness or emphasis is through tonal intensity, that is, through an increase of focus in the sound from airy or breathy to focused and clearly pitched.

This is well illustrated in the second verse, where Amos creates a nuanced differentiation between vocal qualities that complements or communicates the interplay of voices that we find in the lyrics "I've got your mind I said / She said I've your voice / I said you don't need my voice girl / You have your own." With this passage, we shift from the third-person narration of a story to a first-person experience in which the Other, the object of the subject's attention, is also invoked. Amos uses a strong, nonbreathy tone quality and clear text articulation for the statement "I've got your mind I said" and then a weaker, quieter voice with muted pronunciation on the line "She said I've got your voice." In the response, "I said you don't need my voice girl," the subject returns to her stronger voice with an intensity of tone, a height of pitch, and a stronger vibrato but then returns to the weaker voice for the remainder of the verse in which once again the voice of the Other is invoked. Thus, Amos's manipulation of vocal quality contributes to a minidialogue inside the story.

Another musical element that allows Amos to develop her narrative is an irregular phrase structure that offsets listener expectations. For the first four phrases of the song (verse 1), the hypermetric structure is not normative but rather has the design illustrated in example 7.1. Phrase 1 is four measures plus two in the piano, phrase 2 is five measures plus one, phrase 3 is five measures plus one, and phrase 4 is six measures plus two. The implied phrase structure (based on an understanding of the hypermetric conventions) would be simply four four-measure phrases (in 3/4 time), each of which would have a vocal cadence. The antecedent-consequent design of the phrase pairs is evident in the pitch structure, which suggests dominant harmony closure for phrases 1 and 3 and tonic closure for phrases 2 and 4. Each of the expected vocal cadences is disrupted by a rhythmic device. In phrase 1, in the expected measure of cadence the last word, "friend," receives a late (syncopated) arrival on beat 2 instead of beat 1. The second phrase disrupts the feeling of closure by avoiding any vocal pitch in the expected fourth measure and waiting until the fifth measure to arrive on the cadential tonic pitch. Phrase 3 modifies the natural flow of the text to introduce half-note syncopations on the second beat of measures two and three, thus extending the phrase until a fifth measure. Phrase 4 abandons rhythmic motivic regularity and distributes the text with syncopations and new rhythmic

Example 7.1. Tori Amos, "Bells for Her," verse 1

diminutions to develop a six-measure vocal phrase. All of this transpires with the prepared piano repeating a tonic–dominant pedal pattern as a grounding counterpoint to the unusual melodic phrase presentation. This detailed level of phrase analysis is valuable because it offers a conventional musical explanation for the sense of destabilization that the listener might feel in response to the vocal expression.

Interpretive Summary: "Bells for Her"

The narrative of this song presents a sense of both historical time and the immediate present. It also offers the command of third-person authority and the sensitivity of first-person intimacy. The music supports and complements these shifting perspectives by establishing a clear melodic and rhythmic phrase structure that is then subjected to the manipulation of certain expectations. The textural/instrumental complement to this narrative setting is the evocative connotation of tolling bells in the prepared piano heard as a backdrop to the lush and nuanced vocal expression.

2. PJ Harvey: "Hook," Rid of Me (Island Records 314-514 696-2, 1993)

VERSE 1

I was blind I was pained
I was nothing 'til you came
you said babe make you sing
make you feel like some queen

CHORUS

said I'll take you Kathleen
to your home and mine
Lord he hooked me
fish hook and line

VERSE 2

and rolled in like him back
with a halo of deep black
'til my love made me gag
called him daddy take my hand

CHORUS

said I'll take you Kathleen
to your home and mine
good lord he hooked me
fish hook and line

BRIDGE

I'm hooked
I'm too far
oh beautiful

VERSE 3

I'm bound and I'm lame
life is nothing with his chain
daddy wait she can't sing
she can't feel she's no queen

CHORUS

said I'll take you Kathleen
to your home and mine
lord he hooked me
fish hook and line
said I'll take you Kathleen
to your home and mine
good lord he hooked me

we are untied

Agency: "Hook"

Polly Jean "PJ" Harvey's text offers a painful look at an abusive relationship. The narrator's first-person claims ("I was blind I was pained") and a reference to a proper name inform us that the speaking subject is named Kathleen. This allows Harvey as *author* to step away from the autobiographical question. The *implied author* also holds a distance from this story and is clearly making a strong statement against the abusive sexual control that Kathleen experiences.

Narrative Voice: "Hook"

The *story* of "Hook" emerges through the tortured musings of Kathleen as she reflects on a degrading sexual relationship. The narrator does not adopt a fixed *stance* but rather shifts between the subject Kathleen and her own imitation of the abusive man. There are statements that derive from Kathleen's perspective and others that quote "him," suggesting Bakhtin's double-voiced discourse in which two perspectives are presented at once. His words are appropriated by Kathleen ("you said babe make you sing") as she tells the story of how she was "hooked." The subject's *identity*, in relation to the ex-lover, is the very thing that is being questioned in this text as she evaluates the consequences of being involved with such a man ("I was nothing 'til you came"). The personal (first-person) expression is consistent except for a brief moment of third-person expression in the bridge ("she can't feel she's no queen"). This third-person reference to the protagonist is a narrative strategy that reveals Kathleen to be no longer able to speak for herself.

Modes of Contact: "Hook"

The *address* of this narrative is private; Kathleen is reflecting ironically on her relationship. When she refers to "you" we understand this person to be her lover, but she also refers to him as "he," suggesting that this reflection is just in her mind. Her *communication* is direct in the sense that the "I/you" relationship is clearly expressed, yet these direct statements are only imagined. The *expression* is ironic and the irony sometimes self-inflicted ("lord he hooked me") and sometimes directed at him ("'til my love made me gag"). The oppositional feelings of love and degradation are juxtaposed throughout; Kathleen immediately opposes a thought such as "I was nothing 'til you came" with "you said babe make you sing."

Listener Engagement: "Hook"

The temporal distance between the events and their telling in combination with the use of irony creates a dissonant form of narration. At first the narrator is able to maintain a critical stance and assess the relationship ("I was blind I was pained"), and the listener is witness to the shifts in stance and the questioning of identity such that we sustain a critical guard as well. As the narrative continues, however, Kathleen's experience seems to be more immediate and urgent ("I'm bound and I'm lame").

Musical Elements: "Hook"

The most prominent musical effect of this song is the highly distorted vocal track. A flange effect on the voice gives it a hollow sound, with the phasing effect blurring the edges. The vocal distortion musically confirms the dissonance that is perceived in the narrative; Kathleen is struggling with this story. In addition to the distortion, the vocal is very far back in the mix, buried behind the guitar. The voice is centered, but the guitar is also centered so that the guitar and voice become interwoven, difficult for the ear to separate and appearing to fight for attention. This might be interpreted as a musical depiction of the double-voiced expression of Kathleen and her lover.

In contrast to the centered voice and guitar are the panned stereo effects of the drums. The hi-hats occupy the entire stereo field, appearing to have the spatial freedom that the voice and guitar lack.

The musical materials depict well the ironic self-reflection that our protagonist is experiencing. The melodic guitar riff turns around a B half-diminished seventh chord, the produced pitch quality dense, heavy, and distorted, with a continuous sustain that does not let up throughout the verse. At the beginning of the verse, the voice sits on a low F3 (the diminished fifth of the dissonant chord), moving up to D4 (the minor third of B) for the lines that quote the ex-lover ("you said babe make you sing"). The higher register and relatively more stable contrapuntal position (the minor third as opposed to the diminished fifth) is ascribed to the ex-lover's confident expression.

The ex-lover's assertiveness continues into the chorus ("said I'll take you Kathleen"). The strong melody is delivered in accented quarter notes (supported by the dry snare and cymbal, as well as by the guitar on D-minor harmony). The voice moves from E4 up to F4, bringing the voice to a full octave above its originating point, before cadencing firmly on D.

The second verse brings back the guitar riff, but the voice does not return to the original low register. Rather, the voice continues from the established upper octave F4, and climbs to A4 for the third line "'til my love made me gag." The rising pitch of the voice over the course of the song represents the increase in tension and frustration. The higher pitch carries over into the second chorus statement, which emphasizes a movement from G to A before cadencing on F.

In what I have labeled as the bridge section, we hear a statement of the verse and chorus material on guitar with no melodic vocal presentation but instead a faintly whispered voice-over ("I'm hooked / I'm too far / oh beautiful") that offers Kathleen's admission that she has been completely hooked, much to her apparent regret. In the "bridge" version of the chorus, in place of PJ Harvey's voice we hear a distorted white noise. I interpret this covering of the voice to represent the ultimate overpowering of Kathleen's identity.

The third verse brings us back to the guitar riff and the competing voice and guitar. However, now the volume of the guitar overtakes the voice, making it very difficult to discern. This "disappearance" of the voice occurs at the moment in the text where Kathleen admits that she is bound and lame and where finally the first person is replaced with the third-person statement "daddy wait she can't sing."

Interpretive Summary: "Hook"

"Hook" is not a pleasant song to hear. Its thematic content features a negative violent image (of being hooked on a line) and is presented by an agonized protagonist who is repenting a degrading relationship. The musical materials and recording strategies that PJ Harvey develops to represent this story are harsh and grating, albeit controlled and crafted. She depicts Kathleen's struggle for power in relation to her overpowering lover through the placement and strength of the vocal and guitar tracks. The listener hears the gradual overtaking of the voice while Kathleen plunges farther into despair, with the bridge and the third verse taking her as far down in this relationship as she can go. The music makes this narrative clearer than the text could alone, especially through the strategies of musical struggle: the competition between guitar and voice and the struggle that is internal to the vocal line between Kathleen's voice and her lover's.

3. Ani DiFranco: "Overlap," Out of Range *(Righteous Babe Records ESP LASERMATRIX 7205, 1994)*

VERSE 1

I search your profile
for a translation
I study the conversation
like a map
'cause I know there is strength
in the differences between us
and I know there is comfort
where we overlap

CHORUS

come here
stand in front of the light
stand still
so I can see your silhouette
I hope
That you have got all night
'cause I'm not done looking,
no I'm not done looking yet

VERSE 2

each one of us
wants a piece of the action
you can hear it in what we say
you can see it in what we do

we negotiate with chaos
for some sense of satisfaction
if you won't give it to me
at least give me a better view

CHORUS

VERSE 3

I build each one of my songs
out of glass
so you can see me inside of them
I suppose
or you could just leave the image of me
in the background I guess
and watch your own reflection
superimposed

VERSE 4

and I build each one of my days out of hope
and I give that hope your name
and I don't know you that well
but it don't take much to tell
either you don't have the balls
or you don't feel the same

CHORUS

VERSE 1 (reprise)

Agency: "Overlap"

Ani DiFranco is an artist whose claim to authority has always been well documented.[36] She is very proud of her independent production label (Righteous Babe Records) and all that this means for her personal and authorial control over her music. In this song, she would appear to be celebrating that right to carve out her own identity. The theme explores individual identity in the context of an Other's influence. As I read the text and hear the song, I understand the *author* DiFranco to be the speaking subject, exploring questions that not only concern her personally but will reach a like-minded audience. The link between *author* and *narrator-subject* is thus very tight, as the authorial "I" persists throughout the song.

Narrative Voice: "Overlap"

This song does not tell a particular *story* but rather explores the question of how an individual relates to another: how one deals with differences and commonalities, how one negotiates power and desire, how one retains one's identity when the Other's is valued, and even how one might look to an Other in order to recognize aspects of one's own image. The narrator-subject speaks from a personal perspective ("I") throughout except for the second verse, where she adopts a more generalized "we." The third verse suggests that it is DiFranco speaking as she explores the process of song composition and reception.

Modes of Contact: "Overlap"

The *address* is at times private ("I search your profile") and at times public ("each one of us / wants a piece of the action"). The use of both modes is in keeping with the sense that we are hearing DiFranco both as private individual and as public composer. The communication is direct (an "I" addresses a "you") and immediate ("I search your profile"), and the expression is sincere ("I build each one of my songs / out of glass").

Engagement: "Overlap"

The narrative of "Overlap" is a good example of engaging narration. There is a sense of immediacy and directness as the narrator-protagonist expresses her thoughts to the narratee. The described situation (the narrator is gazing at the narratee and contemplating their mutual identities in relation to one another) conjures a very specific image and relationship, which suggests the narrator's confidence. She does not have all the answers ("no I'm not done looking yet") and the relationship is far from perfect, yet she is negotiating this personal terrain with self-awareness of the places where agreement and differences occur. (In contrast with the PJ Harvey song "Hook," we can easily see that "Overlap" negotiates the question of power from a very different vantage point.) The concept of the engaged reader is most important in verse 3, where DiFranco the composer clarifies that she is communicating directly with a listener who is able to find the overlap between self and author ("so you can see me inside of them").

Musical Elements: "Overlap"

Compared to the other artists discussed here, Ani DiFranco's self-produced music has the most stripped-down, bare, and straightforward sound. The effect of the recording is that this is intended as a "natural" performance. Both voice and guitar are centered and prominent in a spatial mix that would be realistic in a live performance situation in a small venue such as a club; the tone of the voice is warm and intimate but not "too" close, that is, not having the effect of being inside the listener's head but simply in front as one might view a live performance; we hear the squeaks and percussive hits on the strings of the acoustic guitar; and the reverberation is appropriate to the tempo and scope of the melodic and harmonic materials (these are enhanced with a gentle reverb but not overdone).

These production values are especially evident when one makes a direct comparison between this recording and the others I have analyzed here. Amos's voice enters the listener's ears with intimacy, while Harvey's is disguised behind the distortion and mixing processes; Morissette's voice (to be discussed subsequently) is highly manipulated in full-rock production with tube saturation, high reverberation, stereophonic panning, and so on. DiFranco, comparatively, is straight and natural, maintaining a polite distance from her acknowledged audience.

The structure of the song is relaxed and potentially hypnotic in its repetition of a particular pattern, but it is flexible enough to allow for a nuanced delivery of the lyrics. In 4/4 time, the guitar part comprises a two-bar riff that moves from a downbeat consonant G-major triad through a syncopated passing harmony on A (with a suspended second from the G chord), finally moving to B minor on the last eighth (with a similar added second C♯). The melody moves up in parallel fifths with the bass, and then, once the harmony arrives on B, the melody plays with the dissonant fourth E and second C♯ above that B. There is a sense of jazz harmonic parallelism and a swing feeling to the syncopated rhythms. The introduction offers four statements of this two-bar riff. When the voice enters for the first verse, the same material forms the basis of the vocal phrasing, changing only for the final two bars of each eight-bar vocal phrase. This cadential passage resolves from F-sharp minor to G major. The chorus has the same eight-bar harmonic phrase as the verse, although the voice articulates a new motivic gesture, which appears in measures one, three, and five, and the vocal patterning expands in range and pitch emphasis (the verses worked largely within the span from B3 to F♯4 while the chorus moves within the higher range from F♯3 to A4).

Interpretive Summary: "Overlap"

The repetitive harmonic structure of "Overlap" offers a comfortable support for DiFranco's gently nuanced delivery. There is very little tension in the presentation, which one might understand as the musical equivalent of the consonant, direct, and engaging form of narration in the lyrics. The minor variants in melody and rhythmic delivery over a consistent harmonic pattern are perhaps the musical equivalent of the lyrical questions posed: what is the identity of the self and how closely does it overlap with that of the Other? DiFranco's self-declared songwriting transparency is skillfully demonstrated here.

4. Alanis Morissette: "You Oughta Know," Jagged Little Pill (Maverick CDW 45901, 1995)

VERSE 1

I want you to know that I'm happy for you
I wish nothing but the best for you both
An older version of me
Is she perverted like me
Would she go down on you in a theatre
Does she speak eloquently
And would she have your baby
I'm sure she'd make a really excellent mother

PRECHORUS

'Cause the love that you gave that we made
wasn't able to make it enough for you to be open wide, no
And every time you speak her name
Does she know how you told me you'd hold me
Until you died, 'til you died
But you're still alive

CHORUS

And I'm here to remind you
Of the mess you left when you went away

It's not fair to deny me
Of the cross I bear that you gave to me
You, you, you oughta know

VERSE 2

You seem very well, things look peaceful
I'm not quite as well, I thought you should know
Did you forget about me Mr. Duplicity
I hate to bug you in the middle of dinner
It was a slap in the face how quickly I was replaced
Are you thinking of me when you **** her

PRECHORUS

CHORUS

BRIDGE (INSTRUMENTAL AND TEXTLESS VOCAL)

PRECHORUS 2

'Cause the joke that you laid on the bed that was me
And I'm not gonna fade
As soon as you close your eyes and you know it
And every time I scratch my nails down someone else's back
I hope you feel it . . . well can you feel it

CHORUS

Agency: "You Oughta Know"

Alanis Morissette equates the enormous success of the debut single from her 1995 breakthrough album *Jagged Little Pill,* "You Oughta Know," with her willingness to share very personal stories and emotions:

> It excited people to see someone being that embarrassingly honest. And it validated their seemingly embarrassing emotions. Society does not revere people who admit they were broken-hearted and horrified in that way. When it is poetic and pretty, it is fine to express it. When it is harsh like that experience was, society wants to move away from that. So it may have been refreshing to those that felt how horrified they were by their break-ups.[37]

The song triggered a great amount of speculation about Morissette's personal life at the time. While she has admitted that it was a response to a specific romantic relationship, she does not discuss the identity of the person.[38] She is also quick to dismiss a one-dimensional reading of the song. The video images for "You Oughta Know" do not tell the tale of a broken romance but offer a reflection on her artistic awakening, demonstrating that the song does not have to be merely "about" a broken romance.

This song begs reflection on sexual subordination and an unequal distribution of power (our narrator has been subordinated by her lover). It is here in this ideological domain that the work reveals the values of the *implied author;* the personal story is representative of a broader social problem. The impact of this story is felt through its negotiation of the master plot of male sexual power. But while the raw specifics of this sexual betrayal make us keenly aware of the woman's suffering, in this case the woman does not submit to it but instead resists through her anger and claim of injustice. In this regard, it is interesting that the song lyrics refer to public venues (a theater and a restaurant), taking public what was personal and private.

Narrative Voice: "You Oughta Know"

The *story* in this verse-prechorus-chorus form emerges in a nonlinear fashion. We shift from speculation about the ex-lover's new relationship to accusations to reflections on the past. Over the course of the verses, the protagonist approaches her ex-lover, timidly at first but then with greater disdain and aggression; in the prechorus she reflects on the betrayal of that relationship and how that betrayal impacts the next relationship; and the chorus is the protagonist's resultant claim of injustice and accusation.

This is the narrator's story. She adopts the *stance, status,* and *identity* of the protagonist throughout, and her claim on the story is personal. The voice does not shift to anyone else's perspective but remains true to the protagonist. The ex-lover's voice is mentioned by the narrator through the prechorus lines "And every time you speak her name" and "Does she know how you told me you'd hold me." The new girlfriend's voice is similarly questioned in verse 1 ("Does she speak eloquently"). Do we question the reliability of this narrator? The perspective is certainly one-sided, and we have no way to evaluate whether or not the protagonist is being "fair" to the actual situation.

While the narrative voice adopted here is clearly understood as the personal voice, this classification risks a reductive evaluation, such as follows: the song is nothing but her personal anger, and then, even further, it is nothing but Morissette's anger, thus making this personal voice an autobiographical, "confessional" voice. I am only content to ascribe the personal voice to this narrative if I am able to grant *authority* to that voice (intellectual credibility, ideological validity, aesthetic value). I have already identified ways in which this narrator resists the normative master plot, doing so by using direct, confident, even aggressive forms of address, and by invoking public display, thus refusing the invisibility of the merely private.

Modes of Contact: "You Oughta Know"

The narrator's *address* is confident and aggressive. She addresses a specific narratee in a very direct and revealing style of language. The narrator refers to herself in the first person, "I," and refers to the narratee using the second person pronoun "you" throughout. The events she describes are very intimate, thus disrupting any sense of formality between narrator and narratee, on the contrary revealing a degree of contempt for his privacy. The first two lines of verses 1 and 2 ("I want you to know that I'm happy for you" and "You seem very well, things look peaceful") reveal a measure of generosity that is in stark contrast to the rest of the text, thus appearing disingenuous. The account of intimate details that should remain private creates a sense of immediacy while the address to the narratee is most likely to be perceived as *mediated* by an actual distance between narrator and narratee. The *expression,* while a response to her sincere feelings of abandonment, is confrontational, ironic, and oppositional.

Listener Engagement: "You Oughta Know"

The narrator and the protagonist are blended into one very strong persona, and her anger is immediate and sincere. However, the narrator/protagonist introduces a great deal of critical judgment on her past situation, creating an example of dissonant first-person narration. Temporal shifts—from reflections in the moment to accounts of the past—create a sense of distance and thus ensure the reader's awareness of the constructed nature of the story. Although the listener is not inside this story, he or she is conveyed information about the past relationship, which provides the context for the intense anger that is the theme of this song.

Without that context, the listener would not understand the source of the anger and would not be sympathetic. The strategies of temporal shifting and narrator-narratee irony actually serve the function of providing the listener with some critical strategies for evaluating the relationship. The listener becomes engaged with the exposed emotional problem rather than seemingly with the narrator/protagonist herself.

Musical Elements: "You Oughta Know"

"You Oughta Know," produced by Glen Ballard, is notable for its very slick and controlled production style. The technical, as well as structural, elements of the vocal and instrumental sound are manipulated to articulate a dramatic change in each section of the song (verse, prechorus, chorus), and these shifts in musical sound have a dramatic impact on the narrative.

The song opens with a sparse and dry presentation of the first two lines of the verse, the lines I mentioned earlier for their unique deferential mode of address. Morissette's vocal *quality* might be described as timid in the sense that the vowels come forward with some hesitation. The melodic space that she occupies is from the fifth of the scale down to the tonic, with the outline of that fifth having a fairly hollow feeling due to the fact that it is only complemented by the fourth degree as a lower neighbor to the fifth and by the warmer minor third only in one statement (at "best"). The syllables are given a sparse (and timid) metric/rhythmic placement as well, with pulses happening only at the level of the half note at the beginning of each phrase. The background support is a quiet snare brush and a heavily processed, high-pitched synth sound that adds an eerie feeling. Ballard recorded her voice with a vintage C-12 mic, a tube mic that gives an overall warmth but at the same time a crisp sound for the diction and good detail in the high end. In these opening lines, the voice is very forward in the mix but also very dry, which creates an intimate effect. These elements combine to suggest a hesitant approach to her ex-lover, signifying his sexual power over her.

The third line of the first verse offers a textural and expressive shift. Morissette's voice increases in volume and allows more nasal resonances, as well as a more insistent, edgier tone. In melodic *space,* she opens up the higher register, now moving between the fifth degree and the upper octave of the tonic, with its neighboring reiterative pattern between the natural seventh degree and the tonic. The text is still offered syllabically, but there is a more active rhythmic presentation of eighth notes. The musical shape of her rhythmic *articulation* is simply reiterative at the level of that eighth note, to the extent that it does not seem natural to the text, with little or no variety in the pace of syllabic presentation. The rhythmic interest lies in the drum kit, which is now fully engaged, with the backbeat hits giving a cold, hard punch on beats 2 and 4. The bass has a rather funky riff that sits on a low tonic, while the electric guitar offers unusually placed melodic fills with a high reverb effect.[39] The voice remains centrally placed, but these *instrumental* effects contribute to a sense of tension and unease. This unease depicts musically the unease the narrator would feel in addressing him now with increased disdain. The opening pleasantries have been set aside.

The prechorus offers a remarkable shift in all musical parameters. The vocal quality is affected by a processing technique that creates a more aggressive sound. Whereas the vocals have been given a mono feed and central placement until this moment, the prechorus pans a doubled statement of the text both hard right and hard left so that two versions of Morissette's voice are heard, each with its own physical placement and power. It is a very dramatic effect due to the clear presence of two different "voices." The melodic shape and rhythmic articulation also contribute to the affective shift. The melody of the verse had been rather hollow, with points of reference on the fifth and first degrees but not much filled in. Now, beginning on the natural seventh degree, she moves down a Dorian scale to return to the lower tonic. The rhythmic articulation for her continued syllabic treatment of the text is now a motivic eighth and sixteenth pattern, once again increasing her level of activity. The bass begins to move, offering a melodic riff from a repeated low tonic, through the third and fourth degrees, leaping down to the natural seventh before repeating the pattern. In the middle register the rhythm guitar and organ blend into the background. The last line of the prechorus brings her voice back into the centered placement. In the prechorus, the protagonist reflects on the betrayal and even speculates about the potential betrayal of the next victim, transferring her own situation to a broader context. The double-voiced presentation during this part of the text is one of the critical moments for the listener in the evaluation of the narrative voice; for me it is a signal that this narrator is not merely addressing a personal situation but is speaking for a larger community.

It is in the chorus that the protagonist clearly picks up the gauntlet. While the lyrics can be understood as her direct address to her ex-lover, certain lyrical codes contribute to the sense of a larger impact ("the cross I bear" and "you oughta know"). The dramatic, edgy quality of Morissette's voice intensifies in the chorus as she moves into the higher part of the melodic range. The motivic "call" that is repeated throughout the chorus is a leap from the higher octave tonic to its upper fourth with a fall back to a chromatically raised third. This gesture introduces a dissonance into the otherwise diatonic Dorian melody, but despite its chromaticism it is eminently singable, certainly a gesture that invites audience participation. The effect of this call is most keenly felt at the end of the chorus when she hesitates on the text "you, you, you" with an upward melodic skip from tonic to minor third, before she makes it to the motivic call on "oughta know," the major third sounding very dissonant and painful after the effort to get there. The instrumental background for the chorus is more unified, with the bass and the rhythm guitar moving in clearer support of her vocal rhythms. Notably, her voice is unaccompanied for that final text call, and the recording process of tube saturation creates an evident distortion as her voice rings out. It is surely a gesture that commands its own discursive power.

Interpretive Summary: "You Oughta Know"

In this song, the narrator/protagonist confronts male sexual dominance that she wishes to resist, not only on her own part but on the part of a larger community that shares in this experience. The ideologies embedded in the story inform the listener that the implied author, in her critique of this master plot, holds feminist values. The real author, Alanis Morissette, may herself be a member of the same community, and she may have a story to tell, but we cannot fool ourselves into thinking that "You Oughta Know" is a factual account of her personal experience. The highly controlled technical production enhances the contrived and public portrayal of what may have originated as a personal story.

Vocal Authority: Critical Conclusions

I could continue with many more examples and demonstrate ever more the variety of musical and narrative expressions in this genre. Each of these artists has her own musical style and sound, and each song in her repertoire explores a unique situation. The four examples I have chosen capture the expressive diversity that is possible within the genre. I have commented on the contrasting aesthetics of musical production and the impact of that stylistic element on the reception of the vocal communication. The musical strategies can bring the artist closer or establish a sense of distance; thus, the artist can be felt to be "inside" the listener's consciousness or at a social distance. The private content can make for comfortable intimacy or social discomfort. The story that is told might appear to speak for only one individual, but it might also be revealed to be pertinent to a larger community with shared values. The artist might lay personal claim to the story or relay a story of broader social significance. Through all of these narrative strategies, artistic authority is retained, especially if one ascribes that authority to the *personal* and *communal* in addition to the more traditional *authorial* narrative mode.

The approach employed here need not be restricted to the repertory I have chosen to discuss. Indeed, much of what can be found in these four songs occurs across a vast range of songs in many repertories throughout popular music. While my specific claim in this chapter is that the analytical approach discussed here provides a useful approach to the music of female pop-rock artists in the 1990s, the consideration of issues of vocal authority and listener engagement, which unpacks the multiple layers of authorship, musical artist, and musical persona, may also provide a new perspective on many other styles. The idea expressed by Simon Reynolds and Joy Press at the beginning of this chapter—that the existence of confessional music and poetry is a myth—has helped frame this narrative, but it could likely frame many more as well.

NOTES

Earlier versions of this chapter were presented at the International Association for the Study of Popular Music (Canada) conference at Carleton University in May of 2004 and at Queen's University in November of 2005. I would like to thank Marc Lafrance, Jada Watson, Shannon Cole, Tamar Dubuc, and Alyssa Woods for their comments on earlier drafts. The research for this essay was supported by a grant from the Social Sciences and Humanities Research Council of Canada.

The epigraph that opens this chapter is from Simon Reynolds and Joy Press, *The Sex Revolts: Gender, Rebellion, and Rock 'n' Roll* (Cambridge: Harvard University Press, 1996), 256.

1. Bonnie Gordon, "Kate Bush's Subversive Shoes," *Women and Music: A Journal of Gender and Culture* 9 (2005): 38.

2. Significant contributions to this area of study include Will Straw, "Authorship," in *Key Terms in Popular Music and Culture*, ed. Bruce Horner and Thomas Swiss (Malden, MA: Blackwell, 1999); Richard Middleton, "Work-in(g)-Practice: Configurations of the Popular Music Intertext," in *The Musical Work: Reality or In-*

vention?, ed. Michael Talbot (Liverpool: Liverpool University Press, 2000); and Allan F. Moore, "Authenticity and Appropriation," *Popular Music* 21, no. 2 (2002): 209–23. See also Andrew Flory's essay on Marvin Gaye in chapter 4 of this volume.

3. Theories of narrative authority are explored, for example, in Susan Sniader Lanser, *Fictions of Authority: Women Writers and Narrative Voice* (Ithaca: Cornell University Press, 1992); Amy Lawrence, "Staring the Camera Down: Direct Address and Women's Voices," in *Embodied Voices: Representing Female Vocality in Western Culture,* ed. Leslie C. Dunn and Nancy A. Jones (New York: Cambridge University Press, 1994); Anna Wilson, *Persuasive Fictions: Feminist Narrative and Critical Myth* (Lewisburg: Bucknell University Press, 2001); and Andrea Schwenke Wyile, "The Value of Singularity in First- and Restricted Third-Person Engaging Narration," *Children's Literature* 31 (2003): 116–41.

4. Such topics have been advanced, for example, in Allan F. Moore, *Rock: The Primary Text,* 2nd ed. (Aldershot and Burlington: Ashgate, 2001); Albin J. Zak, *The Poetics of Rock: Cutting Tracks, Making Records* (Berkeley: University of California Press, 2001); John Covach, "Pangs of History in Late 1970s New-Wave Rock," in *Analyzing Popular Music,* ed. Allan F. Moore (New York: Cambridge University Press, 2003), 173–95; and Walter Everett, "Pitch Down the Middle," in *Expression in Pop-Rock Music: Critical and Analytical Essays,* 2nd ed., ed. Walter Everett (New York: Routledge, 2008), 111–74.

5. See Susan Sniader Lanser, *Fictions of Authority,* excerpt available in *Narrative/Theory,* ed. David Richter (New York: Longman, 1996), 182–94.

6. Significant contributions to this area can be found in Seymour Chatman, *Story and Discourse: Narrative Structure in Fiction and Film* (Ithaca: Cornell University Press, 1978); Dorrit Cohn, *Transparent Minds: Narrative Modes for Presenting Consciousness in Fiction* (Princeton: Princeton University Press, 1978); Mikhail Bahktin, *The Dialogic Imagination,* trans. Caryl Emerson and Michael Holquist (Austin: University of Texas Press, 1981); Mieke Bal, *Narratology: Introduction to the Theory of Narrative* (Toronto: University of Toronto Press, 1985); Richter, *Narrative/Theory;* Wilson, *Persuasive Fictions;* H. Porter Abbott, *The Cambridge Introduction to Narrative* (New York: Cambridge University Press, 2002); and Schwenke Wyile, "The Value of Singularity."

7. Reynolds and Press, *The Sex Revolts,* 377.

8. Adrian Deevoy, "Hips. Tits. Lips. Power: PJ Harvey, Björk, Tori Amos," *Q,* May 1994.

9. Ibid.

10. See Holly Kruse, "Gender," in *Key Terms in Popular Music and Culture,* ed. Bruce Horner and Thomas Swiss (Malden, MA: Blackwell, 1999), 87.

11. Simon Frith, *Performing Rites: Evaluating Popular Music* (New York: Oxford University Press, 1998), 198–99.

12. The themes in this genre have been explored in quite a number of musicological studies. The dark titles of these studies reveal a response to the thematic content of the music: "'Rip Her to Shreds': Women's Music According to a Butch-Femme Aesthetic" (Judith Peraino's article on PJ Harvey, in *repercussions* 1, no. 1 [1992]: 19–47); "Revisiting the Wreck: PJ Harvey's *Dry* and the

Drowned Virgin-Whore" (Mark Mazullo's study of PJ Harvey's debut album *Dry*, in *Popular Music* 20, no. 3 [2001]: 431–47); and *Popular Music, Gender, and Postmodernism: Anger Is an Energy* (Neil Nehring's study of alternative rock forms [London: Sage, 1997]).

13. Sniader Lanser, *Fictions of Authority*, 6.

14. Stephen Thomas Erlewine, "Alanis Morissette," on *All Music Guide*, http://www.allmusic.com/cg/amg.dll?sql=10:w9foxquhldhe.

15. Sniader Lanser, *Fictions of Authority*, 6.

16. Ibid., 8.

17. I have elsewhere examined in more general terms the notion of the voice as a subject in a lyrical narrative and the voice as a vehicle of social communication. See Lori Burns and Alyssa Woods, "Authenticity, Appropriation, Signification: Tori Amos on Gender, Race, and Violence in Covers of Billie Holiday and Eminem," *Music Theory Online* 10, no. 2 (2004). This chapter takes that concept further and opens up the categories for narrative content and perspective.

18. Chatman, *Story and Discourse*, 148.

19. Wayne Booth, *The Rhetoric of Fiction* (Chicago: University of Chicago Press, 1961), excerpted in Richter, *Narrative/Theory*, 146.

20. Abbott, *The Cambridge Introduction to Narrative*, 77.

21. Sniader Lanser, *Fictions of Authority*, 8.

22. Susan Sniader Lanser, *The Narrative Act: Point of View in Prose Fiction* (Princeton: Princeton University Press, 1981), 184.

23. For the interested reader, Serge Lacasse explores Genette's theory of intertextuality and its application to popular music recordings in his essay "Intertextuality and Hypertextuality in Recorded Popular Music," in *The Musical Work: Reality or Invention?*, ed. Michael Talbot (Liverpool: Liverpool University Press, 2000), 35–58.

24. Sniader Lanser, *Fictions of Authority*, 16.

25. Ibid., 19.

26. Sniader Lanser, *The Narrative Act*, 154.

27. Sniader Lanser, *Fictions of Authority*, 21.

28. Ibid., 15.

29. Sniader Lanser, *The Narrative Act*, 174.

30. Schwenke Wyile, "The Value of Singularity," 120.

31. Ibid., 117–18; Schwenke Wyile is here quoting Mike Cadden, "The Irony of Narration in the Young Adult Novel," *Children's Literature Association Quarterly* 25 (2000): 148.

32. Cohn, *Transparent Minds*, 145–60.

33. Deevoy, "Hips."

34. Marie Elsie St. Léger, review of Tori Amos, *Under the Pink, Rolling Stone*, 24 February 1994, 59.

35. Tori Amos, interview published in the *Baltimore Sun* in 1994, cited at http://www.hereinmyhead.com/collect/under/utp3.html.

36. Ani DiFranco herself composed an "open letter" published in *Ms.*, November 1997, reproduced in Raffaele Quirino, *Ani DiFranco: Righteous Babe* (Kingston, ON: Quarry Music Books, 2000). Anna Feigenbaum has written ex-

tensively about DiFranco's relationship with the press; see her article "'Some Guy Designed This Room I'm Standing In': Marking Gender in Press Coverage of Ani DiFranco," *Popular Music* 24, no. 1 (2005): 37–56.

37. Paul Cantin, *Alanis Morissette: You Oughta Know* (Toronto: Stoddart, 1996), 147.

38. It is now a well-known urban legend (at least according to the television channel VH1) that Morissette was singing about her breakup with Dave Coulier ("Joey" in the 1990s U.S. sitcom *Full House*) in "You Oughta Know."

39. It is important to note here that the "funky" bass in the recording of "You Oughta Know" was played by Flea of the Red Hot Chili Peppers.

EIGHT ❈ Recombinant Style Topics

The Past and Future of Sampling

REBECCA LEYDON

IN THIS ESSAY I am interested in the manifestation of a digital aesthetic through the practice of sampling in popular music in the 1990s. More specifically, I wish to consider a particular set of creative musical responses to that practice, ambivalent responses in which aspects of the digital aesthetic are at once embraced and rejected. To begin, I briefly review the shifting status of sampling in pop as it has been employed by musicians and as it has been received by critics and fans. I then consider some examples of recent music in which the deployment of "styles" seems to take the place of digital samples in what appears to be both a gesture of one-upmanship directed toward contemporary pop and a reinvigoration of the "craftsmanship" ideals of older classic rock.

Consider the track "Ars Moriendi" from Mr. Bungle's album *California* of 1999. The song demonstrates a mercurial stylistic plurality that was the band's signature device: four thrash-metal guitar chords initiate a toccatalike introductory passage of gypsy fiddle and Hungarian cimbalom flourishes; beguine rhythms morph into klezmer riffs and romungre rhythmic patterns; suddenly an incongruous patch of dark Detroit techno erupts; and a little later a four-on-the-floor, acid-house kick drum undergirds an accordion sequence while a distorted voice howls out a bit of classical Latin text, "Ave atque vale!"[1]

Critical reception of the *California* album focused exactly on the kind of rapid-fire style shifting found in "Ars Moriendi" and throughout the album. Mr. Bungle's trademark "genre hopping," evident on *California* and on their earlier *Disco Volante* of 1995, has met with mixed reactions. Some fans hear the device as unequivocally celebratory, a kind of pageant of musical "abundance" paying homage to an array of influences from Burt Bacharach and Brian Wilson to the Burundi Drummers. Alternatively, other listeners consider the device as sneeringly "transgressive," a subversion of the rigid codes of pop. Mr. Bungle's brand of polystylism has also been received, more ambivalently, as characteristic of a "culture of commotion," as musical Brownian motion, or as postmodern pastiche. In a less generous reading, the music's bewildering stylistic multiplicity serves only to collapse the field of signifiers into an affectively undifferentiated heap, what Fredric Jameson calls, damningly, "blank parody." Far from offering any sort of bold critique, blank parody is a fundamentally conservative artistic stance, Jameson argues; with the evacuation of any generalizing aesthetic positions, the artist abandons any possibility for transformation of the status quo.[2]

Among musicians, the Jamesonian charge of blank parody has been directed, more pointedly, toward the phenomenon of sampling in popular music, that is, the reuse of quotations extracted from previously recorded materials. A practice that first utilized vinyl sources and turntables, with dance-hall disc jockeys mixing records in a live context, the term *sampling* has acquired the more specialized meaning of the recording, storage, manipulation, and retrieval of musical sounds using digital tools. Following the appearance of the first affordable digital samplers (such as the Ensoniq Mirage) in the mid-1980s, sampling quickly became an attribute of many genres of popular music, one both celebrated and maligned by critics. Certainly sampling seemed initially to democratize the act of composition, opening up a vast sonic palette to anyone with a computer. In the sampling practices of the late 1980s and early 1990s, scholars such as Tricia Rose saw powerful modes of irony and recuperative possibilities, especially in hip-hop's mining of the 1970s funk catalog, which revived and celebrated a particular historical trajectory for contemporary black music, and in its ironic incorporation of sounds from television, Hollywood films, and other media largely closed to African Americans.[3] But by the mid-1990s many critics argued that the technique of sampling had become increasingly banal and pedestrian. For some listeners, such as *New York Times* critic Neil Strauss, sampling reached a nadir with Puff Daddy's (Sean Combs's) "Missing You" in 1997, a tribute to slain rapper Notorious B.I.G., which lifted wholesale the main vamp from the Police's 1983 hit "Every Breath You Take."[4] As legal battles heated up over the ownership and use of recorded sounds in the late 1990s, sampling began to be regarded more and more as a form of corporate buyout in which those with sufficient means (like Sean Combs) simply purchased a set of musical skills that they had not themselves acquired.[5] Sampling's reputation was not helped by the curious redundancy of the samples employed in pop—the same bits of Carl Orff or John Bonham appearing again and again on dozens of tracks, for example—nor by dubious borrowings from world musics that suggested ever more insidious strains of "schizophonic mimesis."[6]

The case has been made by several scholars that the particular affordances of digital sampling have not only cultivated a bricolage approach to musical composition but have also brought about broader changes in listening and modes of reception. In an essay entitled "Reflections of a Disappointed Popular Music Scholar," Lawrence Grossberg considered the rise of sampling and its contribution to a "new dominant neo-eclectic mainstream apparatus," which, he argued, has displaced classic rock's valorization of live performance and its stake in authenticity and artistic purity.[7] A sampling logic, Grossberg argues, informs not only the sound and structure of the music itself but also the listening habits of fans, whose tastes now range across disparate musical styles—hip-hop, pop, and rock hybrids—and whose consumption habits tend to isolate individual songs from complete albums, especially in the practice of downloading MP3s. Roger Beebe and Jason Middleton, extending Grossberg's argument, contend that this apparent lack of a "differentiating logic" does not necessarily translate into a broader range of available subject positions for listeners.[8] On the contrary, these "neo-eclectic" listening habits provide the illusion of cultural affiliations across racial and class boundaries. Despite its "aura of hipness," Beebe and Middleton argue, neo-eclectic listening ultimately preserves the privileges of a white, middle-class, male subject position. The authors' assertions here resonate with Jameson's claim that "blank parody" abandons the transformative possibilities of creative work.

Having presented this rather pessimistic account of digital sampling, let me go back now and take a second look at the example of the song by Mr. Bungle with which I began this chapter. "Ars Moriendi" does not, of course, consist of any actual "samples" at all in the sense of excerpts lifted from existing recordings. Rather, the song presents a series of newly made stylistic allusions. The phrase "contains a sample from X, used by permission," now so ubiquitous on compact disc liner notes, appears nowhere on the *California* album. Instead credit is given to a roster of guest virtuosos who play a variety of acoustic instruments, many of them atypical of a rock ensemble: trumpet, French horn, violin, viola, cello, English horn, accordion, harmonica, pedal steel guitar, cimbalom, timpani, and mallet percussion. Here the musicians themselves stand in, so to speak, for the digital sample. Might we think about "Ars Moriendi," then, as a musical work that is in dialogue with a sampling culture without participating unreservedly in that culture? While the song is certainly illustrative of a kind of sampling logic, there is surely a way in which Mr. Bungle seems to *trump* the sample here. For one thing, the band members can all play their instruments extremely well, and in the performers' virtuosity there is a level of traditional musical labor to which many listeners powerfully respond. The music seems to reinvigorate and extend notions of rock craftsmanship and its ideals of collaborative musical labor.[9] This reinvigoration takes place not only in the performances but also in the recording and production of the album, an old-fashioned and laborious analog process involving three twenty-four-track tape recorders, creating a sound that critics have described as "sprawling and warm."[10] While Beebe and Middleton might consider Mr. Bungle's eclecticism as a reassertion of classic rock's white homosocial dominant, it is also possible to hear in this music an oppositional stance, one that employs sheer technical virtuosity as a kind of antidote to the digital dominant.

The "samplelike" elements on *California* are smartly constructed stylistic references. In order to highlight the distinction between the use of digital samples and whatever it is Mr. Bungle is doing, I find it useful to invoke Leonard Ratner's notion of stylistic *topoi,* the term used in his influential book *Classic Music.*[11] Ratner's now familiar lexicon of eighteenth-century topoi includes generic dance types (both courtly and rustic), military and hunting music, "learned" music, and various orientalist codes (especially Turkish and *style hongrois*), all of which were recognized as discrete styles by eighteenth-century listeners. In the present popular music context, Ratner's term *topoi* provides a useful way to distinguish between an overt *quotation*—such as a sample extracted from a preexisting recording—and a *topic,* a newly composed, newly performed stylistic allusion of the sort we find in Mr. Bungle. Certainly one of the virtues of sampling is that it demystifies the cult of musical authorship; it manifests and promotes what Jason Toynbee calls "social authorship," the idea of the author as editor, mediator, parodist, and hybridizer in contradistinction to the romantic conception of the autonomous artistic genius.[12] But for many performing musicians the deployment of style topics, in place of explicit samples, accomplishes much the same thing while still preserving a space for virtuosic display, compositional skill, musical humor, stylistic competence, and authorial agency, all of which continue to matter very much to individual musicians immersed in a practice. It is unsurprising, then, that in the recent work of a number of artists we can observe a shift away from explicit sampling and toward a greater reliance on style topics. I believe this shift can be read as a kind of "second-generation" engagement with the digital aesthetic, an effort to react imaginatively to the technological practices of cut-and-paste that became so ubiquitous in the 1990s.

As one indication of the declining role of sampling, we can look at the trajectory of Beck Hansen's career through the 1990s and his use of sampling techniques as they evolve over the course of his albums from *Odelay* to *Midnite Vultures*. Beck's 1996 album *Odelay* contains samples from about a dozen credited works. The hit song "Devil's Haircut," for instance, uses looped samples of the drummer Bernard Purdie from his *Soul Drums* album, excerpts from James Brown's "Outa Sight," and other samples from Van Morrison's band Them. The salience of the sampling techniques for listeners is suggested by reviews of the album that proclaimed "Long Live Sampledelica!" and other celebratory remarks such as these:[13]

> Beck and his co-producers, the Dust Brothers shuffle and sling purloined drum licks, classy cameo appearances (jazz bassist Charlie Haden) and very obscure samples (hands up, everybody who remembers the early '70s funk band Rasputin's Stash) with a blithe self-assurance that belies the combustible potential of their juxtapositions.[14]

> Beck samples from every possible wacky source imaginable (and unimaginable), which just makes the ride crazier. There are sounds from all sorts of old records, including one from Dick Hyman's classic Moog record and, on "High 5 (Rock the Catskills)," an obscure early 8os bit where listeners are commanded to scream out the names of their favorite designer jeans. ("Everybody in the house say 'Jordache!'")[15]

Clearly, part of the fun for many listeners at the time was the sleuth work of identifying the obscure sample sources and hearing the detritus of popular culture resurrected and put to surprising new uses. But for Beck the musical point seems to have had as much to do with the sheer abundance of the sources and the battiness of their juxtapositions as with the particular identity of the quotations. Indeed, Beck's approach to sampling on *Odelay* has been characterized by Robert Fink as representative of a "post-canonic" stance in which recorded sounds become "decontextualized, culturally neutral shards" drifting through "a Baudrillardian mediasphere."[16] Fink argues that sampling in much music of the 1990s is best characterized, as he puts it, by "that all-purpose '90s interlocution: 'Uh, yeah; whatever.'"[17] This "whatever" approach means that samples drawn, say, from the masterworks of classical music lose their connotations of prestige or even pretentiousness. Thus, Fink cautions that when Beck samples a passage from Schubert's "Unfinished" Symphony along with bits of bossa nova, rap, and soul in "High 5 (Rock the Catskills)" it would be wrong to assume that the Schubert quote is necessarily of a different quality or status than the other samples despite its special salience for musicologically trained listeners. Fink by no means intends to lament the demise of the classical canon but simply to point out that sources of stylistic authority have long ceased to reside in the academy or other prestigious sites of cultural legitimacy. The back catalog of classical and pop alike is just "stuff," material available for reassembly.

Fink's reading is apt for *Odelay* with its incorporation of a multitude of recorded samples. But Beck's approach to appropriated samples seems to take a different turn in his subsequent work. In comparison with *Odelay*, Beck's *Midnite Vultures* album, released three years later in 1999, contains only two credited samples, and these segments are so subtly interwoven into the musical fabric that the distinction between the band and the sample is difficult to discern.[18] Beck's declining use of samples after *Odelay* may have been partly motivated by the actions of the Illegal Art label, which produced an album in 1998 called *Deconstructing Beck*. The thirteen songs on this compilation are collages, each made entirely using Beck samples, samples taken from works that were themselves made up of other people's samples. Production of this CD was funded by a grant from ®™ark (pronounced "art mark"), a subversive organization that funds creative acts of corporate sabotage, whose support of the *Deconstructing Beck* project was meant to draw attention to the increasing difficulty artists face in obtaining the use of recorded samples without paying hefty royalty fees.[19] The point was to challenge pop music's sampling hierarchy, in which only artists with enough money can afford to buy the rights to any sound they want.

Whether or not Illegal Art's activities influenced Beck directly (it is reported that he actually applauded the project), his own work subsequently seemed to take a decisive turn away from sampling. The mostly acoustic and more stylistically homogeneous *Mutations* album followed *Odelay* in 1998. With *Midnite Vultures* in 1999, however, Beck returned to the multistylistic mode of *Odelay*. But this time, rather than lifting samples wholesale from existing recordings, Beck now cooked up almost everything "from scratch." *Midnite Vultures* features an array of stylistic topoi, newly composed, newly performed passages that allude to a range of recognizable styles. In the opening track, "Sexx Laws," for example, banjo and pedal steel guitar, played by country musicians Herb Pederson and Jay Dee Maness, combine with a horn section reminiscent of the "Stax Records" sound, juxtaposing old-timey bluegrass with southern soul. Throughout the album Beck favors a pared-down approach, usually employing style topics in simple, more austere pairs. He is especially fond of creating a sudden textural vacuum in which all the parts of an established musical texture abruptly halt as an entirely new style and (usually much sparser) texture appear, seemingly out of thin air. The two contrasting styles are subsequently layered and combined in a way that is always unexpectedly congenial. On "Peaches and Cream," for instance, the prevailing guitar-based hard-rock sound is suddenly interrupted by an Isicathamiya vocal ensemble singing the enigmatic phrase "Keep your lamp light trimmed and burning." And on "Get Real Paid," a Kraftwerk-inspired study in retro-electronica, the multiple layers of bleeping synthesizers, beat box, and "talking robot" sounds suddenly dissipate to reveal the heavily reverberant voices of the Arroyo Tabernacle Chorale. These stylistic contrasts are, more specifically, topical "opposites" brought together in a manner that suggests a kind of comic equilibrium, something like the topos of "the well-formed tune that arrives out of nowhere" that Wye Allanbrook highlights in the Mozart K. 466 piano concerto and other examples of the composer's "comedic" instrumental works.[20] Beck's stylistic shifts and recombinations on *Midnite Vultures*, then, seem to be less about inverting the cultural meanings of styles or ironically repositioning pop cultural waste products; rather, the pairs of style topics in these songs seem to be motivated by the contrasts that obtain between opposites and extremes.

I read Beck's approach in his later work as a kind of "second-generation" sampling technique, and as such it resonates with what can be regarded as a broader transformation of sampling culture, a shift motivated by the new creative possibilities of digital media, as well as their particular limitations. A number of scholars have recently begun to explore the ways in which artists confront, personalize, and otherwise grapple with now-dominant digital practices like audio sampling. Simon

Waters, for example, considers the emergence of new creative tactics as musicians confront the particular affordances and constraints of the digital dominant.[21] In his thoughtful essay "The Musical Process in the Age of Digital Intervention," Waters asks whether "digital technology introduces new aesthetic possibilities which are identifiable as responses to that technology . . . and whether the shift in the storage and retrieval systems of music which results from digital technology is significant enough to warrant an addition to Simon Frith's useful taxonomy of music's previous stages of development."[22] Here Waters refers to Frith's tripartite folk-, art-, and pop-culture schema in which music's storage sites shift over time from body to text to recordings.[23] Waters proposes a fourth phase, one in which "music is stored everywhere, in diffuse, virtual space, accessible as material for the performing out of individual preferences."[24] Since Frith's three phases closely correspond to Jacques Attali's stages of "sacrifice," "representation," and "repetition" (in his volume *Noise,* 1977) Waters links the emergence of the digital sampler with the last stage in Attali's scheme, that of "composition," but leaves open to question Attali's utopian predictions about the concomitant overthrow of the commodity-exchange economy.[25] Instead, Waters looks at the particular strategies musicians employ in response to digital audio and how these have changed over time. The ways in which these technologies were first put to use, he claims, suggest an initial "path of least resistance" approach. For example, users initially tended to accept the presets on synthesizers as they came from the factories without much tinkering or experimentation, and digital instruments were simply incorporated into basic analog conceptions of music making.[26]

As users began to grapple with the very digital nature of the new tools, however, the nature of the creative process itself underwent a variety of changes. Waters enumerates several of these "second-wave" responses, one of which is a deliberate turn by some musicians to self-consciously "lo-tech" resources, to obsolete "garage electronics" and archaic synthesizers, for example. Another response is a renewed interest in collaborative work, a consequence of the "networking possibilities" of digital tools but also a compensatory "resocializing" of the process of music making, which computers have rendered increasingly solitary. Related to this is a concern for interactivity. Waters sees this as a reaction to the shortcomings of digital tools in comparison with the "exhilarating immediacy and subtlety of control, and simultaneous capacity for 'out-of-controlness'" of conventional acoustic instruments. "Such demands," he argues, "grow from the long history of intimate familiarity with an extraordinarily rich and malleable set of interactive interfaces for sound production."[27] While this has obviously led to an effort to improve the response times in interactive digital interfaces, it has also led to a renewed interest in and appreciation for traditional skills such as guitar playing and keyboard chops. As I recently heard a composer/pianist colleague remark, "It is certainly fun to play around with samples on a computer, but it is just more *efficient* to play around with notes and chords at the piano."

To return, once again, to the example of Mr. Bungle, I would suggest that several of the strategies that Waters enumerates are operating on the *California* album. The band's embrace of a decidedly "analog" approach in the recording process, the collaborative nature of the compositions and performances, and the strong emphasis on traditional acoustic instruments all attest to a self-conscious refusal to accept the sampling logic that had become so ubiquitous in pop. At the same time, the music readily acknowledges the prevailing "digital" nature of contemporary listening habits, and it engages precisely that listening competence.

In the next part of this essay I want to consider more closely the idea that stylistic allusion in recent pop acts as a kind of displacement of overt sampling. Moreover, I am interested in the ways in which polystylism is already present in certain musics of the past, as are strategies for reconciling stylistic multiplicity with concerns for authorial agency. I suspect that formal strategies comparable to those of historical musics are newly relevant for contemporary pop musicians. Here I look at another of the songs on Mr. Bungle's *California* album that seems to illustrate a concern for both formal coherence and stylistic abundance.

As my use of Leonard Ratner's terminology in connection with recent pop suggests, I am interested in possible parallels between contemporary popular music and the Classical style. Polystylism is usually understood as a key feature of postmodernity, yet, as a musical practice at least, it has a clear historical antecedent in the music of late-eighteenth-century Vienna, the style Ratner investigates in his book. Former Ratner students Kofi Agawu and Wye Allanbrook have likewise emphasized the multiplicity of styles that obtain within what we call *the* classical style.[28] Allanbrook highlights the exposition of Mozart's Piano Sonata K. 332 as a *locus classicus* that vividly demonstrates the mercurial quality of the classical style. Her reading of this passage reveals Mozart's evocations of a "singing style," learned counterpoint, minuet figures, *Jagdmusik,* and Sturm und Drang, following one another in rapid succession. Allanbrook views the piece as "a miniature theater of gestures and styles," a "pell-mell succession of topical representations." The presentation of disparate styles, she says, "seems to be a theme and organizing principle" in itself.[29]

Style topics in Allanbrook's Mozart example function as the thematized components within the overarching discourse of sonata form. Music theorists occasionally fall into the habit of imagining sonata form as somehow prior to the thematic constituents, but Charles Rosen has argued that the form itself emerged precisely as a consequence of the deployment of disparate styles within the same piece; the sonata process develops as a formal syntax that teleologizes the topical allusions and weaves the shifting style references into a cohesive narrative.[30] Rosen's ideas gain support from the words of eighteenth-century listeners themselves, for whom the most striking feature of the sonata was not necessarily its form per se but precisely its variegated sonic and expressive palette. A contemporary of Mozart's, for instance, wrote:

> Just as the subjects of the ode are uncommonly diverse and treated at quite different lengths, so is this true of the sonata. The composer is therefore in no instrumental composition less restricted—as far as character is concerned—than in the sonata, for every emotion and passion can be expressed in it. For the more expressive a sonata is, the more the composer can be heard, as it were, to speak.[31]

Accordingly, many scholars have come to understand "sonata form" as a product of the sheer variety and diversity that existed within the Viennese musical language. The typical four-movement scheme of the sonata and symphony, likewise, can be understood as a modular structure that evolved precisely in order to contain the multiplicity of expressive stances of the classical style, as James Hepokoski and Warren Darcy claim in their account of the expressive logic governing multimovement classical instrumental forms.[32]

As a parallel in American popular music, it is the infusion of a whole miscellany of styles that marks the historical moment at which "rock" as a "style" seems, paradoxically, to coalesce. Sociologist Randal Doane has described the emergence of the classic rock *album* as a "form," loosely analogous to "sonata form" and having emerged for similar reasons. The "album form" organizes the burgeoning stylistic languages of rock in the 1960s within the playback duration afforded by the technology of the long-playing record. Doane considers the particular sequencing of tracks on classic rock albums such as the Rolling Stones' *Beggars Banquet* and the Beatles' *Rubber Soul.* The order of tracks, he suggests, is determined by a kind of "sequencing logic" that derives from the sequence of movements of a classical symphony. Doane considers various determinants—ranging from direct intervention by classically trained producers such as George Martin to the democratization of liberal arts education during the 1950s and 1960s—all of which contributed to the development of a basic "listening competence" in which a particular sequence of expressive styles and tempi would be heard as "natural" and "artful." "Album rock," Doane argues, encompasses a multiplicity of expressive styles in a manner similar to multimovement instrumental forms of the eighteenth and nineteenth centuries. Moreover, this resemblance served as a powerful source of artistic legitimacy within the auteur tradition of classic rock.[33]

Moving beyond the classic rock moment to more recent popular music, we might understand the emerging forms of contemporary rock as continuing the tendency to incorporate a multiplicity of styles but now with a digital twist; within the logic of the digital dominant, styles begin to be juxtaposed in much closer proximity in a manner that is perhaps closer in spirit to the structure of Mozart's K. 332 exposition than to album rock's multimovement modular layout. Attention to the details of musical form *within* a single track has become more conspicuous, perhaps, as popular musicians have become less bound to the constraints of album rock formats and radio distribution and more attuned to the affordances of Internet distribution in which single songs, rather than albums, are the primary unit of consumption.

The concern to reconcile multiple styles with displays of compositional virtuosity is most pronounced among musicians who see themselves as heirs to the auteur tradition of classic rock. This concern can motivate such musicians to take considerable care with the formal coherence of their songs. Trevor Dunn of Mr. Bungle, for instance, spoke of the formal integrity in his music in a recent interview:

> There is definitely a difference between us and, say, Naked City, which is a band that is into intentional, abrupt changes of style and genre-shifting—like digital switching through different CDs or something. But we definitely try to make a *song* work as a *song*.[34]

The "difference" that makes the song "work" for Mr. Bungle has to do with carefully thought out song structures and a kind of "*il filo*" technique in which certain motivic elements are retained across a series of topical transformations. We can see how this plays out in their song "Golem II, the Bionic Vapor Boy," another of the ten tracks on the *California* album (fig. 8.1).

Section (timings)	Style topic	Text	Key	Theme
R1 (0:00)	antique mechanical	\<winding sound> \<music box > \<pause> \<winding sound>	?	X+
R2 (0:10)	carnival retro-futurisitic	\<music box> \<robotic voice> \<pause>	(V of B)	X+ X+
A (0:23) (0:37) (0:44)	carnival bubblegum carnival bubblegum (with funk background layer)	\<instrumental intro> *Golem II: the self-perfecting* *Lie-rejecting* *Human mind-correcting* *(Self-organized, wrought from the clay* *Our king by night, our slave by the day)*	B	X+ X Y Y X+ X Y Y
B (0:52) (1:05) (1:09)	retrofuturistic (funk break)	*Giga-giga-gilgamesh* *What do you know?* *Watch the human life show* *OK let's go* *O my double* *He can pop your bubble* *That means trouble*	G♯	 Z X Z Z X Z
R3 (1:15)	carnival	*Stronger than a lion* *Golem II: the bionic paper boy*	F♯	X X+
C (1:22)	funk	*Self-perfecting* *World-inspecting* *Lie-detecting* *Our instructions* *His induction* *Big production*	G♯	(new)
R4 (1:38)	retro-futuristic	*Golem II: the bionic puppet boy*	F♯	X+
D	antique mechanical	*Ah.. . .* *Ah. . . .* Giga-gilgamesh	B G♯	Z Z

Figure 8.1. Mr. Bungle, "Golem II, the Bionic Vapor Boy"

Section	Style topic	Text	Key	Theme
A′ (1:50)	retro futuristic + bubblegum	*Gigagigagigagiga* *Beast of burden*	B	X+ X Y
(1:57)		*Golem II: the self-perfecting* *Lie-rejecting* *Human mind-correcting*		X+ X
(2:11)	bubblegum (with background funk layer)	*(Self-organized, wrought from the clay* *Our king by night, our slave by the day)*		Y Y
B′ (2:21)	retro futuristic funk break	*Giga-giga-gilgamesh* *Spirit lifting* *Master of shape-shifting* *Seamless drifting*	G♯	 Z X Z
(2:31)	(ride cymbal appears)	*Shining spotlight* *Screaming mobs and stage fright* *You get it right*		Z X Z
R5 (2:41)	cool jazz	*Building a new Zion* *Golem II: the bionic vapor boy*	F♯	X X+
C′ (2:49)	funk	*War-directing* *Mind-inspecting* *Man-correcting* *Our instructions* *His induction* *Big production*	G♯	
R6 (3:05)	carnival music (funk drum pattern continues)	*Golem II: the bionic vapor boy*	F♯	X+
D′ (3:09)	antique mechanical	<scratchy recording of piano>	B G♯	X+ Z Z

Figure 8.1 (continued)

The song is in two halves: two "rotations" through a sequence of themes, the second of which recaps the material of the first, with different text and some variations in instrumentation. In the figure the two pages represent the two halves of the song; subdivisions of the two main parts are marked A, B, C, D in part 1 and A′, B′, C′, D′ for their repetitions in part 2, and approximate timings within the track are given for each of these subdivisions. A brief distinctive refrain recurs throughout the song, marked R1, R2, R3, and so forth on the chart. Despite the diversity of styles within the song—which I shall enumerate—only a small number of melodic elements recur in various combinations throughout the piece. Themes X, Y, and Z in example 8.1 show the main ones. Theme X is a chromatic-neighbor figure followed by an upward leap of a major sixth; this fragment is sometimes presented alone, at different transpositions, and sometimes with the addition of a descending chromatic tag, designated as X+ on the chart. Theme Y is a short sequence of fourths followed by a blues-infected tag. Theme Z is a descending [0147] tetrachord. Together X, Y, and Z represent the motivic elements that are retained from topic to topic and make the song's transitions sound "rational."

Four relatively distinct style topics recur throughout the song plus a fifth, which appears only once. The first topic is really a pair of closely related styles, which I call *antique mechanical* and *carnival music*, respectively. The antique-mechanical style involves the sounds of a music box, a player piano, and scratchy old gramophone recordings, the nostalgic sounds of extinct music-making machines.[35] Carnival music is a subset of

Example 8.1. Melodic figures in "Golem II, the Bionic Vapor Boy"

this style, as it involves reference to sounds of the circus calliope, but it has more specific connotations of "grotesquery" and "carny" weirdness, a favorite trope of Mr. Bungle (and one that might lead listeners to hear strong similarities between the work of Mr. Bungle and that of Frank Zappa).[36] Though not strictly indigenous to the pop/rock vocabulary, this has been an element of pop's repertory of styles since the mid-1960s; think of Smokey Robinson's "Tears of a Clown" or the *Sgt. Pepper* album, where carnival sounds appear in "Being for the Benefit of Mr. Kite" and elsewhere. In "Golem II" the carnivalesque serves as the primary musical topic, a backdrop with which the other stylistic allusions are contrasted.

A second topic is one I'll call *retro-futuristic*. Like the first topic, this one also alludes to obsolete musical instruments but those of more recent decades; here the allusions are to the synthetic sounds of Casio keyboards, "unsubtle" drum machines, "talking robot" sounds, and random electronic blips and squawks. These sounds are today associated principally with 1980s dance pop, that is, with the "first wave" of the digital aesthetic when musicians more readily accepted the factory presets of electronic instruments. Here, as in Beck's "Get Real Paid," which makes use of this same set of associations, these distinctive instrumental timbres suggest a naive and optimistic embrace of state-of-the-art technology that has since been rendered obsolete. Throughout the song, the retro-futuristic topic returns to punctuate the beginnings of the main sections and always appears in conjunction with the strangely hybridized kabbalistic references in the text ("giga-giga-Gilgamesh").

A third topic is the 1960s era *bubblegum* pop style, characterized by references to the Farfisa organ and its bouncy melodic riffs, typical of bands such as the 1910 Fruitgum Co. and the Strawberry Alarm Clock. The riff used in the Mr. Bungle song is consistently associated with the Y theme shown in example 8.1. This sunny bubblegum style continues to turn up quite frequently in hybrid pop (e.g., the music of Smashmouth relies heavily on this style). It appears elsewhere in Mr. Bungle's oeuvre where it typically blends with doo-wop vocals, as in the harmonically eccentric "Vanity Fair," on the *California* album (in which an anomalous Neapolitan chord disrupts the opening doo-wop bass arpeggio).

Stylized 1970s *funk* comprises the fourth topic in "Golem II." Its most distinctive signature here is the inimitable sound of the electric clavichord—the Hohner Clavinet—the favorite keyboard of Stevie Wonder, whose 1972 hit "Superstition" and his "Higher Ground" of 1973 established the clavinet as an enduring signifier for funk.[37] In "Golem II" the funk topic emerges by increments through the first half the song, ini-

tially appearing as a subtle background element in the prevailing bubblegum passage in section A; it subsequently develops into a more insistent instrumental break in the middle of section B and finally erupts into
a fully foregrounded figure in section C.

Indeed, one factor that seems to make the "song work as a song" (to
use Dunn's words) is the manner in which new topics seem to percolate
up from concealed layers in the texture. For example, the final topos is
one that appears only briefly in the song in the fifth refrain (R5): a *cool
jazz* reference encapsulated in a passage featuring a fast walking-bass line
and a double-time swing pattern on a ride cymbal ("shing shing-a shing
shing-a"). This style seems to be reserved for a kind of "point of furthest
remove" toward the end of the second half of the song. The stylistic allusion that is foregrounded at this point, however, is foreshadowed by the
ride-cymbal element, which subtly emerges in the previous passage at the
end of section B'.

There is a great deal of overlap and mixing up of the styles in the
piece, but the basic sequence of the most prominent topical references
can be traced in figure 8.1, where I have correlated the style topics in the
second column with the song's text, given in the third column. Key areas
are shown in the fourth column, and thematic elements (keyed to the
melodic figures in example 8.1) appear in the last column. The latter
represent the motivic connections among the various sections, which
create a sense of continuity in the design of the song. Except for the Y
motive, which is consistently associated with the bubblegum style, the
other recurring motives are adapted to the topics at hand and serve as a
thread that ties together otherwise disparate materials.

In place of a set of samples drawn from existing musical texts, then,
"Golem II" incorporates a set of style topics that can be freely manipulated, reorchestrated, and recombined over the course of the song and
molded into a deliberate formal architecture. In this sense, the topic
proves more flexible than the sample at the same time that it permits,
like sampling, a set of highly charged communicable signs and codes to
come into play. The parallels with the workings of classical stylistic topoi
in, say, Mozart's K. 332 are close in many ways, although I anticipate several objections that might be raised to my use of Ratner's concepts in the
context of this song. The first is that each of the style topics I have isolated in Mr. Bungle's "Golem II," with the possible exception of the cool
jazz style, has been identified primarily by means of a characteristic instrumental timbre rather than any distinctive melodic "figures." Certainly the melodic and rhythmic profile of, say, the clavinet passages

serves as an important signifier of style. Yet it is likely the instrument it-self that bears the bulk of the semiotic burden.

In this sense my classification of particular style topics differs markedly from Ratner's understanding of topoi. While some eighteenth-century styles do correlate closely with certain instruments, or at least the evocation of certain instrumental idioms such as "hunting-horn" fifths or musette drones, Ratner's topics are largely matters of melody, harmony, and rhythm rather than timbres per se. In popular music, however, it is not unusual for single instruments to serve as tokens for style—the banjo standing in for "bluegrass" or the Roland transistor bass for "house," for instance—and it may be one of its key features that genre and instru-mentation are so closely connected.[38] As historians of rock have noted, the continual incorporation of new sounds and instruments is virtually an obligation for rock in order for it to retain its vitality and continued relevance for the youth market. Consequently, instrumentation serves as a reliable and sufficient index for rock's historical styles.

But a second objection stems from the first in that each of the style topics I have identified is a *historical* style. Again, this is not exactly the way eighteenth-century style topics seem to have operated. While some topics, such as the "learned style," were references to "old-fashioned" musical practices, the greater part of classical style topics seems to have been "contemporary" rather than historical. Seeking a close parallel in con-temporary popular music raises a problem, however: because of the very "digital" nature of late twentieth- and early-twenty-first-century pop, its codes are wholly dissimilar to those of the eighteenth century. With the ease of digital storage and retrieval systems, contemporary musical styles are produced and reproduced at such a rapid rate that, arguably, they fail to develop stable meanings. This is utterly unlike eighteenth-century style topics, in which a given musical style could be clearly linked to a geo-graphical locale, a social class, or a fairly stable expressive message.

This problem brings us back to the Jamesonian critique with which I began this discussion. How might one even begin to compile a lexicon of pop style topics given the relentless proliferation of new genre categories created by listeners and practitioners to define and classify contempo-rary popular music? The dozens of subgenres of electronica are only the most extreme case of this microdifferentiation. On the other hand, one of the unexpected consequences of the digital revolution has been the emergence of a detailed collective knowledge of popular music *history* among networks of fans and practitioners. The impulse to classify and differentiate may itself reflect a heightened self-consciousness of pop genealogies and past practices, as does the construction of countless personal Web sites devoted to musical esoterica and arcana of decades past, not to mention the continued popularity of peer-to-peer file sharing of primary sources.[39] At its height the practice of sampling has frequently stimulated excursions into music history on the part of both musicians searching for usable material and fans hunting down the obscure sources of the samples in their favorite new songs. Perhaps this, then, explains the preponderance of historically defined styles in the music I've been discussing (1960s bubblegum, 1970s funk, and 1980s new wave). Fans availing themselves of the storage and retrieval systems provided by digital tools have subjected pop's history to intense research, and it is pop's historical styles that have emerged as the stable musical signifiers in a lexicon of style topics.

In the examples by Beck and Mr. Bungle that I have discussed, I believe that the deployment of "stylistic topoi" has taken the place of quotation and sampling and that stylistic allusion in many ways "exceeds" those technologies. This polystylistic music accomplishes many of the same kinds of ironies, inversions, and recuperative functions that sampling did at its best at the same time that it opens up a space for authorial agency and virtuosity, musical values that remain relevant for artists and fans alike. Meanwhile, musicians who continue to make extensive use of digital sampling seem to have moved on to more interesting projects such as "mashups." As older slice-and-dice sampling techniques begin to sound clichéd, I expect that sampling itself will eventually act as a marker for a stylized topos. Perhaps something like this is already happening on the albums *Midnite Vultures* and *California.*

NOTES

An earlier version of this chapter was presented at the annual meeting of the Society for Music Theory in Philadelphia, November 2001.

1. The Latin text is from an elegy by Gaius Valerius Catullus, a Roman poet of the first century BCE, written following the death of the poet's brother.

2. See Fredric Jameson, *Postmodernism, or, the Cultural Logic of Late Capitalism* (Durham: Duke University Press, 1991).

3. Tricia Rose, *Black Noise: Rap Music and Black Culture in Contemporary America* (Middletown, CT: Wesleyan University Press, 1994).

4. See Neil Strauss, "Sampling is (a) Creative or (b) Theft?" *New York Times,* 14 September 1997. Tim Hughes provides a more nuanced reading of Combs's treatment in "'Now' Sandwiches: The Use of Quotation in Rap Music," paper presented at the annual meeting of the Society for Music Theory, Atlanta, No-

vember 1999. In Combs's defense, his use of the song differs little from the Sugar Hill Gang's much-celebrated appropriation of Chic's "Good Times" in 1979 and thus participates in a reputable tradition of rapping over popular songs.

5. The artist Beck acknowledges this explicitly in a recent interview: "[On the album *Odelay*] it was basically me writing chord changes and melodies and stuff, and then endless records being scratched and little sounds coming off the turntable. Now it's prohibitively difficult and expensive to justify your one weird little horn blare that happens for half of a second one time in a song and makes you give away seventy percent of the song and $50,000" (Matt Fink, "Breaking the Narrative," *Paste*, 1 June 2005). The rapid inflation of the costs of copyright clearance in the late 1990s was promptly acknowledged by legal scholars. Tyrone McKenna, for example, noted, "It is apparent that found elements, or brief fragments of media packed into a new work, absolutely violates the copyright of the owner in law. But to get permission for each and every one of the collage fragments used in an appropriated work may result in fees which can reach into hundreds of thousands of pounds. . . . It is no surprise that these clearance fees are set for the lucrative inter-corporate trade. . . . Signed artists will use sampling less and less often as the costs come out of their royalties" (Tyrone McKenna, "Where Digital Music Technology and Law Collide: Contemporary Issues of Digital Sampling, Appropriation, and Copyright Law," *Journal of Information, Law and Technology* [2000, vol. 1]). http://ww2.warwick.ac.uk/fac/soc/law/elj/jilt/2000_1/mckenna.

6. For a discussion of the ways in which sound recordings become unmoored from their sources as they work their way through networks of circulation and consumption, see Steven Feld, "Pygmy POP: A Genealogy of Schizophonic Mimesis," *Yearbook for Traditional Music* 28 (1996): 1–35.

7. Lawrence Grossberg, "Reflections of a Disappointed Popular Music Scholar," in *Rock Over the Edge: Transformations in Popular Music Culture*, ed. Roger Beebe, Denise Fulbrook, and Ben Saunders (Durham: Duke University Press, 2002), 25–59.

8. Roger Beebe and Jason Middleton, "Hybridity and 'Neo-eclecticism' in Contemporary Popular Music," *Popular Music* 21, no. 2 (2002): 159–72.

9. For a fine study of the tensions between "corporate" and "craftsman" models of digital music making, see Christophe Den Tandt, "From Craft to Corporate Interfacing: Rock Musicianship in the Age of Music Television and Computer-Programmed Music," *Popular Music and Society* 27, no. 2 (June 2004): 139–60.

10. Without the aid of computers, the recording process was apparently so complex that Trey Spruance, Mr. Bungle's guitarist, intends to write an entire monograph on the subject.

11. Leonard Ratner, *Classic Music: Expression, Form, and Style* (New York: Schirmer, 1980).

12. Jason Toynbee, *Making Popular Music: Musicians, Creativity, and Institutions* (New York: Oxford University Press, 2000).

13. Joshua Ostroff, "Fantastic Plastic Machine Amazes!" *Ottawa Sun*, 4 April 1999.

14. David Fricke, "The Year in Recordings," *Rolling Stone*, 26 December 1996–9 January 1997, 183.

15. Ryan Schreiber, *Pitchfork Review* online record reviews, June 1996, http://www.pitchforkmedia.com/article/record_review/15358.

16. Robert Fink, "Elvis Everywhere: Musicology and Popular Music Studies at the Twilight of the Canon," *American Music* 16, no. 2 (1998): 135–79, reprinted in *Rock Over the Edge: Transformations in Popular Music Culture,* ed. Roger Beebe, Denise Fulbrook, and Ben Saunders (Durham: Duke University Press, 2002), 60–109.

17. Ibid., 141.

18. In addition to the two samples acknowledged in the sleeve notes, Beck in "Get Real Paid" almost certainly borrows a short passage from Kraftwerk's "Home Computer" from the 1981 album *Computer World,* a segment that, if not an actual sample, is an accurate reconstruction of the original. My thanks to Mark Spicer for pointing out this close resemblance.

19. Similar protests have been mounted more recently by the organization Downhill Battle, including the Grey Tuesday project, a day of Internet activism designed to promote the illegal "mashup" work on DJ Danger Mouse's *Grey Album* (2004), an album that remixes the Beatles' "White Album" with Jay-Z's *Black Album.* Similarly, the recent 3 Notes and Runnin' campaign was an online music compilation commemorating and protesting a court ruling that found that members of the hip-hop group N.W.A. had violated copyright law when they sampled three notes of a guitar riff from Funkadelic's "Get Off Your Ass and Jam" for their song "100 Miles and Runnin'." Participants each made their own works using the same three-note sample.

20. Wye Allanbrook, "Comic Issues in Mozart's Piano Concertos," in *Mozart's Piano Concertos: Text, Context, Interpretation* (Ann Arbor: University of Michigan Press, 1996), 75–105.

21. Simon Waters, "The Musical Process in the Age of Digital Intervention," *Ariada Texts* 1 (December 2000), http://www.ariada.uea.ac.uk/ariadatexts/ariada1/.

22. Ibid.

23. Simon Frith, *Performing Rites: On the Value of Popular Music* (New York: Oxford University Press, 1996), 226–27.

24. Waters, "The Musical Process in the Age of Digital Intervention."

25. Jacques Attali, *Noise: The Political Economy of Music,* trans. Brian Massumi (Minneapolis: University of Minnesota Press, 1985). Translation of *Bruits: essai sur l'économie politique de la musique* (Presses Universitaires de France, 1977).

26. In a recent article Mark Spicer confirms this "first-wave" approach with respect to the Yamaha DX7:

> Retailing for just under $2,000, the Yamaha DX7 quickly became the most popular synthesizer on the market after it was introduced in 1983, and remained the industry standard for some years following. The DX7 featured the then brand-new technology of digital FM synthesis, yet since this required some advanced understanding of physics, it was notoriously hard for musicians to program their own sounds. Most keyboardists, myself included, relied mainly on the stock factory timbres that came packaged with the instrument, and one therefore hears these distinctive sounds all over pop and rock records from 1984 to c. 1987.

See his review of Walter Everett, *The Beatles as Musicians: The Quarry Men through Rubber Soul*, in *Music Theory Online* 11, no. 4 (October 2005): n. 21.

27. Waters, "The Musical Process in the Age of Digital Intervention."

28. See Kofi Agawu, *Playing with Signs: A Semiotic Interpretation of Classic Music* (Princeton: Princeton University Press, 1991); Wye Allanbrook, "Two Threads through the Labyrinth," in *Convention in Eighteenth- and Nineteenth-Century Music: Essays in Honor of Leonard G. Ratner,* ed. Wye Allanbrook, Janet M. Levy, and William P. Mahrt (Stuyvesant, NY: Pendragon, 1992), 125–72; and Wye Allanbrook, "Theorizing the Comic Surface," in *Music in the Mirror: Reflections on the History of Music Theory and Literature for the 21st Century,* ed. Andreas Giger and Thomas J. Mathiesen (Lincoln: University of Nebraska Press, 2002), 195–216. Going back even farther into the eighteenth century, the music of J. S. Bach has likewise been considered as a compendium of disparate styles, by scholars such as Robert Marshall.

29. Allanbrook, "Two Threads through the Labyrinth," 127.

30. Charles Rosen, *The Classical Style: Haydn, Mozart, Beethoven* (New York: Viking, 1971).

31. Daniel Gottlob Türk, quoted in Agawu, *Playing with Signs,* 29.

32. See James Hepokoski and Warren Darcy, *Elements of Sonata Theory: Norms, Types, and Deformations in the Late-Eighteenth-Century Sonata* (New York: Oxford University Press, 2006).

33. Randal Doane, "Class, Music, and Cultural Competence in the Post-war Suburb," paper presented to a conference of the American Sociological Association, Atlanta, 2003.

34. Walter Scharold, unpublished interview with Trevor Dunn, Oberlin College, 2000. Dunn refers here to John Zorn's band Naked City.

35. For a discussion of the particular expressive effects of obsolete technologies, see Joseph Auner, "Making Old Machines Speak: Images of Technology in Recent Music," *ECHO* 2 (fall 2000), http://www.humnet.ucla.edu/echo/volume2-issue2/auner/auner.html.

36. Zappa's own use of rapid-fire "genre switching" became a signature device of his live band performances from the mid-1960s onward and should certainly be understood as a direct "predigital" antecedent to Mr. Bungle.

37. See Tim Hughes, "Groove and Flow: Six Analytical Essays on the Music of Stevie Wonder," PhD diss., University of Washington, 2003, for a detailed account of Wonder's use of the clavinet.

38. Kevin Holm-Hudson investigates this issue in "The Future Is Now . . . and Then: Sonic Historiography in Post-1960s Rock," *Genre* 34, nos. 3–4 (2001): 243–64.

39. Access to a truly exhaustive data bank of pop music's back catalog may have peaked with the heyday of the file-sharing network Napster, which many users employed to locate otherwise hard to find "oldies" rather than simply to avoid the hefty price tag of new CDs, as was widely reported. See Randal Doane, "Digital Desire in the Daydream Machine," *Sociological Theory* 24, no. 2 (2006): 150–69.

NINE ❧ "I'm Not Here, This Isn't Happening"

The Vanishing Subject in Radiohead's Kid A

MARIANNE TATOM LETTS

POP AND ROCK AFICIONADOS tend to think of many post–*Sgt. Pepper* albums not as loosely organized collections of individual songs but as artistic utterances that develop deeper insights as their song sequences unfold. Although an album may not present as cohesive a narrative as one might expect of, say, a novel or film, the listener can be tempted—even encouraged—to look for a similar development of meaning, particularly when the singer assumes a narrative persona. The perceived cooperation among various musical agents deployed over the course of an album can produce the image of a unified subject whether through an explicit narrative, a broad lyrical and/or musical theme, recurring lyrical and/or musical motives, or some combination of these factors. Radiohead's album *Kid A* (2000), though seemingly concerned with this common theme of subject formation, nevertheless resists conventional notions of cohesion associated with so-called concept albums, offering instead a subject that collapses, almost as soon as he is fully formed, in the song "How to Disappear Completely (And Never Be Found)." My goal in this chapter is to trace—through close analysis of the music and lyrics—the path of *Kid A*'s subject leading up to the moment of his first dissolution.[1]

The idea of the concept album is not well defined. Both scholarly writing and mainstream music reviews often treat the term as self-evident, trusting that most people know what a concept album is without needing a formal definition.[2] I suggest that concept albums essentially fall into two broad categories: *narrative* or *thematic*. Whereas narrative concept albums attain their cohesion through presenting a more or less straightforward plot with characters, thematic concept albums may be further divided into those that rely on lyrics and those that employ musical elements for their unity. A lyrically thematic album is similar to a collection of poems on a given topic, whereas a musically thematic album could be likened to an opera or a symphonic work that uses different melodies or genre styles to stand for characters or emotions. The following chronological list includes representative examples of each category of concept album.

- The Moody Blues' *Days of Future Passed* (1967; thematic, mainly lyrical, although the "classical" orchestrations also mark the album's unity)
- The Who's *Tommy* (1969; narrative, with both lyrical and musical cohesion)
- Jethro Tull's *Aqualung* (1971; thematic in orchestration and lyrics for at least the duration of an album side)[3]
- Pink Floyd's *The Dark Side of the Moon* (1973; thematic, with recurring lyrical and musical elements)
- Pink Floyd's *The Wall* (1979; both narrative and thematic, with recurring lyrical and musical elements to the point of overload and almost of parody)
- Nick Cave's *Murder Ballads* (1996; thematic, but only at the lyrical level, with the unifying musical elements stemming from Cave's overall style rather than an album-specific artistic choice)
- Liz Phair's *Exile in Guyville* (1999; thematic at the lyrical level)
- Green Day's *American Idiot* (2004; thematic at the lyrical level)
- The Decemberists' *The Hazards of Love* (2009; narrative and thematic in both lyrics and music)

There are, however, certain concept albums that attain their impression negatively, as it were, by consistently resisting one or the other of these categories. Perhaps best thought of as a strategy rather than a type in the pure sense, a "resistant" concept album stretches the parameters that traditionally define a concept album (i.e., a clearly articulated narrative or a unifying musical/lyrical theme) while still projecting some kind of overarching concept beyond that of being merely a sequence of organized tracks. The important point to remember here is that a concept album need not be strictly narrative to present a cohesive "concept" to the listener, nor should we necessarily be looking for one. As I will show, Radiohead's *Kid A* is an exemplar of a resistant concept album. Rather than deliberately avoiding narrative or musical unity, a given artist, here Radiohead, may instead create a work that is open to multiple interpretations, including, perhaps, discontinuity. Resisting interpretation is the flip side of encouraging multiple readings. Equally important is the notion that no single reading of a given album should be taken as the "only" or "correct" one; analytical interpretations are just that, interpretations, and it is likely that the artist had a different vision in mind when creating the work than the one that the audience—even the musical analyst—ultimately comprehends.

"Anyone can play guitar": The Origins of Radiohead

The band that would become Radiohead was formed in 1982 by five friends (Thom Yorke, Phil Selway, Ed O'Brien, and brothers Jonny and Colin Greenwood) at the exclusive Abingdon School in Oxford, England. Various members had played together in other bands, but by 1986 the present lineup had jelled into a performing unit. The band exhibited fairly steady stylistic growth from its first album, *Pablo Honey* (1993), through *The Bends* (1995) to *OK Computer* (1997), adding increasingly complex layers of production effects to an essentially guitar-driven sound. After the transatlantic success of the single "Creep" from *Pablo Honey* and the tepid reception of the album's other singles,[4] some predicted that Radiohead would be simply a one-hit wonder,[5] but instead the band's popularity increased immensely over the course of *The Bends* and *OK Computer*. Radiohead was named a "band to watch out for" by *Melody Maker* and *New Musical Express* (*NME*) in 1993,[6] and Martin Clarke notes the success of *The Bends* as "the start of a remarkable growth in commercial success and critical applause that transformed Radiohead from a band that was highly revered into one that was being talked of as a historically classic group."[7]

The band's subsequent album, *OK Computer*, was recognized as Album of the Year (1997) by the British magazines *Q* and *NME*, and Radiohead garnered Band of the Year accolades from *Rolling Stone* and *Spin* as well as receiving a Grammy for Best Alternative Music Performance.[8] *OK Computer* has received a great deal of analytical attention from music scholars, most of whom have treated the work as a concept album, at least in part.[9] James Doheny argues that the song order rather than just the sub-ject makes this album a "song cycle"—that is, a "cohesive focused group of songs with an underlying theme"—and compares it to Pink Floyd's *The Dark Side of the Moon.*[10] *OK Computer*'s theme of technological alien-ation is clearly articulated through such songs as "Karma Police," "Para-noid Android," and "Climbing Up the Walls." Nadine Hubbs calls *OK Computer* a "concept album that immerses the listener in images of alien-ated life under techno/bureau/corporate hegemony. . . . [A] vivid flavor of alienation and disaffectedness . . . is built up by layers over the course of twelve album tracks."[11] Rather than presenting a straightforward nar-rative, as one might expect from a concept album, the lyrics of the album are, Hubbs says, "already oblique in their written form" and "often intel-ligible only in fragments." She goes on to say that because of this treat-ment of the words as "vowel and consonant sounds . . . molded, shifted, stretched in shadings of the texture-color," the "audible effect of these songs [is] one approaching pure musicality."[12] Allan F. Moore and Anwar Ibrahim note that *OK Computer* "gain[ed] its 'age-defining' status through a combination of both musical and sonic exploration, with lyrics concerning the themes, simultaneously universal and personal, of alienation, information overload, and fear of an imminent new millen-nium. It is both a timely and a timeless record, unmistakably Radiohead but still managing to express sentiments shared by people in all walks of life."[13]

Members of the band have discounted the significance of *OK Com-puter* and view it as perhaps less unified. Jonny Greenwood, for example, has stated, "I think one album title and one computer voice do not make a concept album. That's a bit of a red herring." Colin Greenwood was re-portedly "horrified" by *Rolling Stone*'s description of *OK Computer* as a "stunning art-rock tour de force," saying, "What a ghastly thought. That makes it sound like Rick Wakeman and his Knights of the Round Table On Ice."[14] Indeed, the band claims not to have intended the album to be what it was ultimately perceived as, a "concept piece about the age-old fear of the mechanized world being dehumanised by computers and technology."[15] Guitarist Ed O'Brien has acknowledged some degree of musical exploration, or of toying with listeners' expectations, stating, "'Paranoid Android' is the song we play to people when they want to know what the album's like, 'cos it should make them think, 'What the fuck is going to happen on the rest of the album?' "[16] If listeners were confused by the musical experimentation on *OK Computer,* they were in for a shock with *Kid A.*

"Don't get sentimental, it always ends up drivel":
Life after OK Computer

Given the seriousness with which *OK Computer* was treated, it seemed logical for Radiohead's next album also to make a huge statement about the condition of modern man or to extend the notion of the concept album to one that was perhaps easier to follow. After the global success of *OK Computer*, the band seemed "tantalizingly close to rock deification. According to conventional wisdom, one more similar album, one more tour, would get them there for certain."[17] The band faced the artistic challenge of either duplicating its known formula for success or proceeding in a new direction. Thom Yorke apparently was also having "deeply ambivalent feelings about the direction of the group as a whole, and his role within it," including "considerations about how to progress as a band and as a human being with any integrity, in the face of the massive success that subsumed Radiohead into the world of commerce."[18] He also wanted to integrate wider influences into the band's sound, moving beyond a simple guitar and vocals formula.[19] Rather than recording material designed to live up to the commercial success of its previous three albums, the band, or perhaps its management, decided to release an album with no promotional singles and fewer immediately catchy tunes than any of its previous albums.[20]

The result was *Kid A,* an "eerily comforting blend of rock riffs, jazz chords, classical textures, and electronic noise."[21] It drew "a line under the band's previous output and completely re-imagine[d] what Radiohead were all about in this post–*OK Computer* world."[22] Because of advance sales based on the huge buzz from fans and critics alike, *Kid A* soared into the *Billboard* album charts at number 1, selling two hundred thousand copies in its first week of release.[23] During the second week the album dropped to number 10, and two months after its release *Kid A* had fallen off the *Billboard* Top 100 altogether. The drastic fall in chart positions suggests that the album could not maintain its level of sales beyond the band's dedicated core fan base once the reviews started coming in. Fan reactions at the time were varied, with some saying they appreciated the fact that Radiohead was striking out in a new, more innovative direction yet others complaining that they missed the old sound (and, no doubt, the hit singles) of *The Bends* and *OK Computer.*[24] Critical response was also mixed, with *Melody Maker* stating that the band had "created a monument of effect over content, a smothery cataclysm of sound and fury signifying precisely f*** all." *Q* magazine called the album "about as experimental as a major rock record could get within the corporate straight-jacket that Radiohead despise."[25] Nick Hornby wrote in the *New Yorker,* "You have to work at albums like *Kid A.* You have to sit at home night after night and give yourself over to the paranoid millennial atmosphere as you try to decipher elliptical snatches of lyrics and puzzle out how the titles . . . might refer to the songs."[26] *Billboard* called it "the first truly groundbreaking album of the 21st century." *Spin* called it "a post-rock record" and "not only Radiohead's bravest album but its best one as well." *All Music Guide* wrote, however, "*Kid A* never is as visionary or stunning as *OK Computer,* nor does it really repay the intensive time it demands in order for it to sink in." The *Village Voice* perhaps summed it up best, observing, "It's . . . really different. And oblique oblique oblique: short, unsettled, deliberately shorn of easy hooks and clear lyrics and comfortable arrangements. Also incredibly beautiful."[27]

The band members themselves seemed determined not to yield to the commercial pressure of promoting the album, choosing only to release several "antivideos" of animations set to short segments of the album's songs in lieu of any full-length videos, singles, interviews, or a tour.[28] MTV and numerous music Web sites screened these short antivideos, which were also made available for viewing on the band's own Web site, itself a study in obfuscation.[29] Rather than presenting fans with easily navigable areas from which to glean data (even such basic information as the release dates of new material), the Web site instead contained links labeled "waitingroom," "trapdoors," and "testspecimens."[30] These links led the viewer through galleries of cartoons and obscured photos of the band with underlying politicized text, intriguing images and words but no useful facts for anyone seeking concrete information.[31]

The booklet enclosed with the CD release of *Kid A* continued the mystery, containing pages of computer-generated and -manipulated art rather than customary photos of the band.[32] The only human figures appear in a photo in the middle of the booklet, in which a stereotypical "nuclear family" stands with its back to the camera, staring at what appears to be a wall of graffiti. This wall is covered with faintly recognizable words and images of ice and snow, which also permeate the other pages of artwork. An additional booklet, containing pages of text arranged like handbills with artwork reminiscent of cartoonist R. Crumb, was concealed behind the back of the jewel case in the initial pressing of the CD and was later made available for downloading through the band's Web site. Some of the booklet's text is recognizable as lyrics from the songs of *Kid A,* but for the most part it merely serves to evoke, like the computer art, a feeling of desolation in a neoapocalyptic wasteland.[33] This cold, alienating landscape can be viewed as the backdrop to the songs of *Kid A* if not the literal space within which the subject dwells. *Kid A* does continue the themes of *OK Computer* (alienation amid the onslaught of technology), but it challenges the band's earlier methods of narrative cohesion by suggesting a hopeless, self-negating subject that disintegrates at the midpoint of the album at the moment of the subject's maximum articulation. The second half of the album is then spent reconstructing the subject and presenting him with a second chance to overcome life's challenges, which is likewise rejected. This "death" is analytically intriguing because it occurs at a surprising point in the narrative, immediately after the subject has finally been "made flesh" rather than at the end of the album as the listener might expect.[34] In fact, the subject does seem to expire—for a second time—at the end of the album; the first death is an internal one, an existential crisis, rather than an external event recognizable to the outside world.

Kid A presents a compelling challenge for the listener to interpret or even discern narrative personae. Because the album's songs do not, for the most part, stand on their own as discrete three-minute pop "singles," the listener attempts instead to find meaning in the song sequence, which, rather than presenting a straightforward plot with characters from the opening song onward, builds up the subject gradually and then abruptly erases him. Whereas the singer and various other musical agents (piano, orchestra, etc.) are typically viewed as working together to construct a complete musical subject,[35] or, as Edward T. Cone has put it, a "unified utterance of the composer's voice,"[36] on *Kid A,* to my ear, these elements engage instead in a constant struggle for dominance. Rather than assisting the singer toward his goals, the other instruments seem to be working actively against him.[37] Much of the musical sparring in *Kid A* can be heard as a conflict between nature and technology, between sense and nonsense, between music and noise.[38] Figure 9.1 shows how some elements from the first half of *Kid A* fit into these categories.

According to Jacques Attali, "noise" represents an ambiguous intrusion that disrupts the musical texture yet can also create new order and meaning. If a network's existing codes cannot repress the attacking noise, the network will be destroyed and replaced with another that can organize the noise into a culturally accepted form. The noise thus precipitates a sacrificial crisis in order to "transcend the old violence and recreate a system of differences on another level of organization."[39] Attali is speaking of music in general historical terms, but we might explore

Song	Sense	Nonsense	Organic	Technological	Music	Noise
"Everything in Its Right Place"	lead vocals ask for clarification	sampled voice in background	voice is sampled from live performance	keyboards, sampled voice	repeating keyboard motive	voice cuts off like tape failing
"Kid A"	distorted lead vocals	birth cry at end of song	blowing wind, marimbas, strings (all sampled)	filtered voice, sampled music box	music box, marimbas (sampled)	birth cry, filtered voice
"The National Anthem"	lead vocals	horn glissandi, vocal cries, orchestral coda	horns, voice	Ondes Martenot	bass, horns	horn glissandi, distorted voice, orchestra tape winding down
"How to Disappear Completely"	lead vocals	strings, vocalese	acoustic guitar, strings, tambourine	electric guitar	voice, acoustic guitar, bass	strings
"Treefingers"		vocalese		filtered guitars		ambient sound

Figure 9.1. Binary oppositions in the first half of *Kid A*

the possibility that the process can also occur in microcosm at the song or album level. The first half of *Kid A* can be understood in these terms as a fracturing of the musical structure that builds to a crisis point at which the singer is purged from the texture; the album then attempts to build a new structure, which the subject either fails to negotiate successfully or intentionally abandons.

The members of Radiohead seem to have been conscious of subverting these opposing categories of musical sound when making *Kid A*. Guitarist Jonny Greenwood has commented that "a voice into a microphone onto a tape, onto a CD and through your speakers is all as illusory and as fake as any synthesizer. . . . But one is perceived as 'real,' the other somehow 'unreal.' It's the same with guitars versus sampler. It was just freeing to discard the notion of acoustic sounds being truer."[40] By calling into question the perception of acoustic instruments as being somehow more "real" or "authentic" than electronic media, Greenwood further destabilizes these categories. The album presents an unfamiliar sonic space that normally might represent the unreal (in the form of distorted and/or nonacoustic instruments) but here must be treated as the only true, and thus real, space available to the subject. Yearning for the unattainable ideal of the unconstructed real, the subject finds that the only way to reach this state is to "disappear completely." Rather than escaping into a "more real" sonic environment, however, the subject ends up in the gray nothing space of "Treefingers," another nonacoustic soundscape, and must start his journey anew on the second half of the album.[41] The sub-

ject's attempted suicide thus becomes not an empowering act but instead the ultimate failure. Viewed this way, the story of *Kid A* can be understood as the resolution of an existential crisis.

"Everything in its right place": Key Associations in *Kid A*

Regardless of whether a convincing traditional narrative can be assigned
to *Kid A*, the large-scale key plan for the song sequence implies that some
thought went into assembling the album so that it would flow harmonically from song to song.[42] Given the modal ambiguity of many pop songs,
with chord progressions that often do not project a clearly defined tonic,
it is somewhat misleading to force each of the songs on *Kid A* into a conventional major or minor key, and Radiohead's tendency to use pedal
tones and oscillate between two chords related by a third further mud-
dies the tonal waters. Example 9.1 nevertheless shows the overall tonal
plan for the album. "Everything in Its Right Place" moves back and forth
between competing tonal centers on C and F. "Kid A" is ostensibly in F,
one of the keys of the previous song.[43] "The National Anthem" is in D;
"How to Disappear Completely" sounds mainly in F-sharp minor, with
competing passages that center on D and A; and "Treefingers," the midpoint of the album, is also ostensibly in F-sharp. "Optimistic" returns to
D, which could be heard as a large-scale dominant to the G of the next
song, "In Limbo." "Idioteque" is composed around a single unfolding
harmony (an E-flat major seventh chord), yet it seems to alternate between tonal centers on G and E-flat. "Morning Bell" is (loosely) in A, the
upper-neighboring key to G, and "Motion Picture Soundtrack" finally
"resolves" to G in a high voice with overblown harp and choir accompaniment (suggesting a dramatically forced resolution), although the final
G major tonic chord is presented only in a coda after the main song has
faded out. The ultimate resolution is thus represented as beyond the
scope of the actual song or album.

Reducing the album to a single overarching harmonic progression
seems too pat a solution, however, when the songs are examined more
closely. Rather than one large progression in G, the album can best be
grouped into a series of three songs each, plus a separate concluding
song, as shown in example 9.2. Each group is linked by lyrics or style and
is supported by harmonic underpinnings if not functionally dictated by
them. Each grouping also forms a dialectic triad, presenting a thesis, an
antithesis, and a synthesis (though often a weak one). The first group
("Everything," "Kid A," and "The National Anthem") tentatively builds

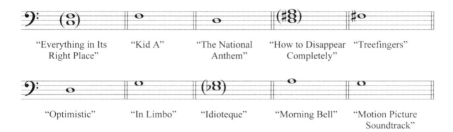

Example 9.1. *Kid A,* overall tonal plan. Songs with two or more competing key centers are indicated in parentheses.

"Everything in Its Right Place," "How to Disappear Completely," "In Limbo," "Idioteque," "Motion Picture
"Kid A," "The National Anthem" "Treefingers," "Optimistic"   "Morning Bell"   Soundtrack"

Example 9.2. *Kid A,* three-song groupings

up the emerging subject of the album, where the ambiguous F tonic of the first two songs is followed by a third song that is squarely in D. Before the subject even appears, the stage is set for "everything" to be "in its right place." When the subject, "Kid A," emerges in the title track, however, he finds it difficult to fit into the world. "The National Anthem" forcibly integrates him into a society of alienation.

The next three songs ("How to Disappear Completely," "Treefingers," and "Optimistic") articulate, destroy, and then reconstitute the subject. Similar to the key plan of the first group, the ambiguous F-sharp tonic of the first two songs is followed by a third song that again sits squarely in the third-related key of D. The subject finally finds his voice in "How to Disappear Completely," but he immediately loses it again in the violent musical texture and then is merely a ghost figure in the landscape of "Treefingers." He resurfaces as a more pessimistic entity in "Optimistic," continuing to exist only because he has failed to erase himself.

The third group presents the renewed subject's continued struggles with modern existence, through "Idioteque" and "In Limbo," and concludes with a sort of wake-up call, or "Morning Bell," that he is not having any greater success in this second incarnation. The A of the third song lifts the tonic G of the first two songs to a higher pitch level. The final song ("Motion Picture Soundtrack") ends with the subject's second death and furnishes a forced resolution and coda (the last a reminder

that the music, and thus the world, continues to exist apart from the subject) along with a parting shot from the subject ("I will see you in the
next life").

A further musical link occurs between those songs that signify the
first death and the reconstitution of the subject. Example 9.3 illustrates
how the closing notes of "How to Disappear Completely" (A–F♯) are
echoed in the opening notes of "Optimistic" (A–B–F♯) after the interlude of "Treefingers," indicating that the subject is essentially picking up
where he left off following his unsuccessful suicide attempt. The would-
be suicide of "How to Disappear Completely" is present again in "Optimistic" with renewed energy and the opportunity for a fresh outlook on
life, and the anguished "aahs" of "How to Disappear Completely" have
been transformed into the soothing "oohs" of "Optimistic." We soon dis-
cover, however, that the negative attitude of the subject is still present, although it seems to have been turned outward onto society instead.
"Treefingers," rather than a literal beyond-death experience, could represent simply an act of "checking out" on the part of the subject, a time
to regroup and refocus his self-denigration as a criticism of society. The
technological soundscape of the song also represents a constructed
"real" or "nature" that exists apart from and is thus superior to the subject. Because of the continued existence of the stage on which the dramatic action has taken place, the final judgment of the album does not
have to occur upon the death of the subject; instead, the subject can be
revived and given a second chance.[44]

The songs of *Kid A* are also tied together with lyrics, but rather than
constructing a clear narrative the words simply drop clues about the setting and the subject's state of mind. In particular, similar lyrics are present on each half of the album, providing a bridge across the subject's attempted suicide. The statement "I slipped away on a little white lie" in
"Kid A" returns in "Motion Picture Soundtrack" as "they fed us on little
white lies," a comment on the paranoid environment that precipitated
the album. The statement in "How to Disappear Completely" that "this
isn't happening" is countered in "Idioteque" with "this is really happening," another instance of the real battling with the unreal. Rather than

"Aah..." (Track 4: 5:22–5:34)   "Ooh..."(Track 6: 0:00–0:10)

Example 9.3. The end of "How to Disappear Completely" and the beginning of "Optimistic"

trying to negate himself in order to reach some imagined reality, the subject seems in the latter song to be trying to force himself to accept reality. The Orwellian reference "living on animal farm" in "Optimistic" can be linked to the dystopian "stop sending letters, letters always get burned" in "Motion Picture Soundtrack."[45] The "dinosaurs roaming the earth" of "Optimistic" are recalled in the apocalyptic "ice age coming" in "Idioteque." The calmly uttered command "rats and children follow me out of town" in "Kid A" returns as the hysterical stutter "who's in bunker . . . women and children first" in "Idioteque," as the subject must face his fate instead of trying to escape it. The words "laugh until my head comes off" in "Idioteque" indicate that even a moment of levity has dire consequences in Radiohead's apocalyptic wasteland. Here laughter negates reason, as the convulsing body literally loses its head. The lyric can also be linked to the "heads on sticks" in "Kid A," which have already been separated from their bodies and must rely on "ventriloquists" for their message.

"Here I'm allowed everything all of the time": Musical Elements in *Kid A*

Let us now turn to the specific musical elements of *Kid A* to try to construct dramatic action or at the very least a clearer understanding of the subject. As I noted earlier, the album's first three songs gradually build up the shaky picture of a protagonist who is defined in negative space by his reactions to his environment. The instability of this structure (and the subject) makes it easier for noise (whether emanating from an internal or external source) eventually to rip it apart. Despite what its title suggests, "Everything in Its Right Place" presents a musical scenario in which expectations of resolution are constantly thwarted. The song has a preludelike quality, as though its purpose is merely to hint at what is to come later rather than to present a clear statement of the album's thesis.[46] The formal sections of the song can be labeled as intro, chorus, verse, chorus, verse, and coda, respectively.[47] The lack of transitional material, or a bridge, suggests an inability to move forward, which foreshadows the feel of the whole album.[48]

"Everything in Its Right Place" is essentially in 10/4, with the bass drum providing the quarter-note pulse. Such a large metric grouping produces a suspended feeling in the music that is furthered by the voice's slow melody being somewhat disconnected from the meter. The chord progressions can be grouped into three larger harmonic motions as shown in figure 9.2a. Note that a pedal tone C sounds in an upper voice throughout the song regardless of the underlying chords (variously C major, D-flat major, E-flat major, and F major), and, although the voice's initial statement introduces the melodic motion F–C–F, the pedal C should not necessarily be construed as having a dominant function to the F, as we might expect in traditional Western art music. Indeed, apart from presenting a stepwise motion of all major chords, the harmonic function remains vague and unsettled, with F and C competing for status as the underlying tonic.[49] Figure 9.2b shows how the three harmonic motions are deployed in each formal section.

The tenuous stability of the song's initial keyboard motive is immediately threatened by the intrusion of a sampled voice babbling nonsensically in alternating speakers. The voice in one channel breaks up lyrics that are heard slightly later ("yesterday I woke up sucking on a lemon"), while the voice in the other channel announces the album title and possibly the lead character, "Kid A." The singer's undistorted, or rational, voice then enters in the center of the stereo field with the word "everything." At first impression the lead vocal, as "acoustic" (although, as

Harmonic Motion	Chord Progression (number of beats)
a	C (4) D-flat (2) E-flat (4)
b	F (2) C (2) D-flat (2) E-flat (4)
c	D-flat (6) C (2) E-flat (2)

Figure 9.2a. Chord progressions of "Everything in Its Right Place"

Section	Harmonic Motion
Introduction	*a*
Chorus 1	*b* and *a*
Verse 1	*c*
Chorus 2	*b* and *a*
Verse 2	*c*
Coda	*b*

Figure 9.2b. Harmonic and formal structure of "Everything in Its Right Place"

Jonny Greenwood has stated, this is a faulty comparison), seems to represent unadulterated "nature," as well as music, and the babbling vocals "technology," as well as noise, yet the relationship grows more complicated as we realize that one has been created from the other; the words of the main vocal (derived from live performance) have been spliced and rearranged into the babbling one.[50] The noise element produces disharmony here by turning one of the musical elements back on itself, suggesting already the triumph of technology over nature.

In the second verse of "Everything in Its Right Place," the phrase structure mutates slightly so that each lyrical idea is repeated twice. The statement "there are two colors in my head" implies that at some level the subject is aware of a fracture. These "two colors" are vividly represented in the sound world of the track itself through the battle for tonal dominance between C and F, the split between the two speaker channels, and an apparent split between a rational, "conscious" voice and a babbling subconscious. As the rational voice tries to interact with the babbling one—asking, "What is that you tried to say? What was that you tried to say?"—it receives only nonsense in return. Significantly, the move from present to past tense here suggests passing action rather than an event that has already taken place outside the song.

The second song on the album, the title track, "Kid A," continues to blur the categories of technology and the organic, opening with the synthesized sound of blowing wind followed by a slow, four-bar repeating keyboard pattern that sounds like a music box being wound. A counter-rhythm played on a marimbalike keyboard then enters and alternates between channels along with occasional percussive tapping. The feel of the song is one of technology trying to replicate natural sounds, much like the blurred distinction between computer-generated and hand-drawn art in the booklets accompanying the CD. When the voice enters, it is distorted and mechanized, as though it is being projected through radio static. Doheny notes, "The character, the 'spirit' perhaps, of Thom's voice, has been electronically superimposed on the 'artificial' pitches of the [Ondes Martenot]."[51] The aural incomprehensibility of the lyrics moves the main vocal into the nonsense category and maps it onto noise.

The opening "music-box" chords of "Kid A" present an interlocking pitch collection that changes the color of the harmony over the course of each measure and produces a "diatonic fog" of constantly thickening and thinning layers of harmonic ambiguity. Example 9.4a shows an approximation of this four-bar pattern, the harmonic complexity of which is furthered when the synthesized marimba is layered into the texture. The "marimba" plays a slower series of first-inversion chords (not transcribed here) that clash with the music-box riff, which continues to repeat.[52] When these marimba chords are coupled with the underlying music-box riff, up to six adjacent pitches of the F major diatonic collection are present at any given time. The effect of these chord clusters is to blur any sense of real tonal stability while building up a sonic background for the entrance of the voice. Thom Yorke's processed and distorted vocal, which enters about a minute into the song, presents yet a third melodic layer, which seems to fit more with the marimba chords than with the music box. In what serves loosely as a "chorus" for the song (the four-times-repeated statement "standing in the shadows at the end of my bed"), a bass guitar is added to the texture and the drums grow much louder in the mix. At the end of the chorus, the bass introduces, in tandem with the drums, a repeated rhythmic motive centering on the dominant C (see example 9.4b), a riff that is similar to the bass riff that begins the next song, "The National Anthem."

About three minutes into "Kid A," a brief interlude of held synthesized string chords interrupts the surface rhythmic flow, seemingly in an attempt to saturate the texture with a reversion to nature's unorganized sound. Although stringed instruments normally provide a humanizing (or "sweetening") effect, here the fabricated sound seems sinister and unnatural, foreshadowing the use of strings as noise in "How to Disappear Completely." The original music-box riff finally returns under the strings, and the voice sings the final verse, again centering on C and A

a) "Music-box" chords

(Track 2: 0:11–0:19)

b) Bass riff

(Track 2: 4:09–4:26)

Example 9.4. "Kid A"

rather than F. The strings fade out as the singer comes back in for the last verse, but it seems that they are simply lying in wait to capture the voice, as they immediately rise in the mix again. The final words of the verse, "rats and children follow me out of town," could perhaps refer to Radiohead's feeling about its audience: that they will naively follow the band anywhere, Pied Piper–like. The singer's halfhearted delivery of the closing words, "c'mon kids," suggests that he is a reluctant leader ready to cast off his role. The unresolved C from "Everything in Its Right Place" finally triumphs here, though seemingly only after being abandoned by (or cutting off) the voice. The strings ultimately fade out under an anguished vocal cry, which blends into high keyboard effects that are abruptly cut off with the onset of the bass riff of the next song. Although the voice itself is in the nonsense category this time, it is again overcome by the nonvocal sounds. Technology has again triumphed over nature, albeit a faux nature since all the sounds are synthetic.

The third song on *Kid A,* "The National Anthem," brings a sense of irony in its topic and lyrics while still expressing the subject's feelings of alienation. Traditionally, a national anthem is conceived as a heroic song that speaks of the unity and pride of a nation's people, but Radiohead's "The National Anthem" speaks instead of terror: "Everyone is so near, everyone has got the fear, it's holding on." Despite the nearness of the crowd, the subject still feels alone, perhaps even more so because of this stifling press of humanity. As a musical representation of the subject's confinement, the song begins with an aggressive wedge-shaped bass riff (the pitches of which are confined entirely within the major third D–F♯), which repeats relentlessly throughout the song (see example 9.5a).

One of the hallmarks of Radiohead's musical style is a strong "groove," defined by Mark Spicer as "the tapestry of riffs . . . that work together to create the distinctive rhythmic/harmonic backdrop which identifies a song."[53] Timothy Hughes notes that *groove* can refer also to the "various backdrops that support different parts of the song" and specifically to "a figure . . . designed to be repeated."[54] Dai Griffiths has noted the band's striking and complex "layering of the guitars and drums" on *OK Computer*.[55] Alex Ross has stressed the importance of the band's interlocking sound, writing, "Take away any one element—Selway's flickering rhythmic grid, for example, fierce in execution and trippy in effect—and Radiohead are a different band."[56] Spicer has discussed Radiohead's use of an "accumulative beginning" for the opening track on *Amnesiac,* "Packt Like Sardines in a Crushd Tin Box," in which, as he puts it, "the addition of each new component seems to be a delib-

a) Bass riff

b) Horn riff

(Track 3: 2:39)

Example 9.5. "The National Anthem"

erate attempt to surprise the listener . . . so that when the groove ultimately does crystallize it sounds as if it has 'emerged' out of a state of
rhythmic, metric, and tonal confusion."[57] Radiohead plays with this technique of accumulation in "The National Anthem" by having instruments
drop out and come back in after the groove is established, lending emphasis to the voice (see figure 9.3).

The instruments punctuate the voice, dropping out on the word
"everyone" at the beginning of each verse as though they are listening to
the singer. The musical texture is built up by the guitar and the vocal
babbling (evocative of the crowd noise on *Sgt. Pepper*) that recurs later in
the song when the lead vocal drops out. The vocal line has slight feed-
back behind it, emphasizing the synthesized element, and its initial pitch
content is limited also to the same D–F♯ major-third range of the bass riff.
As the vocalist sings "it's holding on," he seems to grow more hysterical,
as though he himself is barely holding on or is trying to hold the song together. His wordless "aahs" on A and G♯ foreshadow the "aahs" in "How
to Disappear Completely" that signify the loss of the subject in the noise
of the strings and guitar. In the second verse, the natural sound of
Charles Mingus–style horns presents a challenge to the technological su-
premacy of the synthesized sounds (Ondes Martenot, filtered voice, keyboard effects) heard thus far on the album.[58] The horns begin a rhythmic, seesawing, minor-seventh riff (see example 9.5b) overlaid with free

Intro: CD timings	0:02	0:09	0:13	0:23	0:25	0:39	0:46	0:49	0:53	1:01	1:04	1:17
Bass	X											
Drums			X	O	X							
Ondes Martenot (melody)				X								
Horns											X	
Noise (babble, Ondes, or electric guitar)		X	O			X	O	X	O	X	O	

Verse: CD timings	1:36	1:57	2:18	2:21	2:26	2:27	2:35	2:36	2:39	3:20	3:21	3:30	3:31	3:41	3:42
Voice	X	O	X						O	X	O	X	O	X	O
Bass	(X)														
Drums	(X)		O	X											
Ondes Martenot (melody)		X	O						X						
Horns									X						
Noise (babble, Ondes, or electric guitar)		X	O		X	O	X	O	X						

Outro: CD timings	3:43	3:53	4:00	4:50	4:53	5:11	5:30	5:46
Voice		X	O					
Bass	(X)					O		
Drums	O		X	O	X	O		
Ondes Martenot (melody)	O							
Horns	X					O		
Noise (orchestral snippet; tape winding down)							X	O

Figure 9.3. The groove in "The National Anthem"

improvisation by a trumpet and saxophone representing babble or nonsense. The horns' riff never "resolves" but serves as a confining frame from which the higher sounds try to escape.[59] In effect the other instruments are closing in on the singer, furthering his paranoia. Here the category of nature has been remapped onto noise. The nature element seems to triumph when the horns finally break free. After several repetitions of "holding on," we are left with the bass, isolated horns, and vocal cries evocative of the Ondes Martenot. Noise takes over the texture in the end, when the horns let loose with screeching glissandi. Again babble has had the last word, although this time it is a purely instrumental one. After the horns are cut off, a snatch of orchestral melody reminiscent of Edward Elgar's music is heard. This melody is distorted to sound like a tape being wound down, as if to represent the failure of technological society.

After a moment's pause, a high string cluster is introduced just before the strummed acoustic guitar that opens the next song, "How to Disappear Completely (And Never Be Found)." Once again the synthesized strings seem to be simply lying in wait to engulf the singer. A single high B♭ is left to sound above the guitar, a subtle yet discordant noise over alternating D major and F-sharp minor chords (recalling, not coincidentally, the same boundary pitches in the bass riff and vocal line of "The National Anthem"). The B♭ sounds above the melody until the beginning of the chorus, while the alternating third-related chords and pentatonic bass line (see example 9.6a) evoke a sense of tonal ambiguity that provides an unstable background on which the noise can readily encroach.

Example 9.6b presents an analytical reduction of "How to Disappear Completely" that illustrates how the music and noise elements interact.[60] The noise intrusions are represented on the top staff, with the boxes indicating notes or patterns that repeat throughout a section. The song can be heard as building to a crisis at which the noise that has been threatening the musical texture over the course of the album forces things to the breaking point. Although "How to Disappear Completely" presents the most complete construction of our hypothesized subject thus far, with its

(Track 4: 0:21)

Example 9.6a. "How to Disappear Completely," tonally ambiguous pentatonic bass riff

Example 9.6b. "How to Disappear Completely," reduction

coherent lyrics and relative lack of vocal distortion, the singer seems to be denying his very existence and challenging notions of the real and the un-real: "That there, that's not me." In a sense, the singer could be speaking of his recorded voice from outside the song, calling to mind Attali's no-tion of reproduction, in which the original is supplanted by its copy.[61] The singer describes a dreamlike situation: "I go where I please, I walk through walls, I float down the Liffey."[62] The live performance of an ear-lier version of this song, as seen in the 1999 Radiohead tour documentary *Meeting People Is Easy*, evokes the feeling of the unreality of being on the concert stage and the singer's apparent disconnection from the public persona created for him by his audience.[63] Thom Yorke has stated that the song refers to a dream in which he was flying around Dublin, and the vocal line reflects this dream by sounding more disembodied as the song progresses.[64] The bass line also plays a "two against three" feel against the "fast three" of the guitar's rhythmic pattern, which contributes to the ef-fect of being out of time. The descending A–F♯ minor-third motive (har-monized alternately by both the D major and F-sharp minor chords) dominates the texture, stated by the electric guitar before the voice comes in and eventually moving to the other instruments.

The drums and tambourine enter for the second verse, in which the singer seems to contradict his earlier assertion of nonexistence: "In a lit-tle while, I'll be gone." The strings reenter during this section, following the dynamics of the vocal line. With the next chorus, the singer's claim that "this isn't happening" begins to ring hollow, as hornlike ascending and descending scalar patterns (spanning B to F♯) begin to permeate the texture along with more insistent minor thirds. The singer seems no longer to be able to deny the reality of the intrusion of the noise. As the strings and electric guitar fight for dominance in the third verse, the cri-sis point is described by the singer as cataclysmic scenes of the concert stage and the outdoors (or technology and nature): "Strobe lights and blown speakers, fireworks and hurricanes." In the final chorus, the singer grows yet more insistent, holding out the ends of lines and enun-ciating more clearly. He vehemently denies his existence, just before what seem to be his death throes, when he transcends the increasingly vi-olent texture and climbs into a higher tessitura with vocalese ("aah"), claiming the minor third as his own. At first the strings support him, but as he holds out a suspension they grow discordant and finally drop out to leave the voice hanging precariously alone. When the strings return, they are in unison with the electric guitar, proclaiming the minor third until the end. The forces have been joined, but it is an uneasy truce that has come only with the elimination of the singer. As Cone has stated, the accompaniment "symbolically suggests both the impingement of the outer world on the individual represented by the vocal persona, and the subconscious reaction of the individual to this impingement."[65] Given the enormous pressure under which the members of Radiohead found themselves during the production of this album, trying to live up to audience and market demands after the colossal success of their previous two albums, one can guess that they might literally have wanted to "disappear completely and never be found."[66] The subject himself seems to be unable to cope with the soul-draining alienation of modern society and longs for release.

Our tenuous subject does disappear, nearly completely, in the next song, "Treefingers," which marks the space between the two halves of the album. The singer's words are entirely absent, and his voice is present only in stray "aahs" heard in the distance of the ambient texture.[67] The previously battling instrumental forces seem to be absent from this song as well, as the only sounds present are New Age–style filtered guitars, the chords of which change quite slowly. Jonny Greenwood's acknowledged influence of Messiaen on his compositional style—which we saw already, for example, in his use of one of Messiaen's favorite instruments, the Ondes Martenot, on previous tracks—is apparent in the chord voicings here (see example 9.7). The chords of "Treefingers" are tonally unstable with their added sixths and ninths, but they do follow a regular pattern. The position of the song halfway through the album saps what little momentum has finally been built. The subject seems to have destroyed himself and must be resurrected for the second half of the album. After experiencing a dichotomy between nature and the ego over the first few songs of *Kid A*, the subject attempts to quell his internal struggle by domesticating his anxieties as musical sound. He fails to keep his demons at bay, and they erupt as noise, sporadically until "How to Disappear Completely" but then taking over the texture. The explosion of noise dislocates the subject so that he is ungrounded for "Treefingers." This "new order" created after the intrusion of noise into the previous musical structure is musically flat. When the noise is pushed out of the subject's psyche, it becomes the new field of nature on which he can act. Because this new realm exists apart from the subject, he can be reinvented and come back into play; indeed, the structure of the recording demands it since only half the time allotted for the CD has passed.

The second half of *Kid A* forms something of an opposition with the first, yet the mood created by the tentative sound of the songs leading up

Example 9.7. "Treefingers," chords

to "Treefingers" both permeates and sets the stage for the rest of the album. As discussed previously (see example 9.3), "Optimistic" picks up
where "How to Disappear Completely" left off, with wordless "oohs" and
a similar melody. Our subject has seemingly regained control of his situation; rather than making statements about the unreality of his circumstances, he makes harsh, hyperreal statements about the human condition. "Optimistic" ends with an instrumental vamp that leads straight
into the spiraling triplet feel of "In Limbo." The subject of this song does
appear humanized ("I'm on your side"), but we soon learn that he cannot help even himself ("trapdoors that open, I spiral down"). The song
ends with vocal howls that are eventually distorted and then grind down
to a computer-generated tone.

"Idioteque" is dominated by heavy drums that serve, perhaps, as a
ghost of the bass riff in "The National Anthem." The quickly changing
keyboard chord clusters (4 + 4 + 4 + 8 beats, respectively) present an an-
imated contrast to the languorous chords of "Treefingers." The harmonic rhythm, however, is static, as the chords simply reiterate all the different inversions of an E-flat major seventh chord one after the other
(third inversion, second inversion, first inversion, and root position, respectively), with the upper and lower voices expanding outward with
each new inversion.[68] The other instruments drop out as the vocalist
sings "we're not scaremongering, this is really happening," marking a
sign of the real and refuting his denial in "How to Disappear Completely" that "this isn't happening." The penultimate song on the album,
"Morning Bell," suggests a further humanizing of the protagonist with
an opening up of the melody and a rise in tessitura. Over and over the
singer plaintively asks "release me," although it is not clear whom he is
beseeching.[69] In the album's final song, "Motion Picture Soundtrack,"
the protagonist seems to be on his way to achieving this release. With the
song's closing words, "I will see you in the next life," marking the second
death on the album, the singer's voice climbs to an even higher tessitura,
which is subsumed into a heavenly chorus against a billowing harp. This
forced, theatrical ending turns the song into an epitaph to the whole al-

bum but leaves the listener wanting more, a salvation that comes only with an attempt to forget the trauma of *Kid A* on its follow-up, *Amnesiac.*

NOTES

An earlier version of this chapter was presented at the annual meeting of the Society for Music Theory in Philadelphia, November 2001. Thanks to Mark Spicer, James Buhler, Richard Letts, and Bryan Sale for their advice and comments on various drafts.

1. The second half of *Kid A* is dealt with in a fuller form in my dissertation, "'How to Disappear Completely': Radiohead and the Resistant Concept Album," PhD diss., University of Texas at Austin, 2005; and in my forthcoming book on Radiohead from the University of Indiana Press.

2. For a recent book-length study devoted to the topic, see David O. Montgomery, "The Rock Concept Album: Context and Analysis," PhD diss., University of Toronto, 2002. The Beatles' monumental *Sgt. Pepper's Lonely Hearts Club Band* (1967) is still widely considered to be the "first" concept album, although Frank Zappa and the Mothers of Invention's debut (double) album *Freak Out!* (1966)—a stylistic potpourri of songs that are unified because they all take satirical jabs at American popular culture—was released in the United States almost a year earlier. See Allan F. Moore, *The Beatles: Sgt. Pepper's Lonely Hearts Club Band* (Cambridge: Cambridge University Press, 1997), particularly the last chapter, "Legacy" (70–82). One might also make a case for the Beach Boys' *Pet Sounds* (released in May 1966) as an earlier exemplar of a "thematic" concept album. See Philip Lambert, "Brian Wilson's *Pet Sounds,*" *twentieth-century music* 5, no. 1 (2008): 109–33.

3. For a detailed study of this album, see Allan F. Moore, *Jethro Tull: Aqualung* (New York: Continuum, 2004).

4. "Anyone Can Play Guitar" peaked at number 32 on the U.K. singles charts. "Creep" had failed to reach the Top 40 on its initial U.K. release in September 1992, but its U.K. re-release a year later, following the success of the song in the United States in the summer of 1993, peaked at number 7. See James Doheny, *Radiohead: Back to Save the Universe: The Stories Behind Every Song* (New York: Thunder's Mouth, 2002), 142.

5. *Pablo Honey*'s success was due in large part to "Creep," and touring in support of one single wore the band members down. Jonny Greenwood noted, "We joined this band to write songs and be musicians, but we spent a year being jukeboxes instead. We felt in a creative stasis because we couldn't release anything new" (in *Q* magazine, quoted in Martin Clarke, *Hysterical and Useless* [London: Plexus, 2003], 56). *Melody Maker* called *Pablo Honey* "promisingly imperfect" (quoted in Clarke, *Hysterical and Useless,* 44). "Creep" reached number 4 on the *Billboard* charts for Modern Rock Tracks of 1993 and ranked number 1 or 2 in various *Rolling Stone, Melody Maker,* and *NME* polls for that year. See William Stone, *Radiohead: Green Plastic Wateringcan* (London: UFO Music, 1996), 37.

6. Stone, *Radiohead,* 27.

7. Clarke, *Hysterical and Useless,* 100.

8. Doheny, *Radiohead*, 141. Radiohead also won the Grammy for Best Alternative Music Album for *Kid A* in 2001.

9. Joseph Tate notes that drummer Phil Selway complained about the "over-intellectualization of Radiohead's music by fans and critics alike," declaring, "we don't want people twiddling their goatees over our stuff. What we do is pure escapism" (Joseph Tate, "Introduction," in *The Music and Art of Radiohead*, ed. Joseph Tate [Aldershot and Burlington: Ashgate, 2005)], 1). The Selway quote is from Alex Ross, "The Searchers: Radiohead's Unquiet Revolution," *New Yorker*, August 2001, 115.

10. Doheny, *Radiohead*, 78.

11. Nadine Hubbs, "The Imagination of Pop-Rock Criticism," in *Expression in Pop-Rock Music: Critical and Analytical Essays*, 2nd ed., ed. Walter Everett (New York: Routledge, 2008), 225.

12. Ibid., 226.

13. Allan F. Moore and Anwar Ibrahim, "Identifying Radiohead's Idiolect," in *The Music and Art of Radiohead*, ed. Joseph Tate (Aldershot and Burlington: Ashgate, 2005), 139.

14. The Greenwood brothers are quoted in Clarke, *Hysterical and Useless*, 128. The keyboardist Rick Wakeman (while on hiatus from Yes) famously staged his concept album *The Myths of King Arthur and His Knights of the Round Table* as an Ice Capades show in the 1970s.

15. Ibid.

16. Ibid., 117.

17. Doheny, *Radiohead*, 84.

18. Clarke, *Hysterical and Useless*, 141.

19. Ibid., 142.

20. In a November 2000 article in *Spin*, Zev Borow quotes the reaction of a "Capitol Records insider" on first hearing *Kid A:* "[I]t's amazing, but weird, there aren't any radio singles, and they hate doing press. . . . Roy Lott [Capitol president] is going to shit" (Zev Borow, "The Difference Engine," *Spin*, November 2000, quoted in Erin Harde, "Radiohead and the Negation of Gender," in *The Music and Art of Radiohead*, ed. Joseph Tate [Aldershot and Burlington: Ashgate, 2005], 53). Although some radio stations apparently chose to promote "Optimistic" as if it were a single, no singles from *Kid A* were officially released.

By comparison, *Pablo Honey* had spawned three singles: "Creep," "Anyone Can Play Guitar," and "Stop Whispering" (United States only). *The Bends* and *OK Computer* yielded six each, equivalent to half of the twelve songs that appeared on each album. *The Bends* produced the singles "My Iron Lung" (U.K. number 24), "High and Dry" (U.K. number 17, U.S. number 78), "Fake Plastic Trees" (U.K. number 20), "Just" (U.K. number 17 or 19), "Street Spirit (Fade Out)" (U.K. number 5), and "The Bends" (U.K. number 6), and *OK Computer* included "Paranoid Android" (U.K. number 3), "Karma Police" (U.K. number 8), "Let Down," "No Surprises" (U.K. number 4), "Lucky," and "Airbag." *Amnesiac* (2001), the follow-up album to *Kid A*, yielded two singles: "Pyramid Song" (U.K. number 5) and "Knives Out" (U.K. number 13). Interestingly, "Creep" remains the only Radiohead single to have reached the Top 40 in the United States.

21. Ross, "The Searchers," 112.

22. Doheny, *Radiohead*, 84.

23. This total was four times what *OK Computer* sold in its first week. *Kid A* also debuted at number 1 on the U.K. album chart, where it was certified platinum within a week of its release; similarly, *Amnesiac* would debut at number 1 in the United Kingdom and number 2 in the United States the following year. Richard Menta notes that the availability of *Kid A* in its entirety on Napster did not deter fans from buying it. See his "Did Napster Take Radiohead's New Album to Number 1?" *MP3newswire.net*, 28 October 2000, quoted in Davis Schneiderman, "'We Got Heads on Sticks/You Got Ventriloquists': Radiohead and the Improbability of Resistance," in *The Music and Art of Radiohead*, ed. Joseph Tate (Aldershot and Burlington: Ashgate, 2005), 25.

24. This was evinced by a 2000 discussion on America Online's Radiohead message board. Erin Harde takes the position that Radiohead's experimental phase occurred during the making of *Pablo Honey* and *The Bends*, and that the band began the transition to its present state with *OK Computer* (Harde, "Radiohead and the Negation of Gender," 52).

25. Clarke, *Hysterical and Useless*, 148.

26. Nick Hornby, "Beyond the Pale," *New Yorker*, 30 October 2000, 104. Curtis White countered Hornby's critique with the statement that rather than being self-indulgent Radiohead actually proves its "artistic and political health" by refusing to bow to the pressures of commodification (Curtis White, "Kid Adorno," in *The Music and Art of Radiohead*, ed. Joseph Tate [Aldershot and Burlington: Ashgate, 2005], 13).

27. The reviews are quoted from http://www.metacritic.com/music/artists/radiohead/kida. *Kid A* would end up having long-term critical appeal; *Rolling Stone* gave the album the top spot on its "50 Best Albums of the Decade [2000–2009]" list, stating that "only 10 months into the century, Radiohead had made the decade's best album—by rebuilding rock itself, with a new set of basics and a bleak but potent humanity" (*Rolling Stone*, 24 December 2009–7 January 2010, 48).

28. These antivideos are available on a DVD collection, *The Most Gigantic Lying Mouth of All Time*, through http://www.waste.uk.com. The collection contains four "episodes" of short films set to Radiohead's music that were originally meant to be screened on the band's streaming Web site, http://www.radiohead.tv. The band had solicited films through its Web site and also filmed some studio performances of its own. See also Joseph Tate, "Radiohead's Antivideos: Works of Art in the Age of Electronic Reproduction," in *The Music and Art of Radiohead*, ed. Joseph Tate (Aldershot and Burlington: Ashgate, 2005), 103–17. Thom Yorke has stated, "What frightens me is the idea that what Radiohead do is basically packaged back to people in the form of entertainment, to play in their car stereos on their way to work" but also "You're lying if you're pretending it's not a product, that you're not trying to sell something" (Clarke, *Hysterical and Useless*, 97, 146).

29. http://www.radiohead.com/deadairspace and its alias, http://www.radiohead.co.uk/deadairspace.

30. http://www.radiohead.com/Archive/Site7/03.html.

31. Even on Radiohead's current (2009) Web site, fans seeking routine facts

about the band are referred to external sites or search engines. Martin Clarke notes that Radiohead had "always been a band with a social conscience, but being trapped inside the commercial machine after *OK Computer* had reinforced their ideals" (Clarke, *Hysterical and Useless,* 145). Indeed, part of Radiohead's marketing strategy appears to be creating riddles for fans to solve. As Alex Ross has put it, "The records, the videos, the official Web site, even the T-shirts all cry out for interpretation" (Ross, "The Searchers," 115).

The band's record company, Capitol, did launch a chatbot (GooglyMinotaur) to promote *Kid A,* which encouraged fans to distribute the album's tracks through the Internet before the official CD release. Indeed, Radiohead has embraced this practice wholeheartedly with its subsequent releases in response to the rapid rise of iTunes and other MP3 distribution sites and the marked decline of conventional CD sales in recent years. Setting a new standard for the record industry, Radiohead's latest album, *In Rainbows* (2007), was made available for downloading in its entirety at the band's Web site (where listeners were asked to pay anything from nothing to whatever they could afford) some three months before the CD was officially released for retail purchase.

32. Greg Hainge discusses the evolution in packaging over the course of Radiohead's albums from a straightforward presentation of band photos with *Pablo Honey* and *The Bends* to the increasing use of artwork and obscure snippets of text. See his "To(rt)uring the Minotaur: Radiohead, Pop, Unnatural Couplings, and Mainstream Subversion," in *The Music and Art of Radiohead,* ed. Joseph Tate (Aldershot and Burlington: Ashgate, 2005), 62–84. See also, in the same volume, Lisa Leblanc, "'Ice Age Coming': Apocalypse, the Sublime, and the Paintings of Stanley Donwood" (85–102).

33. It is interesting to compare this booklet with the elaborate faux-newspaper packaging of Jethro Tull's 1972 concept album *Thick as a Brick,* which Bill Martin describes as a "great send-up of English pomposity, provinciality, and the class system" (Bill Martin, *Listening to the Future: The Time of Progressive Rock, 1968–1978* [Chicago: Open Court, 1998], 211).

34. The subject in Pink Floyd's *The Wall* also undergoes two symbolic deaths, one at the midpoint of the album (the end of side 2) and the other at the end of the album. Both these "deaths" appear to be psychotic breaks.

35. See Edward T. Cone, *The Composer's Voice* (Berkeley: University of California Press, 1974); David Brackett, *Interpreting Popular Music* (Cambridge: Cambridge University Press, 1995); and Mikhail Bakhtin, *The Dialogic Imagination: Four Essays,* ed. Michael Holquist, trans. Caryl Emerson and Michael Holquist (Austin: University of Texas Press, 1988).

36. Cone, *The Composer's Voice,* 13.

37. Kevin J. H. Dettmar notes that this is a hallmark of Radiohead's broader style, "an almost epic battle between Thom Yorke's frail voice and the music which alternatively undergirds and overwhelms that voice. . . . And yet, as the biblical metaphor suggests, it's the little guy who ultimately wins" (Kevin J. H. Dettmar, "Foreword," in *The Music and Art of Radiohead,* ed. Joseph Tate [Aldershot and Burlington: Ashgate, 2005], xv).

38. Dettmar extends the analogy to the albums *OK Computer, Kid A,* and *Amnesiac,* a "triptych which is not quite a trilogy," in which "something of a closet

drama is played out between the voice and the noise" (ibid., xvii). He notes also the band's exploration over the course of these three albums of "whether the human voice can retain its authority and authenticity in the reign of Walter Benjamin's 'age of mechanical reproduction,' through the inhuman processing of human utterance" (xviii). See also Carys Wys Jones, "The Aura of Authenticity: Perceptions of Honesty, Sincerity, and Truth in 'Creep' and 'Kid A,'" in *The Music and Art of Radiohead*, ed. Joseph Tate (Aldershot and Burlington: Ashgate, 2005), 38–51. Erin Harde notes that *Kid A* also presents the dichotomy between "the collective and the singular" (Harde, "Radiohead and the Negation of Gender," 57).

39. Jacques Attali, *Noise: The Political Economy of Music*, trans. Brian Massumi (Minneapolis: University of Minnesota Press, 1985), 34.

40. Greenwood's comments on the Internet are quoted in Doheny, *Radiohead*, 92–93. It is interesting to note the proliferation of "unplugged" performances in the 1990s, which were conducted to illustrate a given band's authenticity. Singer Kurt Cobain committed suicide soon after Nirvana appeared on MTV's *Unplugged* (filmed on 13 November 1993, aired on 16 December 1993). Cobain made an unsuccessful suicide attempt on 4 March 1994 and succeeded on 5 April, almost as though the "real" was too much to cope with. See Steve Dougherty, "No Way Out," *People* 41, no. 15 (25 April 1994), http://www.people.com/people/archive/article/0,,20107919,00.html.

41. See Slavoj Žižek, *Looking Awry: An Introduction to Jacques Lacan through Popular Culture* (Cambridge: MIT Press, 1992), in which Žižek discusses the "grey and formless mist" of the Lacanian real in a Robert Heinlein novel, *The Unpleasant Profession of Jonathan Hoag* (13–15).

42. With earlier concept albums (such as *The Dark Side of the Moon*), the track order was often unified in performance before the album was recorded.

43. The transcribed piano-vocal-guitar score for *Kid A* (Miami: Warner Brothers Publications, 2001) presents a bracketed F above the first measure of music for the title track. Given the limitations of the published score in rock music, particularly when the music is as complex and layered as Radiohead's, the piano-vocal-guitar transcription should be taken as no more than a general road map for what is actually sounding on the recording.

44. See Stanley Cavell, *The World Viewed: Reflections on the Ontology of Film* (New York: Viking, 1971), 160.

45. Erin Harde also links "Kid A" to the "mass-produced, assembly-line Alpha children" of Aldous Huxley's *Brave New World* (Harde, "Radiohead and the Negation of Gender," 56).

46. The anticipatory feel of "Everything in Its Right Place" should not be misconstrued as serving the more conventional purpose of an overture, as, for instance, on the Who's *Tommy*, with its introduction of forthcoming musical themes.

47. John Covach would classify "Everything in Its Right Place" as an example of the "contrasting verse-chorus" form. See his "Form in Rock Music: A Primer," in *Engaging Music: Essays in Musical Analysis*, ed. Deborah Stein (New York: Oxford University Press, 2005), 71–74.

48. This marks a contrast with *The Dark Side of the Moon*, which Shaugn O'-

Donnell interprets as "generat[ing] a continual sense of forward motion" through the "prolongation of an extended melodic arch" over the course of the album. See his "'On the Path': Tracing Tonal Coherence in *The Dark Side of the Moon*," in *"Speak to Me": The Legacy of Pink Floyd's* The Dark Side of the Moon, ed. Russell Reising (Aldershot and Burlington: Ashgate, 2005), 87–103.

49. Walter Everett presents a monotonal Schenkerian reading in F major for "Everything in Its Right Place" in his "Making Sense of Rock's Tonal Systems," *Music Theory Online* 10, no. 4 (2004).

50. http://www.followmearound.com/everything_in_its_right_place.php. Mark B. N. Hansen notes that this song alludes to Yorke's breakdown on Radiohead's yearlong *OK Computer* tour, with its main symptom manifested as an inability to speak (David Fricke, "Radiohead: Making Music That Matters," *Rolling Stone*, 2 August 2001, quoted in Mark B. N. Hansen, "Deforming Rock: Radiohead's Plunge into the Sonic Continuum," in *The Music and Art of Radiohead*, ed. Joseph Tate [Aldershot and Burlington: Ashgate, 2005], 118). Hansen further states that this led to the band's "complex deterritorializations" of the voice and "its instrumental avatar, the guitar" (118).

51. Doheny, *Radiohead*, 92. Invented by Maurice Martenot in 1928, the Ondes Martenot was an early electronic keyboard instrument that employed a series of oscillators to produce its distinctive eerie, wavering tone, of which the player could then manipulate the pitches by sliding from note to note using a ribbon controller. The instrument was a favorite of Olivier Messiaen, whose music Jonny Greenwood has acknowledged as exerting a particular influence on his own compositional style.

52. Mark Spicer defines *riff* as "a distinctive melodic-rhythmic idea—usually longer than a motive but not large enough to constitute a full phrase—which is frequently . . . sounded over and over again in the manner of an ostinato" (Mark Spicer, "[Ac]cumulative Form in Pop-Rock Music," *twentieth-century music* 1, no. 1 [2004]: 30).

53. Ibid.

54. Timothy S. Hughes, "Groove and Flow: Six Analytical Essays on the Music of Stevie Wonder," PhD diss., University of Washington, 2003, 14.

55. Dai Griffiths, *Radiohead: OK Computer* (New York: Continuum, 2004), 49.

56. Ross, "The Searchers," 115.

57. Spicer, "(Ac)cumulative Form in Pop-Rock Music," 33.

58. On Mingus-style horns, see http://www.followmearound.com/national_anthem.php. Colin Greenwood's allusion to Mingus apparently refers only to the sound of his ensemble, but we might also consider Mingus's tendency to present several distinct lines at once so that, although the surface seems cacophonous, each line is credible on its own.

59. The idea of trying to break free from a confining musical frame is discussed in greater detail by Susan McClary in "Excess and Frame: The Musical Representation of Madwomen," chap. 4 of her *Feminine Endings* (Minneapolis: University of Minnesota Press, 1991), 80–111. See also my article "Mining for 'Goldheart': A Sketch Study in Popular Music," *Indiana Theory Review* 21 (spring–fall 2000): 147–67, for a discussion of this effect in a song by indie band Guided by Voices.

60. Note that the graph in the example is not meant to be a true Schenkerian analysis of the song. Nonetheless, some of the tools developed for that method are helpful for examining nonclassical music. For a useful summary of some of the issues surrounding the use of quasi-Schenkerian graphs in the analysis of popular music, see Lori Burns and Mélisse Lafrance, *Disruptive Divas: Feminism, Identity, and Popular Music* (New York: Routledge, 2002), 42–46.

61. "[P]eople originally intended to use the record to preserve the performance, and today the performance is only successful as a simulacrum of the record" (Attali, *Noise*, 85). Joseph Tate points to the literalness of the statement, that the band is not present as the listener is experiencing the music and the performance not only isn't happening but may never have happened (Tate, "Radiohead's Antivideos," 108).

62. By mentioning the Liffey, a river in Dublin, Yorke recalls James Joyce's *Ulysses* and underscores the possibility of multiple levels of interpretation.

63. *Meeting People Is Easy*, dir. Grant Gee, EMD/Capitol, 1999.

64. For Yorke's statement, see http://www.followmearound.com/how_to _disappear_completely.php.

65. Cone, *The Composer's Voice*, 35–36.

66. This is an easy assumption to make after viewing *Meeting People Is Easy*, in which the rabid adulation of the crowds serves merely to alienate the band.

67. Martin Clarke states that the song "comes as close as Radiohead ever could to pure ambience, but . . . still acknowledges their musical foundations: resting on what seem to be synthesisers, the song is actually based on an elongated guitar sample" (Clarke, *Hysterical and Useless*, 149).

68. "Idioteque" stemmed initially from an improvisation around these four chords, which Jonny Greenwood borrowed from an electronic composition by Paul Lansky, *mild und leise* (1972–73). See Paul Lansky, "My Radiohead Adventure," in *The Music and Art of Radiohead*, ed. Joseph Tate (Aldershot and Burlington: Ashgate, 2005), 168–76 (the exact chord progression is shown on page 169).

69. A reorchestrated version of "Morning Bell" appears on *Amnesiac*, lending the song a different interpretation within that context. Mark Hansen observes that because of the albums' order of release, the *Amnesiac* version derives its "true significance . . . if it is heard and analyzed after and in light of the *Kid A* version" (Hansen, "Deforming Rock," 137 n. 5).

Contributors

LORI BURNS is Professor of Music and Vice Dean of Research for the Faculty of Arts at the University of Ottawa. Her work on popular music has been published in *Understanding Rock* (Oxford, 1997), *repercussions* (1999), *Expression in Pop-Rock Music* (Garland, 2000; 2nd ed., Routledge, 2008), *Engaging Music: Essays in Music Analysis* (Oxford, 2005), and *Music Theory Online* (2004, 2005 and 2008), as well as reviews in *Popular Music, Notes,* and the *Canadian University Music Review.* Her book on popular music, *Disruptive Divas: Critical and Analytical Essays on Feminism, Identity, and Popular Music* (Routledge, 2002), co-authored with Mélisse Lafrance, won the Pauline Alderman Award from the International Alliance for Women in Music (2005). Her current program of research, entitled "Subjectivity, Embodiment, and Resistance in Popular Music by Female Artists," is funded by the Social Sciences and Humanities Research Council of Canada (2007–10).

JOHN COVACH is Professor of Music at the University of Rochester and Professor of Theory at the Eastman School of Music, where he teaches classes in traditional music theory, as well as the history and analysis of popular music. He has published dozens of articles on topics dealing with popular music, twelve-tone music, and the philosophy and aesthetics of music. He is the author of the college textbook *What's That Sound? An Introduction to Rock and Its History* (2nd ed., Norton, 2009) and coedited *Understanding Rock* (Oxford, 1997); *American Rock and the Classical Music Tradition* (Harwood, 2000); and *Traditions, Institutions, and American Popular Music* (Harwood, 2000). Covach has performed widely on electric and classical guitar in both the United States and Europe and has recorded with the progressive rock band Land of Chocolate. He is the host of *Radio Rock,* a weekly radio show broadcast on WRUR-FM in Rochester, New York.

ANDREW FLORY is Assistant Professor of Music History at the Shenandoah Conservatory. He completed his PhD at the University of North Carolina at Chapel Hill, where he received the Glen Haydon Award for Outstanding Dissertation in Musicology. His first book, *I Hear a Symphony: Listening to the Music of Motown,* is forthcoming from the University of Michigan Press.

JAMES GRIER is Professor of Music History at the University of Western Ontario. The author of *The Critical Editing of Music* (Cambridge, 1996) and *The Musical World of a Medieval Monk: Adémar de Chabannes in Eleventh-Century Aquitaine* (Cambridge, 2006), he has published on music and liturgy in medieval Aquitaine, on the theory and practice of textual criticism, and on the music of Frank Zappa.

KEVIN HOLM-HUDSON is Associate Professor of Music Theory at the University of Kentucky. He is the author of *Genesis and* The Lamb Lies Down on Broadway (Ashgate, 2008) and editor of *Progressive Rock Reconsidered* (Routledge, 2002). He has published widely on popular music topics ranging from the Carpenters to Sigur Rós in *Music Theory Online, Popular Music and Society, American Music, Journal of Religion and Popular Culture,* and *Genre.* His other research interests include musical semiotics, aspects of musical symmetry, and the music of Karlheinz Stockhausen. He is currently preparing an undergraduate music theory text blending popular, non-Western, and Western art music repertories for Prentice-Hall.

MARIANNE TATOM LETTS holds degrees from the University of North Texas and the University of Texas at Austin. Her dissertation examines Radiohead's *Kid A* and *Amnesiac* as modern concept albums. Her other publications include articles on the Beatles' film *Yellow Submarine,* the indie band Guided by Voices, and John Cameron Mitchell's film *Shortbus.* She has presented papers on these and other topics at conferences worldwide and is working on a book about Radiohead for Indiana University Press.

REBECCA LEYDON is Associate Professor of Music Theory at the Oberlin Conservatory. Her research interests include music and visuality, film music, popular music, and avant-garde movements of the nineteenth and twentieth centuries. She is a contributor to *Music Theory Spectrum, Music Theory Online, Popular Music, Perspectives of New Music,* and the *Journal of the American Musicological Society.* Her essays on postwar "exotica" and science fiction film music appear in the anthologies *Widening the Horizon* and *Off the Planet* (Hayward, 2000 and 2004).

MARK SPICER is Associate Professor and Director of Undergraduate Studies in Music at Hunter College and the Graduate Center, City University of New York. He received his B.Mus. and M.Mus. degrees from the University of North Texas and his PhD in music theory from Yale University. He specializes in the reception history and analysis of popular music, especially British pop and rock since the 1960s, and his writings have appeared in *Contemporary Music Review, Gamut, Music Theory Online, twentieth-century music,* and other scholarly journals and essay collections. He also maintains an active parallel career as a professional keyboardist and vocalist and continues to take the stage most weekends with his own "electric R & B" group, the Bernadettes.

ALBIN ZAK is Associate Professor and Chair of the Department of Music at the State University of New York, Albany. He holds degrees in composition and performance from the New England Conservatory and a PhD in musicology from the City University of New York. His research specialties are popular music studies and the history of sound recording, and his articles and reviews have appeared in the *Journal of the American Musicological Society, American Music, Current Musicology, Notes,* and several volumes of collected essays. He is the author of *The Poetics of Rock: Cutting Tracks, Making Records* (California, 2001), and editor of *The Velvet Underground Companion: Four Decades of Commentary* (Schirmer, 1997). His latest book, *"I Don't Sound Like Nobody": Remaking Music in 1950s America,* is forthcoming from the University of Michigan Press.

Index